Mary Shelley's Frankenstein.

Bloom's Modern Critical Interpretations

Bloom's Modern Critical Interpretations

Bloom's Modern Critical Interpretations

Mary Shelley's
FRANKENSTEIN
Updated Edition

Edited and with an introduction by
Harold Bloom
Sterling Professor of the Humanities
Yale University

CHELSEA HOUSE
PUBLISHERS
An imprint of Infobase Publishing

Bloom's Modern Critical Interpretations: Frankenstein, Updated Edition

©2007 Infobase Publishing

Introduction ©2007 by Harold Bloom

Chelsea House
An imprint of Infobase Publishing
132 West 31st Street
New York NY 10001

Library of Congress Cataloging-in-Publication Data
Mary Wollstonecraft Shelley's Frankenstein / Harold Bloom, editor.—Updated ed.
     p. cm. — (Bloom's modern critical interpretations)
  Includes bibliographical references and index.
  ISBN 0-7910-9303-4 (hardcover)
 1. Shelley, Mary Wollstonecraft, 1797–1851. Frankenstein. 2. Horror tales, English—History and criticism. 3. Frankenstein (Fictitious character) 4. Scientists in literature. 5. Monsters in literature.
 [1. Shelley, Mary Wollstonecraft, 1797–1851. Frankenstein. 2. English literature—History and criticism.] I. Bloom, Harold. II. Title: Frankenstein. III. Series.

  PR5397.F3M38 2006
  823'.7—dc22   2006020214

Contributing Editor: Camille-Yvette Welsch
Cover designed by Ben Peterson
Cover photo: ©Universal/Photofest

Printed in the United States of America

Bang EJB 10 9 8 7 6 5 4 3 2 1

This book is printed on acid-free paper.

Contents

Editor's Note

My introduction relates the novel both to John Milton's *Paradise Lost* and to Perry Bysshe Shelley's *Prometheus Unbound*, finding in all three works the image of the double.

Martin Tropp sees the Monster (whom I would prefer to call "the Daemon") as part of a parable of salvation, after which the eminent Joyce Carol Oates finds in the narrative a "picture of a finite and flawed god at war with, and eventually overcome by, his creator."

The philosopher John Locke's pedagogical stance is invoked by Anne K. Mellor to explain the doom of Frankenstein's creature, while H. L. Malchow relates the unhappy Daemon to problems of "race" in nineteenth-century Britain.

Maureen Noelle McLane finds a defensive "humanism" in Victor Frankenstein, after which Denise Gigante helps redefine the Romantic metaphor of ugliness.

Cynthia Pon employs a Feminist context for understanding the novel, while the symbolic use of the body leads to Mary Shelley's "discourse of disembodiment" for Mark Mossman.

Fred V. Randel demonstrates how Mary Shelley places Gothic horror in the contemporary geopolitics of a repressive Europe, after which Lee Zimmerman concludes this volume by bringing together Victor's hidden inner world with his creature's hopeless contradictions.

HAROLD BLOOM

Introduction

there is a fire
And motion of the soul which will not dwell
In its own narrow being, but aspire
Beyond the fitting medium of desire.
    BYRON. *Childe Harold's Pilgrimage*, canto 3

Ere Babylon was dust,
The Magus Zoroaster, my dead child,
Met his own image walking in the garden.
That apparition, sole of men, he saw.
For know there are two worlds of life and death:
One that which thou beholdest; but the other
Is underneath the grave, where do inhabit
The shadows of all forms that think and live
Till death unite them and they part no more
    SHELLEY. *Prometheus Unbound*, act 1

The motion-picture viewer who carries his obscure but still authentic taste for the sublime to the neighborhood theater, there to see the latest in an unending series of *Frankensteins*, becomes a sharer in a romantic terror now nearly 150 years old. Mary Shelley, barely 19 years of age when she wrote the

1

original Frankenstein, was the daughter of two great intellectual rebels, William Godwin and Mary Wollstonecraft, and the second wife of Percy Bysshe Shelley, another great rebel and an unmatched lyrical poet. Had she written nothing, Mary Shelley would be remembered today. She is remembered in her own right as the author of a novel valuable in itself but also prophetic of an intellectual world to come, a novel depicting a Prometheanism that is with us still.

"Frankenstein," to most of us, is the name of a monster rather than of a monster's creator, for the common reader and the common viewer have worked together, in their apparent confusion, to create a myth soundly based on a central duality in Mary Shelley's novel. A critical discussion of *Frankenstein* needs to begin from an insight first recorded by Richard Church and Muriel Spark: the monster and his creator are the antithetical halves of a single being. Spark states the antithesis too cleanly; for her Victor Frankenstein represents the feelings, and his nameless creature the intellect. In her view the monster has no emotion, and "what passes for emotion ... are really intellectual passions arrived at through rational channels." Spark carries this argument far enough to insist that the monster is asexual and that he demands a bride from Frankenstein only for companionship, a conclusion evidently at variance with the novel's text.

The antithesis between the scientist and his creature in *Frankenstein* is a very complex one and can be described more fully in the larger context of Romantic literature and its characteristic mythology. The shadow or double of the self is a constant conceptual image in Blake and Shelley and a frequent image, more random and descriptive, in the other major Romantics, especially in Byron. In *Frankenstein* it is the dominant and recurrent image and accounts for much of the latent power the novel possesses.

Mary Shelley's husband was a divided being, as man and as poet, just as his friend Byron was, though in Shelley the split was more radical. *Frankenstein; or, The Modern Prometheus* is the full title of Mary Shelley's novel, and while Victor Frankenstein is *not* Shelley (Clerval is rather more like the poet), the Modern Prometheus is a very apt term for Shelley or for Byron. Prometheus is the mythic figure who best suits the uses of Romantic poetry, for no other traditional being has in him the full range of Romantic moral sensibility and the full Romantic capacity for creation and destruction.

No Romantic writer employed the Prometheus archetype without a full awareness of its equivocal potentialities. The Prometheus of the ancients had been for the most part a spiritually reprehensible figure, though frequently a sympathetic one, in terms both of his dramatic situation and in his close alliance with mankind against the gods. But this alliance had been ruinous for man in most versions of the myth, and the Titan's benevolence toward humanity was hardly sufficient recompense for the alienation of man from heaven that he had brought about. Both sides of Titanism are evident in earlier Christian references to the story. The same Prometheus who is taken as an analogue of the crucified Christ is regarded also as a type of Lucifer, a son of light justly cast out by an offended heaven.

In the Romantic readings of Milton's *Paradise Lost* (and Frankenstein is implicitly one such reading) this double identity of Prometheus is a vital element. Blake, whose mythic revolutionary named Orc is another version of Prometheus, saw Milton's Satan as a Prometheus gone wrong, as desire restrained until it became only the shadow of desire, a diminished double of creative energy. Shelley went further in judging Milton's Satan as an imperfect Prometheus, inadequate because his mixture of heroic and base qualities engendered in the reader's mind a "pernicious casuistry" inimical to the spirit of art.

Blake, more systematic a poet than Shelley, worked out an antithesis between symbolic figures he named Spectre and Emanation, the shadow of desire and the total form of desire, respectively. A reader of *Frankenstein*, recalling the novel's extraordinary conclusion, with its scenes of obsessional pursuit through the Arctic wastes, can recognize the same imagery applied to a similar symbolic situation in Blake's lyric on the strife of Spectre and Emanation:

> My Spectre around me night and day
> Like a Wild beast guards my way.
> My Emanation far within
> Weeps incessantly for my Sin.
>
> A Fathomless and boundless deep,
> There we wander, there we weep;
> On the hungry craving wind
> My Spectre follows thee behind.
>
> He scents thy footsteps in the snow,
> Wheresoever thou dost go
> Thro' the wintry hail and rain.

Frankenstein's monster, tempting his revengeful creator on through a world of ice, is another Emanation pursued by a Spectre, with the enormous difference that he is an Emanation flawed, a nightmare of actuality, rather than dream of desire. Though abhorred rather than loved, the monster is the total form of Frankenstein's creative power and is more imaginative than his creator. The monster is at once more intellectual and more emotional than his maker; indeed he excels Frankenstein as much (and in the same ways) as Milton's Adam excels Milton's God in *Paradise Lost*. The greatest paradox and most astonishing achievement of Mary Shelley's novel is that the monster is *more human* than his creator. This nameless being, as much a Modern Adam as his creator is a Modern Prometheus, is more lovable than his creator and more hateful, more to be pitied and more to be feared, and above all more able to give the attentive reader that shock of added consciousness in which aesthetic recognition compels a heightened realization of the self. For like Blake's Spectre and Emanation or Shelley's Alastor and Epipsyche, Frankenstein and his monster are the solipsistic and generous halves of the one self. Frankenstein is the mind and emotions turned in upon themselves, and his creature is the mind and emotions turned imaginatively outward, seeking a greater humanization through a confrontation of other selves.

I am suggesting that what makes *Frankenstein* an important book, though it is only a strong, flawed novel with frequent clumsiness in its narrative and characterization, is that it contains one of the most vivid versions we have of the Romantic mythology of the self, one that resembles Blake's *Book of Urizen*, Shelley's *Prometheus Unbound*, and Byron's *Manfred*, among other works. Because it lacks the sophistication and imaginative complexity of such works, *Frankenstein* affords a unique introduction to the archetypal world of the Romantics.

William Godwin, though a tendentious novelist, was a powerful one, and the prehistory of his daughter's novel begins with his best work of fiction, *Caleb Williams* (1794). Godwin summarized the climactic (and harrowing) final third of his novel as a pattern of flight and pursuit, "the fugitive in perpetual apprehension of being overwhelmed with the worst calamities, and the pursuer, by his ingenuity and resources, keeping his victim in a state of the most fearful alarm." Mary Shelley brilliantly reverses this pattern in the final sequence of her novel, and she takes from *Caleb Williams* also her destructive theme of the monster's war against "the whole machinery of human society," to quote the words of Caleb Williams while in prison. Muriel Spark argues that *Frankenstein* can be read as a reaction "against the rational-humanism of Godwin and Shelley," and she points to the equivocal preface that Shelley wrote to his wife's novel, in order to support this view. Certainly Shelley was worried lest the novel be taken as a warning against the inevitable moral consequences of an unchecked experimental Prometheanism and scientific materialism. The preface insists that:

> The opinions which naturally spring from the character and situation of the hero are by no means to be conceived as existing always in my own conviction; nor is any inference justly to be drawn from the following pages as prejudicing any philosophical doctrine of whatever kind.

Shelley had, throughout his own work, a constant reaction against Godwin's rational humanism, but his reaction was systematically and consciously one of heart against head. In the same summer in the Swiss Alps that saw the conception of *Frankenstein*, Shelley composed two poems that lift the thematic conflict of the novel to the level of the true sublime. In the "Hymn to Intellectual Beauty" the poet's heart interprets an inconstant grace and loveliness, always just beyond the range of the human senses, as being the only beneficent force in life, and he prays to this force to be more constant in its attendance upon him and all mankind. In a greater sister-hymn, "Mont Blanc," an awesome meditation upon a frightening natural scene, the poet's head issues an allied but essentially contrary report. The force, or power, is there, behind or within the mountain, but its external workings upon us are either indifferent or malevolent, and this power is not to be prayed to. It can teach us, but what it teaches us is our own dangerous freedom from nature, the necessity for our will to become a significant part of materialistic necessity. Though "Mont Blanc" works its way to an almost heroic conclusion, it is also a poem of horror and reminds us that Frankenstein first confronts his conscious monster in the brooding presence of Mont Blanc, and to the restless music of one of Shelley's lyrics of Mutability.

In *Prometheus Unbound* the split between head and heart is not healed, but the heart is allowed dominance. The hero, Prometheus, like Frankenstein, has made a monster, but this monster is Jupiter, the God of all institutional and historical religions, including organized Christianity. Salvation from this conceptual error comes through love alone; but love in this poem, as elsewhere in Shelley, is always closely shadowed by ruin. Indeed, what choice spirits in Shelley perpetually encounter is ruin masquerading as love, pain presenting itself as pleasure. The tentative way out of this situation in Shelley's poetry is through the quest for a feeling mind and an understanding heart, which is symbolized by the sexual reunion of Prometheus and his Emanation, Asia. Frederick A. Pottle sums up

Prometheus Unbound by observing its meaning to be that "the head must sincerely forgive, must willingly eschew hatred on purely experimental grounds," while "the affections must exorcize the demons of infancy, whether personal or of the race." In the light cast by these profound and precise summations, the reader can better understand both Shelley's lyrical drama and his wife's narrative of the Modern Prometheus.

There are two paradoxes at the center of Mary Shelley's novel, and each illuminates a dilemma of the Promethean imagination. The first is that Frankenstein *was* successful, in that he did create Natural Man, not as he was, but as the meliorists saw such a man; indeed, Frankenstein did better than this, since his creature was, as we have seen, more imaginative than himself. Frankenstein's tragedy stems not from his Promethean excess but from his own moral error, his failure to love; he *abhorred his creature*, became terrified, and fled his responsibilities.

The second paradox is the more ironic. This either would not have happened or would not have mattered anyway, if Frankenstein had been an aesthetically successful maker; a beautiful "monster," or even a passable one, would not have been a monster. As the creature bitterly observes in chapter 17,

> Shall I respect man when he contemns me? Let him live with me in the interchange of kindness, and instead of injury I would bestow every benefit upon him with tears of gratitude at his acceptance. But that cannot be; the human senses are insurmountable barriers to our union.

As the hideousness of his creature was no part of Victor Frankenstein's intention, it is worth noticing how this disastrous matter came to be.

It would not be unjust to characterize Victor Frankenstein, in his act of creation, as being momentarily a moral idiot, like so many who have done his work after him. There is an indeliberate humor in the contrast between the enormity of the scientist's discovery and the mundane emotions of the discoverer. Finding that "the minuteness of the parts" slows him down, he resolves to make his creature "about eight feet in height and proportionably large." As he works on, he allows himself to dream that "a new species would bless me as its creator and source; many happy and excellent natures would owe their being to me." Yet he knows his is a "workshop of filthy creation," and he fails the fundamental test of his own creativity. When the "dull yellow eye" of his creature opens, this creator falls from the autonomy of a supreme artificer to the terror of a child of earth: "breathless horror and disgust filled my heart." He flees his responsibility and sets in motion the events that will lead to his own Arctic immolation, a fit end for a being who has never achieved a full sense of another's existence.

Haunting Mary Shelley's novel is the demonic figure of the Ancient Mariner, Coleridge's major venture into Romantic mythology of the purgatorial self trapped in the isolation of a heightened self-consciousness. Walton, in Letter 2 introducing the novel, compares himself "to that production of the most imaginative of modern poets." As a seeker-out of an unknown passage, Walton is himself a Promethean quester, like Frankenstein, toward whom he is so compellingly drawn. Coleridge's Mariner is of the line of Cain, and the irony of Frankenstein's fate is that he too is a Cain, involuntarily murdering all his loved ones through the agency of his creature. The Ancient Mariner is punished by living under the curse of his consciousness of guilt, while the excruciating torment of Frankenstein is never to be able to forget his guilt in creating a lonely consciousness driven to crime by the rage of unwilling solitude.

It is part of Mary Shelley's insight into her mythological theme that all the monster's victims are innocents. The monster not only refuses actively to slay his guilty creator, he mourns for him, though with the equivocal tribute of terming the scientist a "generous and self-devoted being." Frankenstein, the modern Prometheus who has violated nature, receives his epitaph from the ruined second nature he has made, the God-abandoned, who consciously echoes the ruined Satan of *Paradise Lost* and proclaims, "Evil thenceforth became my good." It is imaginatively fitting that the greater and more interesting consciousness of the creature should survive his creator, for he alone in Mary Shelley's novel possesses character. Frankenstein, like Coleridge's Mariner, has no character in his own right; both figures win a claim to our attention only by their primordial crimes against original nature.

The monster is of course Mary Shelley's finest invention, and his narrative (chaps. 11–16) forms the highest achievement of the novel, more absorbing even than the magnificent and almost surrealistic pursuit of the climax. In an age so given to remarkable depictions of the dignity of natural man, an age including the shepherds and beggars of Wordsworth and what W. J. Bate has termed Keats's "polar ideal of disinterestedness"—even in such a literary time Frankenstein's hapless creature stands out as a sublime embodiment of heroic pathos. Though Frankenstein lacks the moral imagination to understand him, the daemon's appeal is to what is most compassionate in us:

Oh, Frankenstein, be not equitable to every other, and trample upon me alone, to whom thy justice, and even thy clemency and affection, is most due. Remember that I am thy creature; *I ought to be thy Adam, but I am rather the fallen angel, whom thou drivest from joy for no misdeed.* Everywhere I see bliss, from which I alone am irrevocably excluded. I was benevolent and good; misery made me a fiend. Make me happy, and I shall again be virtuous.

The passage I have italicized is the imaginative kernel of the novel and is meant to remind the reader of the novel's epigraph:

Did I request thee, Maker, from my clay
To mold me man? Did I solicit thee
From darkness to promote me?

That desperate plangency of the fallen Adam becomes the characteristic accent of the daemon's lamentations, with the influence of Milton cunningly built into the novel's narrative by the happy device of Frankenstein's creature receiving his education through reading *Paradise Lost* as "a true history." Already doomed because his standards are human, which makes him an outcast even to himself, his Miltonic education completes his fatal growth in self-consciousness. His story, as told to his maker, follows a familiar Romantic pattern "of the progress of my intellect," as he puts it. His first pleasure after the dawn of consciousness comes through his wonder at seeing the moon rise. Caliban-like, he responds wonderfully to music, both natural and human, and his sensitivity to the natural world has the responsiveness of an incipient poet. His awakening to a first love for other beings, the inmates of the cottage he haunts, awakens him also to the great desolation of love rejected when he attempts to reveal himself. His own duality of situation and character, caught between the states of Adam and Satan, Natural Man and his thwarted desire, is related by him directly to his reading of Milton's epic:

It moved every feeling of wonder and awe that the picture of an omnipotent God warring with his creatures was capable of exciting. I often referred the several situations, as their similarity struck me, to my own. Like Adam, I was apparently united by no link to any other being in existence, but his state was far different from mine in every other respect. He had come forth from the hands of God a perfect creature, happy and prosperous, guarded by the especial care of his Creator; he was allowed to converse with and acquire knowledge from beings of a superior nature; but I was wretched, helpless, and alone. Many times I considered Satan as the fitter emblem of my condition, for often, like him, when I viewed the bliss of my protectors, the bitter gall of envy rose within me.

From a despair this profound, no release is possible. Driven forth into an existence upon which "the cold stars shone in mockery," the daemon declares "everlasting war against the species" and enters upon a fallen existence more terrible than the expelled Adam's. Echoing Milton, he asks the ironic question "And now, with the world before me, whither should I bend my steps?" to which the only possible answer is, toward his wretched Promethean creator.

If we stand back from Mary Shelley's novel in order better to view its archetypal shape, we see it as the quest of a solitary and ravaged consciousness first for consolation, then for revenge, and finally for a self-destruction that will be apocalyptic, that will bring down the creator with his creature. Though Mary Shelley may not have intended it, her novel's prime theme is a necessary counterpoise to Prometheanism, for Prometheanism exalts the increase in consciousness despite all cost. Frankenstein breaks through the barrier that separates man from God and gives apparent life, but in doing so he gives only death-in-life. The profound dejection endemic in Mary Shelley's novel is fundamental to the Romantic mythology of the self, for all Romantic horrors are diseases of excessive consciousness, of the self unable to bear the self. Kierkegaard remarks that Satan's despair is absolute because Satan, as pure spirit, is pure consciousness, and for Satan (and all men in his predicament) every increase in consciousness is an increase in despair. Frankenstein's desperate creature attains the state of pure spirit through his extraordinary situation and is racked by a consciousness in which every thought is a fresh disease.

A Romantic poet fought against self-consciousness through the strength of what he called imagination, a more than rational energy by which thought could seek to heal itself. But Frankenstein's daemon, though he is in the archetypal situation of the Romantic Wanderer or Solitary, who sometimes was a poet, can win no release from his own story by telling it. His desperate desire for a mate is clearly an attempt to find a Shelleyan Epipsyche or Blakean Emanation for himself, a self within the self. But as he is the nightmare actualization of Frankenstein's desire, he is himself an emanation of Promethean yearnings, and his only double is his creator and denier.

When Coleridge's Ancient Mariner progressed from the purgatory of consciousness to his very minimal control of imagination, he failed to save himself, since he remained in a cycle of remorse, but he at least became a salutary warning to others and made of the Wedding Guest a wiser and a better man. Frankenstein's creature can help neither himself nor others, for he has no natural ground to which he can return. Romantic poets liked to return to the imagery of the ocean of life and immortality, for in the eddying to and fro of the healing waters they could picture a hoped-for process of restoration, of a survival of consciousness despite all its agonies. Mary Shelley, with marvelous appropriateness, brings her Romantic novel to a demonic conclusion in a world of ice. The frozen sea is the inevitable emblem for both the wretched daemon and his obsessed creator, but the daemon is allowed a final image of reversed Prometheanism. There is a heroism fully earned in the being who cries farewell in a claim of sad triumph: "I shall ascend my funeral pile triumphantly and exult in the agony of the torturing flames." Mary Shelley could not have known how dark a prophecy this consummation of consciousness would prove to be for the two great Promethean poets who were at her side during the summer of 1816, when her novel was conceived. Byron, writing his own epitaph at Missolonghi in 1824, and perhaps thinking back to having stood at Shelley's funeral pile two years before, found an image similar to the daemon's to sum up an exhausted existence:

> The fire that on my bosom preys
>   Is lone as some volcanic isle;
> No torch is kindled at its blaze—
>   A funeral pile.

The fire of increased consciousness stolen from heaven ends as an isolated volcano cut off from other selves by an estranging sea. "The light of that conflagration will fade away; my ashes will be swept into the sea by the winds" is the exultant cry of Frankenstein's creature. A blaze at which no torch is kindled is Byron's self-image, but he ends his death poem on another note, the hope for a soldier's grave, which he found. There is no Promethean release, but release is perhaps not the burden of the literature of Romantic aspiration. There is something both Godwinian and Shelleyan about the final utterance of Victor Frankenstein, which is properly made to Walton, the failed Promethean whose ship has just turned back. Though chastened, the Modern Prometheus ends with a last word true, not to his accomplishment, but to his desire:

> Farewell, Walton! Seek happiness in tranquillity and avoid ambition, even if it be only the apparently innocent one of distinguishing yourself in science and discoveries. Yet why do I say this? I have myself been blasted in these hopes, yet another may succeed.

Shelley's Prometheus, crucified on his icy precipice, found his ultimate torment in a Fury's taunt: "And all best things are thus confused to ill." It seems a fitting summation for all the work done by modern Prometheanism and might have served as an alternate epigraph for Mary Shelley's disturbing novel.

MARTIN TROPP

The Monster

In the first stage, one deals with the persona, and above all with the
shadow. The patient dreams of a repulsive individual who is always
different but retains certain features throughout, and also shows certain
traits resembling the dreamer. Eventually the time comes for the patient
to understand that this individual is none other than himself, or rather
his shadow, and this enables him to become fully aware of those aspects
of his personality that he has refused to see ... One should of course,
accept the shadow, but at the same time render it harmless.

—HENRI ELLENBERGER

At the center of *Frankenstein* is the Monster's own story. The "horrid
thing" of Mary Shelley's dream, the "filthy mass that moved and talked," has
all the deliciously frightening appeal of the decaying creatures of horror
tales. But at the same time it is the first of a new species—a robot, or more
specifically, an android, programmed to destroy all whom its creator
outwardly loves. Articulate, intelligent, and sensitive, the Monster argues
eloquently for its right to exist, all the while murdering the innocent to
punish the guilty and generally frightening the wits out of anyone it meets.
If Victor Frankenstein's frenzied discovery of the "new alchemy" makes him
the first mad scientist, the existence of the Monster presents him with the
first and most enduring symbol of modern technology. It also poses a

From *Mary Shelley's Monster.* © 1976 by Martin Tropp.

problem that is still with us—what are we to do with our creations, especially when they fail to live up to the promises of their creators? The Monster is, on the deepest and most personal level, a projection of Mary Shelley's feelings of isolation and hatred. On a larger scale it serves the same function. An orphan of science, created and abandoned, the Monster threatens to take out its anger and rejection on the species of man. Readers of *Frankenstein* have, from its first publication in 1818, had to face the Monster's arguments and decide if it has a right to survive or if, indeed, it is a monster at all.

In an early review of his wife's novel, Shelley argued that there is, in effect, no monster in *Frankenstein*. Like many later writers on the subject, he takes the creature at its word, asserting that its crimes are not "the offspring of any unaccountable propensity to evil, but flow irresistibly from certain causes fully adequate to their production. They are the children, as it were, of Necessity and Human Nature ... In this the direct moral of the book consists ... Treat a person wicked and he will become wicked."[1] Shelley's apologetics turn on the word "person." If the Monster is fully human, then mankind's treatment of it is criminal. But as self-projection, Doppelgänger, or infernal machine, it is clear that the Monster has the superhuman power and destructiveness of a creature of myth.

For one thing, it is abominable. The classic monsters of legend, like the Minotaur, Dragon, or Gorgon, grotesquely combine the characteristics of more than one animal. As a result, they stand outside of the normal categories of nature. The Monster is even more horrible. Half human, half machine, it falls somewhere between life and death, a thing so unnatural that any human it meets responds with an instinctive and overwhelming loathing. Even Walton, at the end of Frankenstein's long story, knowing what he will see, confronts the Monster and confesses that "I dared not again raise my eyes to his face, there was something so scaring and unearthly in his ugliness." This unearthliness, which makes human acceptance out of the question, is underscored by the Monster's namelessness. In Genesis 3:19–20, Adam's dominion over plants and animals is demonstrated by his power to name them; knowing the name of something has traditionally conferred magical control over it, as well as giving it a place in an ordered universe. Frankenstein's creation is simply "the Monster"—aptly communicating its total otherness and man's impotence before it.

The physical characteristics of the Monster are inherited from a whole family of humanoid monsters that stalk the world of folklore. As a girl growing up in England and Scotland, Mary Godwin no doubt heard some version of the series of legends of the monstrous offspring of Cain, of whom Grendel is the most familiar. She also probably heard the middle European folk tale of the Golem while on her travels and may even have met a "wild man" as part of a Swiss or Bavarian carnival or mummers play. This fur-covered creature, half man, half animal, was supposed to inhabit the forests and glaciers of Europe. As old as the *Gilgamesh* epic and Genesis (16:12), the story of the wild man is found in medieval art, legend, and literature. An outcast like our Monster, it was said to reach out from the darkness to attack the unwary. In the traditional ritual, which still survives, someone dressed as the wild man appears and causes mock terror among the villagers, who drive out, capture, or "kill" it; a similar episode occurs in *Frankenstein* and has become an obligatory scene in nearly all the Frankenstein films.[2] But more important than the Monster's genetic background is its moral ancestry. For this we must turn to a figure that, like Prometheus, was elevated to heroic status by many Romantic writers. For Blake and Shelley, Milton's Satan was an admirable rebel, a Prometheus gone wrong. For Mrs. Shelley, he was the monstrous double of Lucifer, Arch-angel turned Arch-destroyer, and his story a subtle argument from the Prince of Lies himself.

Paradise Lost (1667) is, like *Frankenstein*, designed to define man's place in the universe and give form to those forces threatening to displace him. Milton tells the apocryphal Christian myth of the Fall of the rebel angels and its effect upon human history. Lucifer, one of the most beautiful of the archangels, jealous of Christ's place in the Divine Family, revolts against his creator and tries to command heavenly power. For their crime he and his legion of followers are cast out of Heaven into Hell and transformed into the hideous Satan and his crew of devils. In the infernal Palace of Pandemonium, they discuss how best to carry on the fight and finally resolve to become the implacable foes of humanity. Satan travels to earth, tempts Adam and Eve from the Garden of Eden, and begins man's long and bloody history. The poem ends with the distant promise of the redemption of Adam's descendants through the sacrifice of God's Son. Although Mrs. Shelley's God was certainly not Milton's, they shared a feeling for a divinely created natural order. Direct evidence of her reading of *Paradise Lost* in both 1815 and 1816 is everywhere in *Frankenstein*, from the epigraph to the Monster's last speech. While her references to the poem may be contradictory in a few places, in general they are not haphazard borrowings. Mrs. Shelley found in *Paradise Lost* a pattern which could give form to her fears and mythic shape to her understanding of what technology threatened for the future.

While planning his experiment, Victor felt like Lucifer: "I trod heaven in my thoughts, now exulting in my powers, now burning with the idea of their effects." Like Lucifer before the Fall, Frankenstein before the Monster is in rebellion against his own creator, jealous of his place in his own family, experimenting with a technological imitation of the heavenly thunderbolt, and planning to invert the natural order of things. The interplay of Frankenstein/Monster is somewhat like the relationship between Lucifer/Satan. Each "monster" is, in outward appearance, a reflection of the inner self of its creator, both separate entity and other self, conceived at the moment of rebellion against God and given form when hoped-for triumph gives way to disaster. Thus, the most beautiful of archangels becomes his own monster, cast into Hell with only his memories and evil intact. Similarly, at the moment the Monster comes to life, Frankenstein remembers:

> His limbs were in proportion, and I had selected his features as beautiful. Beautiful!—Great God! His yellow skin scarcely covered the work of muscles and arteries beneath; his hair was of a lustrous black, and flowing; his teeth of a pearly whiteness; but these luxuriances only formed a more horrid contrast with his watery eyes ... shrivelled complexion and straight black lips ... the beauty of the dream vanished, and breathless horror and disgust filled my heart.

The transformation of beautiful dream to loathsome reality begins Frankenstein's long fall to isolation and death. At the end of his life, he realizes the epic dimensions of his crime and its punishment: "... like the archangel who aspired to omnipotence, I am chained in an eternal hell."

At first, Frankenstein tries to escape his chains. He runs from his creation in terror and, for a time, believes he is free. But, on the icy slopes of Chamounix glacier, he meets it again and hears its story. The Monster documents its slow transformation from would-be Adam, to fallen angel, to modern Satan as a painful self-awakening. It begins its independent life without history—part child, part man, part machine. Only with time will it learn that all of man's world is a garden from which it is excluded, that Nature itself has no place for it, and that its only universe is Milton's "universe of death"—the Hell that is always around it.

Its first days in a forest near Ingolstadt resemble what was, at the time, considered the ideal condition for man—the state of nature. Jean Jacques Rousseau argued in his writings that civilization was a corrupting influence and that man, in his "natural state," was "an animal less strong than some, and less agile than others, but, upon the whole, the most advantageously organized of any; I see him satisfying his hunger under an oak, and his thirst at the first brook; I see him laying himself down to sleep at the foot of the same tree that afforded him his meal and there all his wants completely supplied."[3] This snug vision of the past assumed that all men were at peace, amply supplied with food and shelter and able to learn speech by imitating animal sounds.[4] If Rousseau had been looking, he would have seen the Monster beginning his life in exactly this way—living on acorns, nuts, and berries, drinking from a brook, and sleeping under a tree. Unfortunately, nothing works. It fails to find enough food or adequate shelter; when it tries to imitate the birds' songs, the horrid grunts that emerge frighten it into silence. Its inability to live in what was thought to be the most natural state for man points up its unnaturalness—the world of Nature is hostile to a being that doesn't fit. The landscape the Monster finds himself in is more like the vast wasteland Satan and his legions discover when they awaken from the shock of their own fall into damnation.

The "burning lake" of *Paradise Lost* lies in a "frozen Continent," "dark and wild, beat with perpetual storms"[5] where the fallen angels are punished by being made to feel "fierce extremes by change more fierce / From beds of raging Fire to starve in Ice."[6] Hopeless, lost, and confused, the beaten army

> Viewed first their lamentable lot, and found
> No rest: through many a dark and dreary Vale
> They pass'd, and many a Region dolorous
> O'er many a frozen, many a fiery Alp,
> Rocks, Caves, Lakes, Fens, Bogs, and shades of death.[7]

These waste places have their traditional monstrous inhabitants:

> ... Nature breeds,
> Perverse, all monstrous, all prodigious things,
> Abominable, inutterable, and worse
> Than fables yet have feign'd, or fear conceived.[8]

Clearly, Rousseau's state of Nature is, for the Monster, a Miltonic place of infernal torment. Its first sensations are of the painful alteration of light and ark; it remembers "feeling pain invade me from all sides." Extremes of cold and heat continue to oppress the Monster; half-frozen, it discovers a fire and innocently puts its hand in the embers, with predictable results. Throughout its unnatural existence, the Monster remains in an icy "universe of death" beyond the boundaries of the living world—a place Milton describes as fit for monsters. Yet it is always also associated with fire and lightning. For example, it first appears to Frankenstein after the creation in a flash of lightning that illuminates "the lake, making it appear like a vast sheet of fire," while it ultimately chooses fire as its instrument of self-destruction. But, at the start of its existence, it is unaware of where it is, and what it will become. Wandering in its cold world, it finds its first refuge in a hut abandoned by a shepherd, a place it later calls "as exquisite and divine a retreat as Pendaemonium [*sic*] appeared to the daemons of hell after their sufferings in the lake of fire."

In *Paradise Lost*, after the meeting in Pandemonium, Satan decides to fly to earth to inspect God's latest creation. Taking the form of a cormorant, he perches on a tree in Eden and secretly observes Adam and Eve in the Garden. Their happiness reminds him of his eternal pain, and ultimately he finds the way to tempt them to sin. After the Monster has left the shepherd's hut, traveled to a village, and been driven out in a hail of stones, it hides in a hovel where it can secretly observe the lives of a noble family reduced to poverty. Here, it learns man's language, history, and its own true nature. The episode follows the Miltonic pattern; hidden in this new Eden, the Monster learns its Satanic role as the destroyer of human happiness.

While it was traditional at the time to romanticize the lives of the rural poor, to the Monster's eyes, the world it sees is more than romantic—it is "indeed a Paradise." It first observes a man and woman, Felix and Agatha De Lacey, working in the fields. Although the De Laceys have fallen on hard times, from the Monster's viewpoint they live in a perfect environment: "They possessed a delightful house (for such it was in my eyes) and every luxury; they had a fire to warm them when chill, and delicious viands when hungry; they were dressed in excellent clothes; and, still more, they enjoyed one another's company and speech." The weather, in contrast to the cold and damp of the Monster's first days, is magical: "[Rain] frequently took place; but a high wind quickly dried the earth, and the season became far more pleasant than it had been." The cottage is even surrounded by a garden, where their blind father (God?) walks every day, and which is Felix's job to cultivate.

The Monster frequently peers in the window and watches the son and daughter listen to their father play the violin. It remembers being filled with "a mixture of pain and pleasure, such as I had never before experienced ... I withdrew from the window, unable to bear these emotions." Satan feels a similar torment as he spies on Adam and Eve:

> Imparadis't in one another's arms ... while I to
> 　　　　　Hell am thrust,
> Where neither joy nor love, but fierce desire

Among our other torments not the least
Still unfulfilled with pain of longing pines.[9]

The difference, of course, is that Satan knows he is a devil, condemned to
Hell forever, while the Monster still believes it can find a place in the world
of man and nature, even though the old man's violin makes sounds "sweeter
than the thrush or nightingale" while its own attempts at imitating the birds
frighten it into silence. Though it looks vaguely like a man, the Monster
slowly discovers the great gulf between itself and all things human. It recalls,
"I had admired the perfect forms of my cottagers—their grace, beauty, and
delicate complexions; but how was I terrified when I viewed myself in a
transparent pool! At first I started back, unable to believe that it was indeed
I who was reflected in the mirror; and when I became fully convinced that I
was in reality the monster that I am, I was filled with the bitterest sensations
of despondence and mortification. Alas! I did not yet entirely know the fatal
effects of this miserable deformity." The Monster, at this time only able to
form its concepts, from those around it, looks at the reflection as if it were a
man looking at some hideous thing. It is yet to find a model for the totality
of its being.

The Monster does have one remarkable stroke of luck: it manages to
learn much of human history, as well as how to read and speak, by
eavesdropping on Felix, who is conveniently teaching French from a history
book to an Arabian girl. Unlikely as it might be, the episode does explain the
Monster's literacy, as well as introduce it to the long history of human evil
and duplicity. It also leads the Monster to ask itself,

> And what was I? Of my creation and creator I was absolutely
> ignorant, but I knew that I possessed no money, no friends, no
> kind of property. I was, besides, endued with a figure hideously
> deformed and loathsome; I was not even of the same nature as
> man. I was more agile than they, and could subsist upon coarser
> diet; I bore the extremes of heat and cold with less injury to my
> frame; my stature far exceeded theirs. When I looked around, I
> saw and heard of none like me. Was I then a monster, a blot upon
> the earth, from which all men fled, and whom all men disowned?

The recitation of man's history and culture has taught the Monster the extent
of its isolation; nowhere in the world of men does it find a counterpart.

The Monster soon stumbles upon three books: *Paradise Lost*, a volume
of Plutarch's *Lives*, and Goethe's *Sorrows of Werter* [sic]. In the hero of *Werter*

it sees "a more divine being than I ever beheld or imagined," but the novel leads it again to notice how "I found myself similar, yet at the same time strangely unlike to the beings concerning whom I read ... Who was I? What was I?" In Plutarch it finds "high thoughts" but no answer to its question. But *Paradise Lost*, which it reads as a "true history," contains the solution:

> I often referred the several situations, as their similarity struck me to my own. Like Adam, I was apparently united by no link to any other being in existence; but his state was far different from mine in every other respect. He had come forth from the hands of God a perfect creature, happy and prosperous, guarded by the especial care of his Creator ... but I was wretched, helpless, and alone. Many times I considered Satan as the fitter emblem of my condition; for often, like him, when I viewed the bliss of my protectors, the bitter gall of envy rose within me.

Milton, therefore, provides the Monster with an identity. Although not yet rejected by the De Laceys, it recognizes that, like Satan, the happiness of men only goads it to evil. From this moment on, the Monster begins to wear the Satanic cloak it has found. It finds some papers in its pockets, reads of its human creation, yet still uses Milton's metaphor: "Satan had his companions, fellow-devils, to admire and encourage him; but I am solitary and abhorred." However, the Monster still dreams of Paradise and makes one last attempt to enter its gates.

It has been leaving an appropriate gift at the De Laceys' door each morning—a pile of firewood. One day it enters the cottage when only the blind old man is there and attempts to win his sympathy. It still half believes that it is a monster only in appearance, that "a fatal prejudice clouds [men's] eyes, and where they ought to see a feeling and kind friend, they behold only a detestable monster." The old man listens and replies, "it will afford me true pleasure to be in any way serviceable to a *human* creature" (author's italics). When the family returns, the Monster is, of course, chased out as the old man, sensing its inhuman nature, asks "Great God! ... Who are you?" The Monster has learned; its abominable nature cannot be embraced by the old man's sympathy for all things human.

The Monster's response to this rejection, which also drives the De Lacey family from their Eden, is a final confirmation of its Satanic nature. In *Paradise Lost* Satan ends the Council in Hell by vowing to revenge himself upon God by finding a way to destroy God's favored species,

By sudden onset, either with Hell fire
To waste his whole Creation, or possess
All as our own, and drive as we were driven,
The puny habitants, or if not drive,
Seduce them to our party.[10]

The Monster's first reaction to rejection is to feel "rage and revenge. I could with pleasure have destroyed the cottage and its inhabitants, and have glutted myself with their shrieks and misery." It declares: "I, like the arch-fiend, bore a hell within me; and, finding myself unsympathized with, wished to tear up the trees, spread havoc and destruction around me, and then to have sat down and enjoyed the ruin ... from that moment I declared everlasting war against the species, and, more than all, against him who had formed me, and sent me forth to this insupportable misery." The Monster's response to his rejection is finally to give vent to a cosmic, unchecked, and Satanic fury: "... unable to injure any thing human, I turned my fury towards inanimate objects ... [I] destroyed every vestige of cultivation in the garden ... As the night advanced, a fierce wind arose from the woods, and quickly dispersed the clouds that had loitered in the heavens: the blast tore along like a mighty avalanche, and produced a kind of insanity in my spirits, that burst all bounds of reason and reflection." In its fury, the Monster burns down the cabin and heads out to the Hell of the frozen Continent: "Nature decayed around me, and the sun became heatless; rain and snow poured around me; mighty rivers were frozen; the surface of the earth was hard and chill, and bare, and I found no shelter ... The mildness of my nature had fled, and all within me was turned to gall and bitterness."

The Monster returns to its cold Hell, confirmed in its evil. It goes on systematically to murder Frankenstein's family and friends, strangling his young brother, William, with "exultation and hellish triumph," causing the death of his "step-servant," Justine, his best friend, Henry Clerval, and his bride, Elizabeth. At the beginning of its story, the Monster tells Frankenstein, "I ought to be thy Adam; but I am rather the fallen angel, whom thou drivest from joy for no misdeed. Every where I see bliss, from which I alone am irrevocably excluded." At the end, it realizes that "the fallen angel becomes a malignant devil." The Monster's agony as the hideous product of a scientist's flawed vision gives it no place to turn but to Satan for a mirror. The goal of its existence becomes the damnation of its Maker, as it lures Frankenstein to its own isolated Hell on the ice fields of the Arctic. The Monster's crimes, like its isolation, are irrevocably determined by

Frankenstein's crime of giving awareness to a thing that can never find a place in the world of man and nature. Therefore the importance of Milton's epigraph

> Did I request thee, Maker, from my clay
> To mould me Man? Did I solicit thee
> From darkness to promote me?—[11]

In Milton's poem, Adam asks this of his God; in Mrs. Shelley's novel, Frankenstein's would-be Adam asks it of man. Once given life, the products of an unnatural technology can never fit into the natural world and, in Mrs. Shelley's view, must inevitably come to oppose it. Their methods are Satan's—either direct destruction or the "seduction" of man to their side. Thus the danger inherent in the Monster's eloquent, persuasive, but diabolical arguments for its own survival.

When the Monster finishes its tale, it asks its creator to build it a mate, promising they will go off together to the "wilds of South America" and never bother mankind again. But, Frankenstein has learned the lesson of the Monster's story. In the Council in Hell in *Paradise Lost*, one of the devils, Mammon, argues like the Monster that the devils should abandon their fight against God and build a separate isolated kingdom. But Beelzebub, supporting Satan, replies that it is the devils' unalterable nature to oppose God. Frankenstein similarly replies, "How long can you, who long for the love and sympathy of man, persevere in this exile? You will return, and again seek their kindness, and you will meet with their detestation; your evil passions will be renewed, and you will then have a companion to aid you in the task of destruction." Frankenstein also fears the Monster's Satanic guile: "May not even this be a feint that will increase your triumph by affording a wider scope for revenge?" He is nevertheless almost convinced but destroys the Monster's bride-to-be at the last moment, realizing that by allowing the products of technology to proliferate he will only increase the danger to mankind: "one of the first results of those sympathies for which the daemon thirsted would be children, and a race of devils would be propagated on earth, who might make the very species of man a condition precarious and full of terror."

He ignores the obvious solution—as creator, he could surely leave out a part or two to insure foolproof birth control. But the assumption that they will be fertile helps the technological prophecy. The "new species" created to "bless man" has become a potential race of devils plotting to make the human species extinct. Like any living thing, man's creations will cling to life; their lives must, however, ultimately thrive at the expense of their creators, since both cannot share the same world. Technology need not threaten us by a sudden assault on our world. Instead, it can slowly build its own empire, propagate a "race of devils," and transform earth into a Hell suitable for its existence. At the time Mrs. Shelley worked on *Frankenstein*, what Blake called the "dark Satanic Mills" of the Industrial Revolution were pouring an inferno of smoke and fire over the English landscape and subjecting workers to the relentless rhythm of the machine. Byron's maiden speech in the House of Lords, on February 27, 1812, concerned the mobs of displaced laborers who were threatened by Parliament with execution for wrecking the new machinery. It may indeed have seemed that the old world was crumbling and a new kingdom was taking shape.

At the end of *Paradise Lost* Adam is given a vision of man's future history; he learns that eventually his suffering will end and that, through Christ, he will come to know Paradise again. *Frankenstein* has no such optimistic vision, though it does hold out some hope for a more rational science. The tale told to Walton is a warning—made clear by Frankenstein's final assessment of his treatment of the Monster:

> During these last days I have been occupied in examining my past conduct; nor do I find it blameable. In a fit of enthusiastic madness I created a rational creature and was bound towards him, to assure, as far as was in my power, his happiness and well-being. That was my duty; but there was another still paramount to that. My duties towards the beings of my own species had greater claims to my attention, because they included a greater proportion of happiness or misery. Urged by this view, I refused, and I did right in refusing, to create a companion for the first creature. He showed unparalleled malignity and selfishness, in evil: he destroyed my friends; he devoted to destruction beings who possessed exquisite sensations, happiness, and wisdom; nor do I know where this thirst for vengeance may end. Miserable himself, that he might render no other, wretched, he ought to die."

Frankenstein asks Walton to destroy the Monster, warning him of its Satanic nature: The Monster "is eloquent and persuasive; and once his words had even power over my heart; but trust him not. His soul is as hellish as his form, full of treachery and fiendlike malice." The Monster tells Walton that it was the "slave, not the master of an impulse which I detested, yet could not disobey" and that its murders tortured its heart, even while it was committing them." We are reminded of its subservience to Frankenstein's unconscious wishes, as well as Satan's lament,

> Ay, me, they little know
> How dearly I abide that boast so vain
> Under what torments I inwardly groan
> While they adore me on the Throne of Hell
> The lower still I fall, Only Supreme
>   In misery.[12]

The truth is contained in an even closer paraphrase of Milton, when the Monster admits to Walton that "evil thenceforth became my good ... The completion of my demonical design became an insatiable passion."

Walton at first feels pity, but then, looking at the corpse of his only friend, sees the true face of the Monster. He calls it a "hypocritical fiend," realizing "if he whom you mourn still lived, still would he be the object, again would he become the prey, of your accursed vengeance. It is not pity that you feel; you lament only because the victim of your malignity is withdrawn from your power." The last human being it meets spurns the Monster, with reason. Walton knows that the impossibility of man's acceptance only drives the Monster to "hellish malice," just as the exclusion of Satan from God's love leads him to further damn himself. As a symbol for a demonic technology, the Monster never loses the pathetic quality of an abandoned child that strikes out at a world It can never join. Throughout the Monster's story, the human and natural world was a kind of Paradise from which it alone excluded. When it decides to travel to the North Pole, the farthest point from all of humanity, and there somehow find enough wood to build its funeral pyre, it seeks the culmination of its Satanic identity. Mrs. Shelley was reading Dante while working on *Frankenstein* and, at the bottom of his Hell, at the greatest distance from God, she found Lucifer, locked in ice. The Monster's vision of its own destruction, in the center of a frozen landscape, "exult[ing] in the agony of the torturing flames," brings together the images of cold and fire that accompanied it since its first awakening and finally gives the Monster a place in the mythological cosmos it can call its own.

Born of Frankenstein's megalomania, the Monster through its growing awareness of its identity defines the dimensions of its maker's dangerous madness and ties together the many threads of Mary Shelley's novel. Linked in life and death, Frankenstein and Monster are separate entities and one being, a Lucifer/Satan who play out the Romantic closet drama of the mind, the myth of self-exploration and self-awareness, on a stage that spans the terra incognita of space and time, the unexplored Arctic, and the unexperienced future. The power of technology gives Frankenstein's dream self a concrete reality and a separate existence, allowing it to act out its maker's fantasies with terrible results. That it becomes a devil is determined by the nature of Frankenstein's experiment and his blindness to his own motivations. Both creator and creature are presented to Walton as an object lesson, a warning of where a narcissistic science can lead.[13]

The end of the novel is ambiguous. Frankenstein has been led to the Arctic wastes by his Monster and dies with nothing but his dreams to sustain him. Although he has reminded Walton of his paramount duties toward his fellow man, Frankenstein's last words betray his ignorance of the meaning of his own destruction: "Seek happiness in tranquillity, and avoid ambition, even if it be only the apparently innocent one of distinguishing yourself in science and discoveries. Yet why do I say this? I have myself been blasted in these hopes, yet another may succeed." Walton only turns his ship around at the instigation of his crew, feeling "ignorant and disappointed" and condemning their "cowardice and indecision." But he has learned that his explorations must begin with true concern for his fellow man. Rather than sacrificing human life to his own desire for knowledge and power, he realizes that he cannot lead his crew "unwillingly to danger," that "… it is terrible to reflect that the lives of all these men are endangered through me. If we are lost, my mad schemes are the cause."

Mrs. Shelley leaves Walton on the Polar Sea, heading south, toward the rest of the human race. He has met the Monster and cast it back into the darkness, having seen the demonic results of isolation and monomania. At the start of his journey he believed he could escape his own self through scientific exploration, comparing his feelings as he set out to "the joy a child feels when he embarks in a little boat, with his holiday mates, on an expedition of discovery up his native river." Through Frankenstein's parallel tale, he discovers where that "native river" actually leads—"to the forgotten sources" of the "mountain river" of his past. The insight of *Frankenstein* is that awareness of the self and hope for the future of humanity are inextricably bound together.

In Canto XXXI of the *Inferno*, Dante is shown the Titans, who struggled against God, at the edge of the frozen pool of Cocytus, in the last circle of Hell. Although not mentioned in the poem, Prometheus, a Titan, presumably would be found there as well. When Walton watches

Frankenstein waste away from cold and deprivation on his icebound ship he, like Dante, witnesses the terrible punishment extracted for the crime of pride and rebellion against the natural order. Both travelers journey past suffering to a greater understanding of themselves and the universe. In the fourteenth century, Hell awaited the sinner after death; at the start of the Industrial Revolution, a new Inferno threatened to engulf the future of mankind. The message Walton brings back from the Arctic is directed to "Mrs. Saville" and the modern world, and meant, like Dante's poem, to show the way to salvation. If man is to be saved he must join Mary Shelley in seeking a path out of what she once called "the icy region this heart encircles."

NOTES

1. *Shelley's Prose, or the Trumpet of Prophecy*, ed. David Lee Clarke (Albuquerque: University of New Mexico Press, 1954), pp. 54–55. Some later examples of this reading are Milton Millhauser, "The Noble Savage in Mary Shelley's *Frankenstein*," *Notes and Queries*, 90 (1946), pp. 248–50; Milton Mays, "*Frankenstein*: Mary Shelley's Black Theodicy," *Southern Humanities Review*, 3 (1969), pp. 146–53; Wilfred Cude, "Mary Shelley's Modern Prometheus: A Study in the Ethics of Scientific Creativity," *Dalhousie Review*, 52 (1972), pp. 212–25; George Levine, "Frankenstein and the Tradition of Realism," *Novel*, 7 (fall 1973), pp. 14–30. The argument is neatly summed up in a sample term paper by Anita Brooks, "Frankenstein's Lonely Monster," *Practical English Handbook*, 4th ed., (Boston: Houghton Mifflin, 1974), pp. 291–309.

2. My information on the wild man comes from Richard Bernheimer, *Wild Men in the Middle Ages* (New York: Octagon, 1970). For other possible ancestors of the Monster, see Burton Pollin, "Philosophical and Literary Sources of *Frankenstein*," *Comparative Literature*, 7 (1965), pp. 97–108; Oliver Emerson, "Legends of Cain in Old and Middle English," *PMLA*, 21 (1906), pp. 831–929; Daniel Cohen, *A Modern Look at Monsters*, (New York: Dodd, Mead, 1970). An interesting antecedent for the concept of a technological monster can be found in the "Tales, Fables, and Prophecies" of Leonardo Da Vinci; he writes of a giant from the Libyan desert who tramples men like ants—a vision, perhaps, of the monstrous potential of his military inventions (*The Notebooks of Leonardo Da Vinci*, ed. Robert Linscott [New York: Modern Library, 1957], pp. 415–17).

3. Jean Jacques Rousseau, The Social Contract and Discourse on the Origin and Foundation of Inequality Among Mankind (1762) (New York: Washington Square Press, 1971), p. 179.

4. Lester G. Crocker, *Jean Jacques Rousseau: The Quest (1712–1758)* (New York: Macmillan, 1968), Vol. I, 257.

5. John Milton, *Paradise Lost, Works*, Vol. II, Part One, ed. Frank Allen Patterson (New York: Columbia University Press, 1931). Book II, ll. 587–88.

6. Milton Book II, ll. 598–600.

7. Milton Book II, ll. 615–21.

8. Milton Book II, ll. 624–27.

9. Milton Book II, ll. 506–11.

10. Milton Book II, ll. 364–68.

11. Milton Book X, ll. 743–45.

12. Milton Book IV, ll. 86–92.

13. A point first made by M.A. Goldberg, "Moral and Myth in Mrs. Shelley's *Frankenstein*," *Keats-Shelley Journal*, 8 (1959), pp. 27–38.

JOYCE CAROL OATES

Frankenstein's Fallen Angel

"Am I to be thought the only criminal, when all human kind sinned against me?"

—FRANKENSTEIN'S DEMON

Quite apart from its enduring celebrity, and its proliferation in numberless extraliterary forms, Mary Shelley's *Frankenstein; or, The Modern Prometheus* is a remarkable work. A novel *sui generis*, if a novel at all, it is a unique blending of Gothic, fabulist, allegorical, and philosophical materials. Though certainly one of the most calculated and *willed* of fantasies, being in large part a kind of gloss upon or rejoinder to John Milton's *Paradise Lost*, *Frankenstein* is fueled by the kind of grotesque, faintly absurd, and wildly inventive images that spring direct from the unconscious: the eight-foot creature designed to be "beautiful," who turns out almost indescribably repulsive (yellow-skinned, shriveled of countenance, with straight black lips and near-colorless eyes); the cherished cousin-bride who is beautiful but, in the mind's dreaming, yields horrors ("As I imprinted the first kiss on her lips, they became livid with the hue of death; her features appeared to change, and I thought that I held the corpse of my dead mother in my arms; a shroud enveloped her form, and I saw the grave-worms crawling in the folds"); the mad dream of the Arctic as a country of "eternal light" that will prove, of

From *Critical Inquiry*, Vol. 10, No. 3 (March 1984). © 1984 The University of Chicago Press.

course, only a place of endless ice, the appropriate landscape for Victor Frankenstein's death and his demon's self-immolation.

Central to Frankenstein—as it is central to a vastly different nineteenth-century romance, *Jane Eyre*—is a stroke of lightning that appears to issue in a dazzling "stream of fire" from a beautiful old oak tree ("So soon the light vanished, the oak had disappeared, and nothing remained but a blasted stump"): the literal stimulus for Frankenstein's subsequent discovery of the cause of generation and life. And according to Mary Shelley's prefatory account of the origin of her "ghost story," the very image of Frankenstein and his demon-creature sprang from a waking dream of extraordinary vividness:

> I did not sleep, nor could I be said to think. My imagination, unbidden, possessed and guided me, gifting the successive images that arose in my mind with a vividness far beyond the usual bound of reverie. I saw—with shut eyes, but acute mental vision—I saw the pale student of unhallowed arts kneeling beside the thing he had put together. I saw the hideous phantasm of a man stretched out, and then, on the working of some powerful engine, show signs of life, and stir with an uneasy, half-vital motion.... The student sleeps: but he is awakened; he opens his eyes: behold the horrid thing stands at his bedside, opening his curtains, and looking on him with yellow, watery, but speculative eyes.

Hallucinatory and surrealist on its deepest level, *Frankenstein* is of course one of the most self-consciously literary "novels" ever written: its awkward form is the epistolary Gothic; its lyric descriptions of natural scenes (the grandiose Valley of Chamounix in particular) spring from Romantic sources; its speeches and monologues echo both Shakespeare and Milton; and, should the author's didactic intention not be clear enough, the demon-creature educates himself by studying three books of symbolic significance— Goethe's *Sorrows of Young Werther*, Plutarch's *Lives*, and Milton's *Paradise Lost*. (The last conveniently supplies him with a sense of his own predicament, as Mary Shelley hopes to dramatize it. He reads Milton's great epic as if it were a "true history" giving the picture of an omnipotent God warring with His creatures; he identifies himself with Adam, except so far as Adam had come forth from God a "perfect creature, happy and prosperous." Finally, of course, he identifies with Satan: "I am thy creature: I ought to be thy Adam; but I am rather the fallen angel, whom thou drivest from joy for no misdeed. Everywhere I see bliss, from which I alone am irrevocably excluded. I was benevolent and good; misery made me a fiend. Make me happy, and I shall again be virtuous.")

The search of medieval alchemists for the legendary philosophers' stone (the talismanic process by which base metals might be transformed into gold or, in psychological terms, the means by which the individual might realize his destiny), Faust's reckless defiance of human limitations and his willingness to barter his soul for knowledge, the fatal search of such tragic figures as Oedipus and Hamlet for answers to the mysteries of their lives— these are the archetypal dramas to which *Frankenstein* bears an obvious kinship. Yet, as one reads, as Frankenstein and his despised shadow-self engage in one after another of the novel's many dialogues, it begins to seem as if the nineteen-year-old author is discovering these archetypal elements for the first time. Frankenstein "is" a demonic parody (or extension) of Milton's God; he "is" *Prometheus plasticator*, the creator of mankind; but at the same time, by his own account, he is totally unable to control the behavior of his demon (variously called "monster," "fiend," "wretch," but necessarily lacking a name). Surprisingly, it is not by way of the priggish and "self-devoted" young scientist that Mary Shelley discovers the great power of her narrative but by way of the misshapen demon, with whom most readers identify: "My person was hideous, and my stature gigantic: What did this mean? Who was I? What was I? Whence did I come? What was my destination?" It is not simply the case that the demon—like Satan and Adam in *Paradise Lost*—has the most compelling speeches in the novel and is far wiser and more magnanimous than his creator: he is also the means by which a transcendent love—a romantically *unrequited love*—is expressed. Surely one of the secrets of *Frankenstein*, which helps to account for its abiding appeal, is the demon's patient, unquestioning, utterly faithful, and utterly human love for his irresponsible creator.

When Frankenstein is tracking the demon into the Arctic regions, for instance, it is clearly the demon who is helping him in his search, and even leaving food for him; but Frankenstein is so blind—in fact so comically blind—he believes that "spirits" are responsible. "Yet still a spirit of good followed and directed my steps, and, when I most murmured, would suddenly extricate me from seemingly insurmountable difficulties. Sometimes, when nature, overcome by hunger, sunk under the exhaustion, a repast was prepared for me in the desert, that restored and inspirited me.... I may not doubt that it was set there by the spirits that I had invoked to aid me."

By degrees, with the progression of the fable's unlikely plot, the inhuman creation becomes increasingly human while his creator becomes increasingly inhuman, frozen in a posture of rigorous denial. (He is blameless of any wrongdoing in terms of the demon and even dares to tell Walton, literally with his dying breath, that another scientist might succeed where he had failed!—the lesson of the "Frankenstein monster" is revealed as totally lost on Frankenstein himself.) The demon is (sub)human consciousness-in-the-making, naturally benevolent as Milton's Satan is not, and received with horror and contempt solely because of his physical appearance. He is sired without a mother in defiance of nature, but he is in one sense an infant—a comically monstrous eight-foot baby—whose progenitor rejects him immediately after creating him, in one of the most curious (and dreamlike) scenes in the novel:

> "How can I describe my emotions at this catastrophe, or how delineate the wretch whom, with such infinite pains and care, I had endeavored to form? ... I had worked hard for nearly two years, for the sole purpose of infusing life into an inanimate body. For this I had deprived myself of rest and health. I had desired it with an ardor that far exceeded moderation; but now that I had finished, the beauty of the dream vanished, and breathless horror and disgust filled my heart. Unable to endure the aspect of the being I had created, I rushed out of the room, and continued a long time traversing my bed-chamber, unable to compose my mind to sleep."

Here follows the nightmare vision of Frankenstein's bride-to-be, Elizabeth, as a form of his dead mother, with "grave-worms crawling" in her shroud; and shortly afterward the "wretch" himself appears at Frankenstein's bed, drawing away the canopy as Mary Shelley had imagined. But Frankenstein is so cowardly he runs away again; and this time the demon is indeed abandoned, to reappear only after the first of the "murders" of Frankenstein's kin. On the surface, Frankenstein's behavior is preposterous, even idiotic, for he seems blind to the fact that is apparent to any reader—that he has loosed a fearful power into the world, whether it strikes his eye as aesthetically pleasing or not, and he *must* take responsibility for it. Except, of course, he does not. For, as he keeps telling himself, he is blameless of any wrongdoing apart from the act of creation itself. The emotions he catalogs for us—gloom, sorrow, misery, despair—are conventionally Romantic attitudes, mere luxuries in a context that requires *action* and not simply *response*.

By contrast the demon is all activity, all yearning, all hope. His love for his maker is unrequited and seems incapable of making any impression upon

Frankenstein; yet the demon never gives it up, even when he sounds most threatening: "Beware," says the demon midway in the novel, "for I am fearless, and therefore powerful. I will watch with the wiliness of a snake, that I may sting with its venom. Man, you shall repent of the injuries you inflict." His voice is very like his creator's—indeed, everyone in *Frankenstein* sounds alike—but his posture is always one of simple need: he requires love in order to become less monstrous, but, as he is a monster, love is denied him; and the man responsible for this comically tragic state of affairs says repeatedly that he is not to blame. Frankenstein's typical response to the situation is: "I felt as if I had committed some great crime, the consciousness of which haunted me. I was guiltless, but I had indeed drawn a horrible curse upon my head, as mortal as that of crime." But if Frankenstein is not to blame for the various deaths that occur, who is? Had he endowed his creation, as God endowed Adam in Milton's epic, with free will? Or is the demon psychologically his creature, committing the forbidden acts Frankenstein wants committed?—so long as Frankenstein himself remains "guiltless."

It is a measure of the subtlety of this moral parable that the demon strikes so many archetypal chords and suggests so many variant readings. He recapitulates in truncated form the history of consciousness of his race (learning to speak, read, write, etc., by closely watching the De Lacey family); he is an abandoned child, a parentless orphan; he takes on the voices of Adam, Satan ("Evil thenceforth became my good," he says, as Milton's fallen angel says, "Evil be thou my good"), even our "first mother," Eve. When the demon terrifies himself by seeing his reflection in a pool, and grasping at once the nature of his own deformity, he is surely not mirroring Narcissus, as some commentators have suggested, but Milton's Eve in her surprised discovery of her own beauty, in book 4 of *Paradise Lost*:

> I thither went
> With unexperienc't thought, and laid me down
> On the green bank, to look into the clear
> Smooth Lake, that to me seem'd another Sky.
> As I bent down to look, just opposite,
> A Shape within the wat'ry gleam appear'd
> Bending to look on me, I started back,
> It started back, but pleas'd I soon return'd,
> Pleas'd it return'd as soon with answering looks
> Of sympathy and love; there I had fixt
> Mine eyes till now, and pin'd with vain desire
>
> [ll. 456–66][1]

He is Shakespeare's Edmund, though unloved—a shadow figure more tragic, because more "conscious," than the hero he represents. Most suggestively, he has become by the novel's melodramatic conclusion a form of Christ: sinned against by all humankind, yet fundamentally blameless, and yet quite willing to die as a sacrifice. He speaks of his death as a "consummation"; he is going to burn himself on a funeral pyre somewhere in the Arctic wastes—unlikely, certainly, but a fitting end to a life conceived by way of lightning and electricity:

> "But soon," he cried with sad and solemn enthusiasm, "I shall die, and what I now feel be no longer felt. Soon these burning miseries will be extinct. I shall ascend my funeral pile triumphantly, and exult in the agony of the torturing flames. The light of that conflagration will fade away; my ashes will be swept into the sea by the winds. My spirit will sleep in peace; or, if it thinks, it will not surely think thus."

But the demon does not die within the confines of the novel, so perhaps he has not died after all. He is, in the end, a "modern" species of shadow or *Doppelgänger—the nightmare that is deliberately created by man's ingenuity* and not a mere supernatural being or fairy-tale remnant.

*   *   *

Frankenstein's double significance as a work of prose fiction and a cultural myth—as "novel" of 1818 and timeless "metaphor"—makes it a highly difficult story to read directly. A number of popular misconceptions obscure it for most readers: Frankenstein is of course *not* the monster, but his creator; nor is he a mad scientist of genius—he is in fact a highly idealistic and naive youth in the conventional Romantic mode (in Walton's admiring eyes, "noble," "cultivated," a "celestial spirit" who has suffered "great and unparalleled misfortunes"), not unlike Mary Shelley's fated lover Shelley. Despite the fact that a number of catastrophes occur around him and indirectly because of him, Victor Frankenstein is well intentioned, gentlemanly, *good*. He is no sadist like H. G. Wells' exiled vivisectionist Dr. Moreau, who boasts: "You cannot imagine the strange colorless delight of these intellectual desires. The thing before you is no longer an animal, a fellow-creature, but a problem."[2] Frankenstein's mission, on the other hand, is selfless, even messianic:

"No one can conceive the variety of feelings which bore me onwards, like a hurricane, in the first enthusiasm of success. Life and death appeared to me ideal bounds, which I should first break through, and pour a torrent of light into our dark world. A new species would bless me as its creator and source; many happy and excellent natures would owe their being to me. No father could claim the gratitude of his child so completely as I should deserve theirs.... If I could bestow animation upon lifeless matter, I might in the process of time ... renew life where death had apparently devoted the body to corruption."

It is a measure of the novel's extraordinary fame that the very name "Frankenstein" has long since supplanted "Prometheus" in popular usage; and the Frankenstein legend retains a significance for our time as the Prometheus legend does not.

How many fictional characters, after all, have made the great leap from literature to mythology? How many creations of sheer language have stepped from the rhythms of their authors' idiosyncratic voices into what might be called a collective cultural consciousness? Don Quixote, Dracula, Sherlock Holmes, Alice (in Wonderland), certain figures in the fairy tales of Hans Christian Andersen ... and of course Frankenstein's "monster." Virtually millions of people who have never heard of the novel *Frankenstein*, let alone that a young Englishwoman named Mary Shelley (in fact Godwin) wrote it at the age of nineteen, are well acquainted with the image of Frankenstein popularized by Boris Karloff in the 1930s and understand, at least intuitively, the ethical implications of the metaphor. (As in the expression, particularly relevant for our time, "We have created a Frankenstein monster.") The more potent the archetype evoked by a work of literature, the more readily its specific form slips free of the time-bound *personal* work. On the level of cultural myth, the figures of Dracula, Sherlock Holmes, Alice, and the rest are near-autonomous beings, linked to no specific books and no specific authors. They have become communal creations; they belong to us all. Hence the very real difficulty in reading Mary Shelley's novel for the first time. (Subsequent readings are far easier and yield greater rewards.)

Precisely because of this extraordinary fame, one should be reminded of how original and unique the novel was at the time of its publication. Can it even be read at the present time in a context hospitable to its specific allusions and assumptions—one conversant with the thorny glories of *Paradise Lost*, the sentimental ironies of Coleridge's "Rime of the Ancient

Mariner," the Gothic conventions of tales-within-tales, epistolary frames, and histrionic speeches delivered at length? In a more accomplished work, *Wuthering Heights*, the structural complexities of tales-within-tales are employed for artistic ends: the ostensible fracturing of time yields a rich poetic significance; characters grow and change like people whom we have come to know. In Mary Shelley's *Frankenstein* the strained conventions of the romance are mere structural devices to allow Victor Frankenstein and his demon their opposing—but intimately linked—"voices." Thus, abrupt transitions in space and time take place in a kind of rhetorical vacuum: all is summary, past history, *exemplum*.

But it is a mistake to read *Frankenstein* as a modern novel of psychological realism, or as a "novel" at all. It contains no characters, only points of view; its concerns are pointedly moral and didactic; it makes no claims for verisimilitude of even a poetic Wordsworthian nature. (The Alpine landscapes are all self-consciously sublime and theatrical; Mont Blanc, for instance, suggests "another earth, the habitations of another race of beings.") If one were pressed to choose a literary antecedent for *Frankenstein*, it might be, surprisingly, Samuel Johnson's *Rasselas*, rather than a popular Gothic work like Mrs. Radcliffe's *Mysteries of Udolpho*, which allegedly had the power to frighten its readers. (A character in Jane Austen's *Northanger Abbey* says of this once famous novel: "I remember finishing it in two days—my hair standing on end the whole time.") Though *Frankenstein* and *Dracula* are commonly linked, Bram Stoker's tour de force of 1897 is vastly different in tone, theme, and intention from Mary Shelley's novel: its "monster" is not at all monstrous in appearance, only in behavior; and he is thoroughly and irremediably evil by nature. But no one in *Frankenstein* is evil—the universe is emptied of God and of theistic assumptions of "good" and "evil." Hence, its modernity.

Tragedy does not arise spontaneous and unwilled in so "modern" a setting; it must be made—in fact, manufactured. The Fates are not to blame; there *are* no Fates, only the brash young scientist who boasts of never having feared the supernatural. ("In my education my father had taken the greatest precautions that my mind should be impressed with no supernatural horrors. I do not ever remember to have trembled at a tale of superstition, or to have feared the apparition of a spirit…. A churchyard was to me merely the receptacle of bodies deprived of life, which, from being the seat of beauty and strength, had become food for the worm.") Where *Dracula* and other conventional Gothic works are fantasies, with clear links to fairy tales and legends, and even popular ballads, *Frankenstein* has the theoretical and cautionary tone of science fiction. It is meant to prophesy, not to entertain.

Another aspect of *Frankenstein's* uniqueness lies in the curious bond between Frankenstein and his created demon. Where, by tradition, such beings as doubles, shadow-selves, "imps of the perverse," and classic *Doppelgängers* (like poor Golyadkin's nemesis in Dostoevsky's *Double* [1846]) spring full grown from supernatural origins—that is, from unacknowledged recesses of the human spirit—Frankenstein's demon is *natural* in origin: a manufactured nemesis. He is an abstract idea made flesh, a Platonic essence given a horrific (and certainly ludicrous) existence. Yet though he is meant to be Frankenstein's ideal, a man-made miracle that would "pour a torrent of light into our dark world," he is only a fragment of that ideal—which is to say, a mockery, a parody, a joke. The monsters we create by way of an advanced technological civilization "are" ourselves as we cannot hope to see ourselves—incomplete, blind, blighted, and, most of all, self-destructive. For it is the forbidden wish for death that dominates. (In intention it is customarily the deaths of others, "enemies"; in fact it may be our own deaths we plan.) Hence the tradition of recognizing Faustian pacts with the devil as acts of aggression against the human self—the very "I" of the rational being.

Since Frankenstein's creature is made up of parts collected from charnel houses and graves and his creator acknowledges that he "disturbed, with profane fingers, the tremendous secrets of the human frame," it is inevitable that the creature be a *profane* thing. He cannot be blessed or loved: he springs not from a natural union but has been forged in what Frankenstein calls a "workshop of filthy creation." One of the brilliant surrealist touches of the narrative is that Frankenstein's shadow-self is a giant; even the rationalization for this curious decision is ingenious. "As the minuteness of the parts formed a great hindrance to my speed," Frankenstein explains to Walton, "I resolved, contrary to my first intention, to make the being of a gigantic stature; that is to say, about eight feet in height, and proportionably large." A demon of mere human size would not have been nearly so compelling.[3]

(The reader should keep in mind that, in 1818, the notion that "life" might be galvanized in laboratory conditions was really not so farfetched, for the properties of electricity were not commonly understood and seem to have been bound up magically with what might be called metaphorically the "spark" of life.[4] Again, in 1984, the possibility of artificially induced life, human or otherwise, does not seem especially remote.)

Because in one sense the demon is Frankenstein's deepest self, the relationship between them is dreamlike, fraught with undefined emotion. Throughout the novel Frankenstein is susceptible to fainting fits, bouts of illness and exhaustion, and nightmares of romantic intensity—less a fully realized personality than a queer stunted half-self (rather like Roderick Usher, whose sister Madeleine, *his* secret self, is buried alive). It is significant that as soon as Frankenstein induces life in his eight-foot monster, he notices *for the first time* what he has created. "His limbs were in proportion," Frankenstein testifies, "and I had selected his features as beautiful." But something has clearly gone wrong:

> "Beautiful! Great God! His yellow skin scarcely covered the work of muscles and arteries beneath; his hair was of a lustrous black, and flowing; his teeth of a pearly whiteness; but these luxuriances only formed a more horrid contrast with his watery eyes, that seemed almost of the same color as the dun white sockets in which they were set, his shrivelled complexion, and straight black lips."

Significant too is the fact that Frankenstein retreats from this vision and falls asleep—an unlikely response in naturalistic terms but quite appropriate symbolically—so that, shortly afterward, his demon can arouse *him* from sleep:

> "I started from my sleep with horror; a cold dew covered my forehead, my teeth chattered, and every limb became convulsed; when, by the dim and yellow light of the moon, as it forced its way through the window-shutters, I beheld the wretch, the miserable monster whom I had created. He held up the curtain of the bed; and his eyes, if eyes they may be called, were fixed on me. His jaws opened, and he muttered some inarticulate sounds, while a grin wrinkled his cheeks."

> "Oh! no mortal could support the horror of that countenance. A mummy again endued with animation could not be so hideous as that wretch. I had gazed on him while unfinished; he was ugly then; but when those muscles and joints were rendered capable of motion, it became a thing such as Dante could not have conceived."

Frankenstein's superficial response to the "thing" he has created is solely in aesthetic terms, for his atheistic morality precludes all thoughts of transgression. (Considering that the author of *Frankenstein* is a woman, a woman well acquainted with pregnancy and childbirth at a precocious age, it is curious that nowhere in the novel does anyone raise the issue of the demon's "unnatural" genesis: he is a monster-son born of Man exclusively, a parody of the Word or the Idea made Flesh.) Ethically, Frankenstein is "blameless"—though he is haunted by the suspicion throughout that he has committed a crime of some sort, with the very best of intentions.

Where the realistic novel presents characters in a more or less coherent "field," as part of a defined society, firmly established in time and place, romance does away with questions of verisimilitude and plausibility altogether and deals directly with the elements of narrative: it might be said to be an "easier" form psychologically, since it evokes archetypal responses on its primary level. No one expects Victor Frankenstein to behave plausibly when he is a near-allegorical figure; no one expects his demon to behave plausibly since he is a demonic presence, an outsized mirror image of his creator. When the demon warns Frankenstein (in traditional Gothic form, incidentally), "I shall be with you on your wedding-night," it seems only natural, granted Frankenstein's egocentricity, that he worry about his own safety and not his bride's and that, despite the warning, Frankenstein allows Elizabeth to be murdered. His wish is his demon-self's command, though he never acknowledges his complicity. Indeed, *Frankenstein* begins to read as an antiromance, a merciless critique of Romantic attitudes—sorrow, misery, self-loathing, despair, paralysis, etc.—written, as it were, from the inside, by a young woman who had already lost a baby in infancy (in 1815, a girl), would lose another, also a girl, in 1817, and, in 1819, lost a third—named, oddly, William (the very name of the little boy murdered early in the narrative by Frankenstein's demon).[5] Regardless of the sufferings of others, the romantically "self-devoted" hero responds solely in terms of his own emotions. He might be a lyric poet of the early 1800s, for all his preoccupation with self: everything refers tragically to him; everything is rendered in terms of his experience:

> Great God! Why did I not then expire? Why am I here to relate the destruction of the best hope, and the purest creature of earth? [Elizabeth] was there, lifeless and inanimate, thrown across the bed, her head hanging down, and her pale and distorted features half covered by her hair. Everywhere I turn I see the same figure,—her bloodless arms and relaxed form flung by the murderer on its bridal bier. Could I behold this, and live? (Alas, life is obstinate, and clings closest where it is most hated.) For a moment only, and I lost recollection: I fainted.

Frankenstein grapples with the complex moral issues raised by his demonic creation by "fainting" in one way or another throughout the novel. And in his abrogation of consciousness and responsibility, the demon naturally acts: for this *is* the Word, the secret wish for destruction, made Flesh.

The cruelest act of all is performed by Frankenstein before the very eyes of his demon: this is the sudden destruction of the partly assembled "bride." He makes the creature at the bidding of his demon, who has promised, most convincingly, to leave Europe with her and to live "virtuously"; but, suddenly repulsed by the "filthy process" he has undertaken, Frankenstein destroys his work. ("The wretch saw me destroy the creature on whose future existence he depended for happiness, and with a howl of devilish despair and revenge, withdrew.") Afterward he thinks, looking at the remains of the half-finished creature, that he has *almost* mangled the living flesh of a human being; but he never feels any remorse for what he has done and never considers that, in "mangling" the flesh of his demon's bride, he is murdering the pious and rather too perfect Elizabeth, the cousin-bride whom he professes to love. "Am I to be thought the only criminal," the demon asks, "when all human kind sinned against me?" He might have said as reasonably, *when all humankind conspired in my sin.*

While *Paradise Lost* is to Frankenstein's demon (and very likely to Mary Shelley as well) the picture of an "omnipotent God warring with his creatures," *Frankenstein* is the picture of a finite and flawed god at war with, and eventually overcome by, his creation. It is a parable for our time, an enduring prophecy, a remarkably acute diagnosis of the lethal nature of *denial*: denial of responsibility for one's actions, denial of the shadow-self locked within consciousness. Even in the debased and sensational form in which Frankenstein's monster is known by most persons—as a kind of retarded giant, one might say, with electrodes in his neck—his archetypal significance rings true. "My form," he says eloquently, "is a filthy type of yours."

NOTES

1. The influence of John Milton on *Frankenstein* is so general as to figure on nearly every page; and certainly the very conception of the monumental *Paradise Lost* stands behind the conception of Mary Shelley's "ghost story." According to Christopher Small's excellent *Ariel Like a Harpy: Shelley, Mary, and Frankenstein* (London, 1972), Mary Shelley's book list notes *Paradise Regained* as read in 1815, and in 1816 she and Shelley were both

reading *Paradise Lost* at intervals during the year. At one point Shelley read the long poem aloud to her, finishing it in a week in November of 1816.

2. H. G. Wells' *Island of Dr. Moreau* (1896) is a savage variant on the Frankenstein legend. Moreau experiments on living animals, trying to make them "human" or humanoid; he succeeds in creating a race of Beast Folk who eventually rise up against him and kill him. Moreau's beliefs strike a more chilling—and more contemporary—note than Frankenstein's idealism: "To this day I have never troubled about the ethics of the matter. The study of Nature makes a man at last as remorseless as Nature," boasts Moreau.

3. In Robert Louis Stevenson's *Strange Case of Dr. Jekyll and Mr. Hyde* (1886), the undersized and mysteriously deformed Hyde, Jekyll's deliberately willed alter ego, is sheer pitiless appetite, devoid of any of Frankenstein's demon's appealing qualities. He is ugly, stunted, hateful in appearance—but deliberately hateful, for, much more obviously than Frankenstein's well-spoken nemesis, he represents his creator's violent reaction against the restraints of civilization. Stevenson's novella is fascinating for many reasons, one of them being Jekyll's remarkable voice when he confesses his relationship with Hyde and the gradual usurpation of his soul by Hyde's spirit:

> The powers of Hyde seemed to have grown with the sickliness of Jekyll. And certainly the hate that divided them was equal on each side. With Jekyll, it was a thing of vital instinct. He had now seen the full deformity of that creature that shared with him some of the phenomena of consciousness, and was co-heir with him to death: and beyond these links of community, which in themselves made the most poignant part of his distress, he thought of Hyde, for all his energy of life, as of something not only hellish but inorganic. This was the shocking thing; that the slime of the pit seemed to utter cries and voices; that the amorphous dust gesticulated and sinned; that what was dead, and had no shape, should usurp the offices of life. And this again, that that insurgent horror was knit to him closer than a wife, closer than an eye; lay caged in his flesh, where he heard it mutter and felt it struggle to be born.

4. In Thomas Hogg's *Life of Percy Bysshe Shelley* (1858), Shelley's lifelong fascination with lightning, electricity, and galvanism is discussed at some length. As a boy he owned something called an "electrical machine" with which he amused himself with experiments; as a young man he was mesmerized by lightning and thunder and made it a point to "enjoy" electrical storms.

5. The feminist critic Ellen Moers interprets *Frankenstein* solely in terms of a birth myth "that was lodged in the novelist's imagination ... by the fact that she was herself a mother" ("Female Gothic," *Literary Women* [Garden City, N.Y., 1977], p. 140). Though her argument certainly aids in understanding some of the less evident motives for the composition of *Frankenstein*, it reduces a complex philosophical narrative to little more than a semiconscious fantasy, scarcely a *literary* work at all. Did Mary Shelley's womb, or her brain, write *Frankenstein*? In virtually a parody of feminist mythmaking, Moers argues that Mary Shelley's book is "most powerful" where it is "most feminine": "in the motif of revulsion against newborn life, and the drama of guilt, dread, and flight surrounding birth and its consequences" (p. 142).

ANNE K. MELLOR

Making a Monster

Mary Shelley's waking nightmare on June 16, 1816, inspired one of the most powerful horror stories of Western civilization. It can claim the status of a myth, so profoundly resonant in its implications for our comprehension of our selves and our place in the world that it has become, at least in its barest outline, a trope of everyday life. Of course, both the media and the average person in the street have mistakenly assigned the name of Frankenstein not to the maker of the monster but to his creature. But as we shall see, this "mistake" actually derives from an intuitively correct reading of the novel. *Frankenstein* is our culture's most penetrating literary analysis of the psychology of modern "scientific" man, of the dangers inherent in scientific research, and of the exploitation of nature and of the female implicit in a technological society. So deeply does it probe the collective cultural psyche of the modern era that it deserves to be called a myth, on a par with the most telling stories of Greek and Norse gods and goddesses.

But Mary Shelley's myth is unique, both in content and in origin. *Frankenstein* invents the story of a man's single-handed creation of a living being from dead matter. All other creation myths, even that of the Jewish golem,[1] depend on female participation or some form of divine intervention (either directly or instrumentally through magical rituals or the utterance of holy names or sacred letters). The idea of an entirely man-made monster is

From *Mary Shelley: Her Life, Her Fiction, Her Monsters.* © 1989 by the Taylor and Francis Group.

Mary Shelley's own. And this myth of a man-made monster can be derived from a single, datable event: the waking dream of a specific eighteen-year-old girl on June 16, 1816.[2] Moreover, Mary Shelley created her myth single-handedly. All other myths of the western or eastern worlds, whether of Dracula, Tarzan, Superman or more traditional religious systems, derive from folklore or communal ritual practices.

As myth, Mary Shelley's *Frankenstein*, for all its resonance, has hardly been well explored. While the film industry has exploited and popularized the more salient dimensions of the story, it has ignored the complexity of Mary Shelley's invention—in particular, it has overlooked the significance of the making and unmaking of the female monster. Before Ellen Moers's ground-breaking discussion of *Frankenstein* in *The New York Review of Books* in 1973, literary scholars and critics had for the most part discussed Mary Shelley's career merely as an appendage to her husband's, dismissing *Frankenstein* as a badly written children's book even though far more people were familiar with her novel than with Percy Shelley's poetry. Feminist critics have, of course, noted the injustice of this; in the last fifteen years they have begun to explore the multi-layered significance of *Frankenstein*.[3] In the discussion that follows, I shall look at the novel from several different perspectives—feminist, biographical, psychological, textual, historical, and philosophical. I wish to assess the many ways in which *Frankenstein* portrays the consequences of the failure of the family, the damage wrought when the mother—or a nurturant parental love—is absent.

I have throughout referred to the manuscript and to the first (1818) edition of *Frankenstein*, since these present a more coherent literary vision generated from the most immediate psychological and social experiences of the author. The most often reprinted second edition of 1831 was substantively revised by Mary Shelley in an attempt to interpolate a later and in some ways contradictory concept of nature and the human will, a concept produced by the traumatic deaths of her husband and children. The three versions of *Frankenstein*—manuscript, 1818 edition, and 1831 edition—constitute a text-in-process whose stages differ as much as do the various texts of Wordsworth's *Prelude*, albeit for different reasons.

Perhaps I should explain why *Frankenstein* receives a more extended discussion in this book than do Mary Shelley's other novels. Not only is this novel Shelley's most famous, most complex, and most culturally resonant, but it was also written at a time in her life—before the deaths of her children, Clara Everina and William, and her husband—when her imagination was free to explore and articulate the profound ambivalences in her relationship with Percy Shelley. Her later novels suffer from her obsessive need to idealize her husband and the bourgeois family, the results of which are overly sentimental rhetoric and implausible plot-resolutions. Nonetheless, as I shall try to show, these later novels are fascinating for the ways in which they reveal the development of Mary Shelley's thought and undermine the very ideals they purport to affirm.

From a feminist viewpoint, *Frankenstein* is a book about what happens when a man tries to have a baby without a woman. As such, the novel is profoundly concerned with natural as opposed to unnatural modes of production and reproduction. Ellen Moers first drew our attention to the novel's emphasis on birth and "the trauma of the after-birth."[4] Since this is a novel about giving birth, let us begin with the question of origins, "the question," as Mary Shelley acknowledged in her Introduction to the revised edition of *Frankenstein* of 1831, "so very frequently asked me—'How I, then a young girl, came to think of, and to dilate upon, so very hideous an idea?'" Mary Shelley then tells a story almost as well-known as the novel itself, of how she and Byron and Percy Shelley and Dr. Polidori, after reading ghost stories together one rainy evening near Geneva in June, 1816, agreed each to write an equally thrilling horror story; how she tried for days to think of a story, but failed; and finally, how one night after a discussion among Byron, Polidori, and Percy Shelley concerning galvanism and Erasmus Darwin's success in causing a piece of vermicelli to move voluntarily, she fell into a reverie or waking dream in which she saw "the pale student of unhallowed arts kneeling beside the thing he had put together" and felt the terror he felt as the hideous corpse he had reanimated with a "spark of life" stood beside his bed, "looking on him with yellow, watery, but speculative eyes."[5]

Why did Mary Shelley have such a dream at this point in her life? Affectively, the dream evoked a powerful anxiety in her. Over fifteen years later, she claimed she could still see vividly the room to which she woke and feel "the thrill of fear" that ran through her. Why was she so frightened? Remember that Mary Shelley had given birth to a baby girl eighteen months earlier, a baby whose death two weeks later produced a recurrent dream: "Dream that my little baby came to life again; that it had only been cold, and that we rubbed it before the fire, and it lived. Awake and find no baby." Once again she was dreaming of reanimating a corpse by warming it with a "spark of life." And only six months before, Mary Shelley had given birth a second time, to William. She doubtless expected to be pregnant again in the near future; and indeed, she conceived her third child, Clara Everina, only six months later in December. Mary Shelley's reverie unleashed her deepest subconscious anxieties, the natural but no less powerful anxieties of a very young, frequently pregnant woman. Clearly, in her dream, Mary Shelley lost her distanced, safely external view of "the pale student"—she initially "saw" him kneeling beside his creation, just as she "saw" the "hideous phantasm" stir into life. Gradually her dream-work drew her into a closer identification with the student. Even as she watched him rush out of the room, she knew how he felt, shared his "terror" at his success and his "hope" that the thing would subside back into dead matter. At the end of her dream, nothing separates the dreamer from the student of unhallowed arts. Even though she continues to use the third person—"he sleeps; he opens his eyes"—she has become the student; she is looking up at the "yellow, watery, but speculative eyes" of the "horrid thing." For only from inside the student's drawn bed-curtains could she see those eyes.

This dream economically fuses Mary Shelley's myriad anxieties about the processes of pregnancy, giving birth, and mothering. It gives shape to her deepest fears. What if my child is born deformed, a freak, a moron, a "hideous" thing? Could I still love it, or would I be horrified and wish it were dead again? What will happen if I can't love my child? Am I capable of raising a healthy, normal child? Will my child die (as my first baby did)? Could I wish my own child to die, to destroy itself? Could I kill it? Could it kill me (as I killed my mother, Mary Wollstonecraft)?

One reason Mary Shelley's story reverberates so strongly is because it articulates, perhaps for the first time in Western literature, the most powerfully felt anxieties of pregnancy. The experience of pregnancy is one that male writers have by necessity avoided; and before Mary Shelley, female writers had considered the experiences of pregnancy and childbirth as improper, even taboo, subjects to be discussed before a male or mixed audience. Mary Shelley's focus on the birth-process illuminates for a male readership hitherto unpublished female anxieties, fears, and concerns about the birth-process and its consequences. At the same time, her story reassures a female audience that such fears are shared by other women.

Mary Shelley's dream thus generates that dimension of the novel's plot which has been much discussed by feminist critics, Victor Frankenstein's total failure at parenting. For roughly nine months, while "winter, spring, and summer, passed away," he labours to give life to his child until, finally, on a dreary night in November, he observes its birth: "I saw the dull yellow eye of the creature open; it breathed hard, and a convulsive motion agitated its limbs."[6] But rather than clasping his newborn child to his breast in a nurturing maternal gesture, he rushes out of the room, repulsed by the abnormality of his creation. And when his child follows him to his bedroom, uttering inarticulate sounds of desire and affection, smiling at him, reaching out to embrace him, Victor Frankenstein again flees in horror, abandoning his child completely.

Frankenstein's failure to mother his child results from an earlier failure of empathy. Throughout his experiment, Frankenstein never considers the possibility that his creature might not wish the existence he is about to receive. On the contrary, he blithely assumes that the creature will "bless" him and be filled with "gratitude" (49). Frankenstein's lack of imaginative identification with his creation, his lack of what Keats would have called "negative capability," causes him to make a critical mistake. In his rush to complete his experiment, and because "the minuteness of the parts formed a great hindrance," he resolves to make his creature "of a gigantic stature; that is to say, about eight feet in height, and proportionably large" (49). He never once considers how such a giant will survive among normal human beings. Nor does he carefully contemplate the features of the creature he is making. "I had selected his features as beautiful. Beautiful!—Great God! His yellow skin scarcely covered the work of muscles and arteries beneath; his hair was of a lustrous black, and flowing; his teeth of a pearly whiteness; but these luxuriances only formed a more horrid contrast with his watery eyes, that seemed almost of the same colour as the dun white sockets in which they were set, his shrivelled complexion, and straight black lips" (52). Frankenstein's inability to sympathize with his child, to care for or even to comprehend its basic needs, soon takes the extreme form of putative infanticide. After his next glimpse of his child, he confesses, "I gnashed my teeth, my eyes became inflamed, and I ardently wished to extinguish that life which I had so thoughtlessly bestowed" (87).

Even after the creature reminds Frankenstein of his parental obligation to provide for his child—"I ought to be thy Adam" (95)—Frankenstein still fails to give him the human companionship, the Eve, the female creature, that he needs to achieve some sort of a normal life. The creature's consequent despair is registered in the epigraph which appears on the title page of each of the three volumes of the first edition. It is Adam's cry of misery at being punished for his freely chosen sin, a cry which—given the creature's innocence—reverberates more poignantly, and ironically, with each reappearance:

> Did I request thee, Maker, from my clay
> To mold me man? Did I solicit thee
> From darkness to promote me?
> (*Paradise Lost*, X, 743–45)

Read rhetorically, these questions sharpen our sense of Frankenstein's responsibility to his creature, and his culpable denial of that responsibility. They articulate the cry of an unfairly punished child: "I never asked to be born!"

Frankenstein's refusal to parent his child is both an impulsive emotional reaction and a deliberate decision. Even on his death-bed Frankenstein stubbornly insists that he has acted correctly. As he confesses to Walton:

> During these last days I have been occupied in examining my past conduct; nor do I find it blameable. In a fit of enthusiastic madness I created a rational creature, and was bound towards him, to assure, as far as was in my power, his happiness and well-being. This was my duty; but there was another still paramount to that. My duties towards my fellow-creatures had greater claims to my attention, because they included a greater proportion of happiness or misery. Urged by this view, I refused, and I did right in refusing, to create a companion for the first creature. He shewed unparalleled malignity and selfishness, in evil: he destroyed my friends; he devoted to destruction beings who possessed exquisite sensations, happiness, and wisdom; nor do I know where this thirst for vengeance may end. Miserable himself, that he may render no other wretched, he ought to die. (215)

Frankenstein's statement is a tissue of self-deception and rationalization. He never once considers whether the creature's "malignity" might have been prevented, as the creature himself repeatedly insists, by loving care in infancy; he never asks whether he was in any way responsible for the creature's development. He relies on a Benthamite utilitarian ethical calculus, the greatest good for the greatest number, without first demonstrating that the creature could not have benefited from the companionship of a female, and without proving that the female creature would have been more malignant than the male (as he claimed when he destroyed her partially finished form). And it never occurs to him that he might have created a female incapable of reproduction. Instead he assumes that the two creatures would share his egotistical desire to produce offspring who would bless and revere them. From the moment of the creature's birth, Frankenstein has rejected it as "demoniacal" (53) and heaped abuse upon it. Frankenstein represents a classic case of a battering parent who produces a battered child who in turn becomes a battering parent: the creature's first murder victim, we must remember, is a small child, whom he wished to adopt.

Throughout the novel, Frankenstein's callous disregard of his responsibility as the sole parent of his only child is contrasted to the examples of two loving fathers: Alphonse Frankenstein and Father De Lacey. Both these fathers assiduously care for their motherless children, providing them with loving homes and moral guidance. "My father ... watched me as a bird does its nestling," remarks Victor Frankenstein, in a passage deleted from the manuscript of the novel (at 183:33). No "More indulgent and less dictatorial parent" than Alphonse Frankenstein exists upon earth, acknowledges Victor (150). And Father De Lacey has a "countenance beaming with benevolence and love" (104). They construct what Lawrence Stone has described as the closed domestic nuclear family of the eighteenth century, which is organized around the principle of personal autonomy and bound together by strong affective ties.[7] Such loving fathers as Alphonse Frankenstein and Father De Lacey are rewarded with the genuine gratitude of their children; Felix and Agatha even starve themselves that their father may eat. Mary Shelley promoted this ideal of the loving family in one of the creature's comments upon his reading:

> Other lessons were impressed upon me even more deeply. I heard of the difference of sexes; of the birth and growth of children; how the father doated on the smiles of the infant, and the lively sallies of the older child; how all the life and cares of the mother were wrapt up in the previous charge; how the mind of youth expanded and gained knowledge; of brother, sister, and all the various relationships which bind one human being to another in mutual bonds. (116–17)

Shelley both anticipates and goes beyond Stone's model of the closed domestic nuclear family, however, by introducing a new element, an egalitarian definition of gender-roles within the bourgeois family. Notice that both the father and the mother are equally devoted to their children; that both boys and girls ("youth") are expected to receive an education; that the same bonds mutually bind persons of opposite gender. Shelley's ideological commitment to a mutually supportive, gender-free family functions in the novel as the ethical touchstone by which the behavior of Victor Frankenstein is found wanting.

As she wrote out her novel, Mary Shelley distanced herself from her originating dream-identification with the anxious and rejecting parent and focused instead on the plight of the abandoned child. Increasingly she identified with the orphaned creature. The heart of this three-volume novel is the creature's account of his own development, which occupies all but thirty pages of the second volume of the first edition. And in this volume, Mary Shelley spoke most directly in her own voice: Percy Shelley's manuscript revisions are far less numerous in Volume II than in Volumes I or III. As she described the creature's first experiences in the world and his desperate attempts to establish a bond of affection with the De Lacey family, Mary Shelley was clearly drawing on her own experiences of emotional isolation in the Godwin household. Specific links join the creature's life to Mary Shelley's own. The creature reads about his conception in the journal of lab reports he grabbed up as he fled from Victor Frankenstein's laboratory (125–26); Mary Shelley could have read about her own conception in Godwin's Diary (where he noted the nights on which he and Mary Wollstonecraft had sexual intercourse during their courtship with a "Chez moi" or a "Chez elle", including every night but two between December 20, 1796, and January 3, 1797). Both the creature and Mary Shelley read the same books. In the years before and during the composition of *Frankenstein*, Mary Shelley read or reread the books found by the creature in an abandoned portmanteau—Goethe's *Werther*, Plutarch's *Lives of the Noble Romans*, Volney's *Ruins or, ... the Revolutions of Empire*, and Milton's *Paradise Lost*, as well as the poets the creature occasionally quotes, Coleridge and Byron.[8] Moreover, as a motherless child and a woman in a patriarchal culture, Mary Shelley shared the creature's powerful sense of being born without an identity, without role-models to emulate, without a history.[9] The creature utters a *cri de coeur* that was Mary Shelley's own: "Who was I? What was I? Whence did I come? What was my destination? These questions continually recurred, but I was unable to solve them" (124).

What the creature does know is that a child deprived of a loving family becomes a monster. Again and again he insists that he was born good but compelled by others into evil: "I was benevolent and good; misery made me a fiend" (95). Granted a mate, he will become good again: "My vices are the children of a forced solitude that I abhor; and my virtues will necessarily arise when I live in communion with an equal" (143). Even after the destruction of all his hopes has condemned him to unremitting vengeance, the creature still insists, "I had feelings of affection, they were requited by detestation and scorn" (165).

The creature's argument is derived in part from Rousseau's *Emile*, which Mary Shelley read in 1816.[10] Rousseau claimed that "God makes all things good; man meddles with them and they become evil."[11] He blamed the moral failings of children specifically upon the absence of a mother's love. Attacking mothers who refuse to nurse or care for their own children in early infancy, Rousseau insists, in a comment that self-servingly ignores a father's parental responsibilities (Rousseau abandoned his own children at the local orphanage):

> Would you restore all men to their primal duties, begin with the mothers; the results will surprise you. Every evil follows in the train of this first sin; the whole moral order is disturbed, nature is quenched in every breast, the home becomes gloomy, the spectacle of a young family no longer stirs the husband's love and the stranger's reverence. (13)

Without mothering, without an early experience of a loving education, writes Rousseau in a statement that the creature's experience vividly confirms, "a man left to himself from birth would be more of a monster than the rest" (5).

Mary Shelley powerfully evoked the creature's psychic response to the conviction that he is destined to be forever an outcast, as alone as the Ancient Mariner on his wide, wide sea—a horrifying spectacle that had haunted Mary Shelley's imagination since she heard Coleridge recite the poem in 1806. Again and again the creature cries out:

> Every where I see bliss, from which I alone am irrevocably excluded. (95)
> I had never yet seen a being resembling me, or who claimed any intercourse with me. What was I? (117)
> Increase of knowledge only discovered to me more clearly what a wretched outcast I was.... no Eve soothed my sorrows, or shared my thoughts; I was alone. (127)

Here Mary Shelley unearthed her own buried feelings of parental abandonment and forced exile from her father. Her creature, disappointed in his long-cherished desire for a welcome from the De Lacey family, feels anger, then a desire for revenge, and finally a violent severing from all that is human, civilized, cultural. "I was like a wild beast that had broken the toils; destroying the objects that obstructed me, and ranging through the wood with a stag-like swiftness ... All, save I, were at rest or in enjoyment: I, like the arch-fiend, bore a hell within me" (132). Both the allusion to Milton's Satan and the image of a beast breaking out of harness focus her argument that a human being deprived of companionship, of nurturing, of mothering, is driven beyond the pale of humanity. The creature has crossed the barrier that separates the human from the bestial, the domesticated from the wild, the cooked from the raw. Symbolically, the creature turns his acculturated love-gifts of firewood back into raw fire by burning the De Lacey cottage to the ground while dancing round it, himself consumed in a frenzy of pure hatred and revenge.

Searching for his only legitimate parent, the creature encounters outside Geneva the five-year-old William Frankenstein. Once more thwarted in his desire for a family when the child refuses to accompany him, his anger claims—perhaps unintentionally—its first human sacrifice. Here, as U. C. Knoepflmacher has suggested, Mary Shelley is uncovering her own repressed aggression.[12] For it can be no accident that the creature's first victim is the exact image of her son William, named after his grandfather Godwin. Having felt rejected by her father, emotionally when he married Mary Jane Clairmont and overtly when she eloped with Percy Shelley, Mary had long repressed a hostility to Godwin that erupted in the murder of his namesake. It is actually his double namesake, since Godwin had given the name William to his own son, who was the favored child in the Godwin–Clairmont household, tenderly nicknamed Love-will by his doting mother. This murder thus raises to consciousness one of the most deeply buried fears energizing Mary Shelley's original dream: *might I be capable of murdering my own flesh and blood?* For William Frankenstein is a deliberate portrait of William Shelley: he has the same "lively blue eyes, dimpled cheeks, and endearing manners" (37), the same "dark eyelashes and curling hair" and propensity to take little wives (62), Louisa Biron being William Frankenstein's favorite playmate, where Allegra Byron was William Shelley's choice. The creature's calculated strangling of the blue-eyed, blond-haired, manly boy articulates both Mary Shelley's horrified recognition that she is capable of imagining the murder of her own child—capable of infanticide itself—and her instinctive revulsion against that act. As she suggests, a rejected and unmothered child can become a killer, especially the killer of its own parents, siblings, children. When the nuclear family fails to mother its offspring, it engenders homicidal monsters.

And yet, even without mothering, the creature manages to gain an education. Mary Shelley's allusion to Rousseau's theory of the natural man as a noble savage, born free but everywhere in chains and inevitably corrupted by society, focuses one of the minor concerns of the novel, its theory of education. In the great debate on the relative importance of nature versus nurture, on whether learning achievements should be attributed primarily to innate intelligence or to social environment, Mary Shelley was convinced that nurture is crucial. Her reading of Rousseau's *Second Discourse* had given her insight into the limitations of the natural man as well as the potential evils of civilization.[13] Her creature is Rousseau's natural man, a creature no different from the animals, responding unconsciously to the needs of his flesh and the changing conditions of his environment. He feels pleasure at the sight of the moon, the warmth of the sun, the sounds of bird-song, the light and heat of fire; pain at the coldness of snow, the burning sensation of fire, the pangs of hunger and thirst. In the state of nature, man is free and unselfconscious; insofar as he can gratify his primal desires easily, he is happy. For Frankenstein's creature, a dry hovel is "paradise, compared to the bleak forest, my former residence, the rain-dropping branches, and dank earth" (102). But as Rousseau also emphasized, especially in *The Social Contract*, the natural man lacks much: language, the capacity to think rationally, companionship and the affections that flow from it, a moral consciousness. Peering through the chinks of his hovel, Mary Shelley's creature rapidly discovers the limitations of the state of nature and the positive benefits of a civilization grounded on family life.

Even though she depicts Frankenstein's creature as Rousseau's natural man, even though she echoes Rousseau's *Emile* at critical points, she does not endorse Rousseau's view that the simple gratification of human passions will lead to virtuous behavior. Her account of the creature's mental and moral development is more closely allied to the epistemological and pedagogical theories of David Hartley and John Locke. The associationist David Hartley argued that early sensitive experiences determine adult behavior, and the rationalist John Locke concurred that natural man is neither innately good nor innately evil, but rather a white paper or blank slate upon which sensations write impressions that then become ideas or conscious experience. The creature's moral development closely parallels the paradigm that Hartley laid out in his *Observations of Man, His Frame, His Duty, and His Expectations* (1749)[14] and follows the theories that Locke propounded first in 1690 in his *Essay Concerning Human Understanding* (which Mary Shelley read in 1816) and later in the more pragmatically oriented *Some Thoughts Concerning Education* (1693). The creature first experiences purely physical and undifferentiated sensations of light, darkness, heat, cold, hunger, pain and pleasure; this is the earliest period of infancy when "no distinct ideas occupied my mind; all was confused" (98). Gradually, the creature learns to distinguish his sensations and thus his "mind received every day additional ideas" (99). At the same time he learns the causes of his feelings of pain or pleasure and how to produce the effects he desires by obtaining clothing, shelter, food and fire. The creature's education is completed in just the way Locke advocates, by providing him with examples of moral and intellectual virtue. As Locke insisted:

> Of all the ways whereby children are to be instructed, and their manners formed, the plainest, easiest, and most efficacious, is to set before their eyes the examples of those things that you would have them do or avoid.... Virtues and vices can by no words be so plainly set before their understandings as the actions of other men will show them.[15]

When the creature stares through the chink in the wall of his hovel into the adjoining cottage, he sees before him a living illustration of benevolence, affection, industry, thrift, and natural justice in the actions of the De Lacey family. The De Laceys embody Mary Shelley's ideal of the egalitarian family—with one important exception: they lack a mother. The De Laceys not only stimulate the creature's emotions and arouse his desire to do good to others (which takes the form of gathering firewood for them), but also introduce him to the concept and function of a spoken and written language. Here adopting a referential theory of language, in which sounds or words are conceived as pointing to objects or mental states, Mary Shelley traces the creature's linguistic development from his earliest acquisition of nouns and proper names through his grasp of abstractions to his ability to speak, read, and finally write, the latter processes enabled by his overhearing Safie's French lessons in the next room and by his acquisition of a private library. While Locke's insistence that children learn best from examples now seems commonplace, Peter Gay has rightly reminded us that Locke was the first educator to recognize that human rationality and the capacity for self-discipline evolve gradually in the growing child and that the subject-matter to be learned must be adapted to the differential capacities of children at different stages of development.[16]

The creature learns from sensations and examples; what he learns is determined by his environment. The De Lacey family provides a lesson in almost perfect virtue, grounded in the private domestic affections, together with a treatise on social and human injustice as practiced in the public realm by the law courts of France and Safie's ungrateful Turkish father. The creature's knowledge of human vice and virtue is further enlarged by his reading. From Plutarch's *Lives of the Noble Romans* he learns the nature of heroism and public virtue and civic justice; from Volney's *Ruins, or A Survey of the Revolutions of Empires* he learns the contrasting nature of political corruption and the causes of the decline of civilizations; from Milton's *Paradise Lost* he learns the origins of human good and evil and the roles of the sexes; and from Goethe's *Werther* he learns the range of human emotions, from domestic love to suicidal despair, as well as the rhetoric in which to articulate not only ideas but feelings.

The creature's excellent education, which includes moral lessons garnered from the two books Locke thought essential, Aesop's Fables and the Bible, is implicitly contrasted to the faulty education received by Victor Frankenstein. While Alphonse Frankenstein initially followed Godwin's pedagogical precepts—he inspired his children to learn in a noncompetitive atmosphere by encouraging their voluntary desire to please others and by giving them practical goals (one learns a foreign language in order to read the interesting books in that tongue)—he failed to monitor sufficiently closely the books that Victor Frankenstein actual[ly] read. Instead of the Bible, Aesop, and *Robinson Crusoe* recommended by Godwin, Locke, and Rousseau, Victor devoured the misleading alchemical treatises of Cornelius Agrippa, Paracelsus, and Albertus Magnus, books which encouraged, not an awareness of human folly and injustice, but rather a hubristic desire for human omnipotence, for the gaining of the philosopher's stone and the elixir of life.

Mary Shelley's pedagogy, derived in large part from her father's espousal of Locke, emphasizes the role of the affections in the education of young children. Victor learns because he wishes to please his father, Elizabeth because she wishes to delight her aunt, the creature because he wishes to emulate and be accepted by the De Lacey family. Clearly an unloved child will not learn well—the creature's education is effectively ended when the De Laceys abandon him. But how well does even a much-loved child learn? Victor Frankenstein was such, but his father's indulgence only encouraged his son's egotistical dreams of omnipotence. In this Mary Shelley reveals her nagging doubt whether even a supportive family can produce a virtuous adult. In the successes and failures of both the creature's and Frankenstein's education, Mary Shelley registered a pervasive maternal anxiety: *even if I love and nurture my child, even if I provide the best education of which I am capable, I may still produce a monster—and who is responsible for that?*

Behind Mary Shelley's maternal anxieties lies a more general problem, the problem posed for her by Rousseau's writings. For Rousseau had made it clear that the movement away from the state of nature into the condition of civilization entails a loss of freedom, a frustration of desire, and an enclosure within the prison house of language or what Lacan has called the symbolic order. Civilization produces as much discontent as content. In place of the natural man's instinctive harmony with his surroundings, society substitutes a system of conflicting economic interests and a struggle for individual mastery, an aggressive competition restrained by but not eliminated from Rousseau's favored constitutional democracy. For once the creature has left the state of nature and learned the language and laws of society, he has gained a self-consciousness that he can never lose, the consciousness of his own isolation:

> I learned that the possessions most esteemed by your fellow-creatures were, high and unsullied descent united with riches.... but ... I possessed no money, no friends, no kind of property. I was, besides, endowed with a figure hideously deformed and loathsome; ... When I looked around, I saw and heard of none like me....
>
> I cannot describe to you the agony that these reflections inflicted upon me; I tried to dispel them, but sorrow only increased with knowledge. Oh, that I had for ever remained in my native wood, nor known or felt beyond the sensations of hunger, thirst, and heat! (115–16)

Deprived of all human companionship, the creature can never recover from the disease of self-consciousness; for him, no escape, save death, is possible. In this context, the novel points up the irony implicit in Locke's most famous pedagogical maxim: "A sound mind in a sound body is a short but full description of a happy state in this world" (19). Exercise and good diet can produce the healthy body Locke found so conducive to the development of mental and moral capacities; but can the creature, born with a grotesquely oversized and unsound body, ever develop a sound mind? Or, in the terms posed for Shelley by David Hartley, can an unmothered child whose formative experiences are of pain rather than pleasure ever develop a rational intellect, a healthy moral sense, or a normal personality?

NOTES

1. On the origin and nature of the golem, see Gershom G. Scholem, *On the Kabbalah and Its Symbolism*, trans. Ralph Manheim (London: Routledge & Kegan Paul, 1965), Chapt. 5; and Scholem's witty updating of the idea in his "The Golem of Prague and the Golem of Rehovot," in *The Messianic Idea of Judaism* (New York: Schocken Books, 1971), pp. 335–40.

2. This date is derived from Dr. Polidori's claim, on June 17, 1816, that "The ghost-stories are begun by all but me," in *The Diary of Dr. John William Polidori*, ed. William Michael Rossetti (London: Elkin Mathews, 1911), p. 125.

3. The major feminist readings of *Frankenstein* to date are those by Ellen Moers, in *Literary Women* (Garden City, New Jersey: Doubleday, 1976), pp. 91–99; Marc A. Rubenstein, "'My Accursed Origin': The Search for the Mother in *Frankenstein*," *Studies in Romanticism* 15 (Spring 1976): 165–94; Sandra Gilbert and Susan Gubar, in *The Madwoman in the Attic* (New Haven: Yale University Press, 1979), 213–47; Barbara Johnson, "My Monster/My Self," *Diacritics* 12 (1982): 2–10; Devon Hodges, "*Frankenstein* and the Feminine Subversion of the Novel," *Tulsa Studies in Women's Literature* 2 (Autumn 1983): 155–64; Mary Poovey, *The Proper Lady and the Woman Writer—Ideology as Style in the Works of Mary Wollstonecraft, Mary Shelley and Jane Austen* (Chicago and London: University of Chicago Press, 1984), Chaps. 4–5; Mary Jacobus, "Is There a Woman in This Text?" *New Literary History* 14 (1982): 117–41; Burton Hatlin, "Milton, Mary Shelley and Patriarchy," in *Rhetoric, Literature, and Interpretation*, ed. Harry R. Garvin (Lewisburg, Pa.: Bucknell University Press, 1983), pp. 19–47; Margaret Homans, *Bearing the Word—Language and Female Experience in Nineteenth-Century Women's Writing* (Chicago: University of Chicago Press, 1986), Chap. 5; and the essays by George Levine, U. C. Knoepflmacher, Judith Wilt, and Kate Ellis included in *The Endurance of Frankenstein*, ed. George Levine and U. C. Knoepflmacher (Berkeley and Los Angeles, and London: University of California Press, 1979). For a complete bibliography of research on *Frankenstein* before 1983, see Frederick S. Frank, "Mary Shelley's *Frankenstein*: A Register of Research," *Bulletin of Bibliography* 40 (1983): 163–88.

4. Ellen Moers, "Female Gothic," in *Literary Women*, p. 93. This essay first appeared in *The New York Review of Books* on March 21, 1974.

5. Mary Wollstonecraft Shelley, Introduction to *Frankenstein, or The Modern Prometheus* (London: Colburn and Bentley; Standard Novels Edition, 1831), p. xi.

6. Mary Wollstonecraft Shelley, *Frankenstein, or The Modern Prometheus* (London: Lackington, Hughes, Harding, Mavor and Jones, 1818); all further references to *Frankenstein*, unless otherwise noted, will be to the only modern reprint of the first edition, edited by James Rieger (New York: Bobbs-Merrill, 1974; reprinted, Chicago: University of Chicago Press, 1982), and will be cited by page number only in the text. These phrases occur on pages 51 and 52 of the Rieger text.

7. Lawrence Stone, in *The Family, Sex and Marriage in England 1500–1800* (London: Weidenfeld and Nicolson, 1977), distinguishes three types of family structures: the Open Lineage Family, which he asserts was prevalent for the millennium prior to 1600 and characterized by its "permeability by outside influences" and "members' sense of loyalty to ancestors and to living kin" (p. 4); the Restricted Patriarchal Nuclear Family, which he argues came into dominance between 1530–1700 among the upper and middle classes, and in which the father assumed greater power and determined the nuclear family's particular loyalties to political and religious factions; and the Closed Domesticated Nuclear Family, which he says began to develop after 1640 and was "well established by 1750 in the key middle and upper sectors of English society." (8–9). It manifested four key features: "intensified affective bonding of the nuclear core at the expense of neighbors and kin; a strong sense of individual autonomy and the right to personal freedom in the pursuit of happiness; a weakening of the association of sexual pleasure with sin and guilt; and a growing desire for physical privacy" (p. 8). Alan MacFarlane (*Love and Marriage in*

England, Modes of Reproduction 1300–1840 [Oxford: Basil Blackwell, 1986]), Linda A. Pollock (*Forgotten Children—Parent–Child Relations From 1500–1900* [Cambridge: Cambridge University Press, 1983]), and Randolph Trumbach (*The Rise of the Egalitarian Family—Aristocratic Kinship and Domestic Relations in Eighteenth-Century England* [New York, San Francisco, London: Academic Press, 1978]) have criticized Stone's models on the grounds that the Malthusian marriage-system and the affectional nuclear family existed well before the sixteenth century, but their arguments do not sufficiently take into account the documented changes that occurred within the British family during the modern period. Within the context of Stone's classifications, Victor Frankenstein's attempt to create a family or race entirely dependent upon him is an example of the Restricted Patriarchal Nuclear Family, in which the father is, as Stone comments, virtually "a legalized petty tyrant within the home" (p. 7). The Patriarchal Family was becoming more rather than less prevalent in nineteenth-century England under the impact of the industrial revolution and the rigid separation of the public (wage-earning) from the domestic (unwaged) spheres (see Heidi Hartmann, "Capitalism, Patriarchy, and Job Segregation by Sex," in *Capitalist Patriarchy and the Case for Socialist Feminism*, ed. Zillah Eisenstein [New York and London: Monthly Review Press, 1979], 206–47).

8. Mary Shelley's extensive reading program is documented in her *Journal* (ed. Frederick L. Jones [Norman, Oklahoma: University of Oklahoma Press, 1947]); these books are listed on pp. 47–49, with the exception of Volney's *Ruins*. For knowledge of Volney, she probably relied on Percy Shelley, who read the book in 1814 (Newman Ivey White, *Shelley* [London: Secker and Warburg, 1941; revised edition, 1947], pp. I:277, 292, 419). For the impact of Volney on Percy Shelley's "The Revolt of Islam," which he was working on during the composition of *Frankenstein*, see Kenneth Neill Cameron, *Shelley—The Golden Years* (Cambridge: Harvard University Press, 1974), p. 315.

9. Gilbert and Gubar have emphasized this point in *The Madwoman in the Attic* (New Haven: Yale University Press, 1979), pp. 238, 247. See also Marcia Tillotson, "'A Forced Solitude': Mary Shelley and the Creation of Frankenstein's Monster," in *The Female Gothic*, ed. Juliann E. Fleenor (Montreal and London: Eden Press, 1983): 167–75.

10. *Mary Shelley's Journal*, ed. Frederick L. Jones, p. 72. Claire Clairmont probably first introduced Mary Shelley to *Emile*, which she read during their trip back to England in September, 1814, (*The Journals of Claire Clairmont 1814–1827*, ed. Marion Kingston Stocking [Cambridge: Harvard University Press, 1968], pp. 39–40).

11. Jean Jacques Rousseau, *Emile*, trans. Barbara Foxley (New York: Dutton–Everyman's Library, 1911; repr. 1963), p. 5. All future references to this Everyman edition are cited in the text.

12. U. C. Knoepflmacher, "Thoughts on the Aggression of Daughters," *The Endurance of Frankenstein*, ed. George Levine and U. C. Knoepflmacher, pp. 88–119. William Veeder endorses this view in his *Mary Shelley & Frankenstein—The Fate of Androgyny* (Chicago: University of Chicago Press, 1986), pp. 161–71.

13. For an illuminating discussion of Rousseau's writings in relation to *Frankenstein*, see Paul A. Cantor, *Creature and Creator: Myth-making and English Romanticism* (New York: Cambridge University Press, 1984), pp. 4–25, 119–28.

14. For an excellent discussion of the parallels between David Hartley's model of psychological development and the Creature's formative experiences, see Sue Weaver Schopf, "'Of what a strange nature is knowledge!': Hartleian Psychology and the

Creature's Arrested Moral Sense in Mary Shelley's *Frankenstein*," *Romanticism Past and Present* 5 (1981): 33–52.

15. John Locke, *Some Thoughts Concerning Education*, ed. Peter Gay (New York: Bureau of Publications, Teachers College, Columbia University, 1964), p. 66.

16. John Locke, *Some Thoughts Concerning Education*, pp. 1–3.

H.L. MALCHOW

Frankenstein's Monster and Images of Race in Nineteenth-Century Britain

The Black stripp'd, and appeared of a giant-like strength,
Large in bone, large in muscle and with arms a cruel length.[1]

It is now commonly accepted that the Gothic literary genre of the late eighteenth and early nineteenth centuries represents, if remotely and unconsciously, the central tensions of an age of social liberation and political revolution. The themes of unjust persecution and imprisonment which are central to works like Matthew Lewis's *The Monk*, Charles Maturin's *Melmoth* or Eugene Sue's *The Wandering Jew*, together with the dilemmas of identity facing the liberated which permeate William Godwin's *Caleb Williams* or Mary Shelley's *Frankenstein*, obviously resonate with the events of an age that, as Chris Baldick has finely observed, witnessed humanity seizing responsibility "for re-creating the world, for violently reshaping its natural environment and its inherited social and political forms, for remaking itself".[2] Criticism in this vein has, however, focused almost exclusively on domestic themes—the "demonizing" of the proletariat in an era of industrial and political revolution, or the self-exploration and "nascent feminism" of authors like Mary Shelley and Charlotte Brontë. In contrast this essay will offer a racial reading of Mary Shelley's *Frankenstein* as a third level of interpretation which meshes with the Marxist and the feminist location of the novel in the social and psychological context of the times.

From *Past and Present*, No. 139 (May, 1993). © 1993 by Oxford University Press. Note: Several images relevant to the text have been removed from this article.

The thesis developed here is that Shelley's portrayal of her monster drew upon contemporary attitudes towards non-whites, in particular on fears and hopes of the abolition of slavery in the West Indies, as well as on middle-class apprehension of a Luddite proletariat or Mary Shelley's "birthing trauma".[3] Indeed the peculiar horror of the monster owes much of its emotional power to this hidden, or "coded", aspect, and the subsequent popularity of the tale through several nineteenth-century editions and on the Victorian stage, as well as in satire, derived in large part from the convergence of its most emotive elements with the evolving contemporaneous representation of ethnic and racial "Others". Such an argument necessarily rests on "evidence" that is indirect, circumstantial and speculative. There is no clear proof that Mary Shelley consciously set out to create a monster which suggested, explicitly, the Jamaican escaped slave or maroon, or that she drew directly from any personal knowledge of either planter or abolitionist propaganda. That she did so is certainly not impossible, and there can at least be no doubt that powerful literary images with which Shelley would have been quite familiar—Shakespeare's Caliban or Rousseau's noble savage—also played a significant role in the eighteenth-century image of the Edenic non-white. It is not, in any event, my purpose to prove explicit connections and direct sources. Nor is it my purpose to discover a hidden "key" which will unlock every level of meaning, intended or otherwise, in the novel. What is of interest here is how closely Shelley's fictional creation parallels in many respects the racial stereotypes of the age, and how her exploration of the limits of Rousseau and William Godwin on man and education, surely the most important sub-theme in the novel, mirrors contemporary difficulties in maintaining universal humanistic ideals in the context of the slave-economy of the West Indies and an expanding empire over non-white populations in Asia and Africa.

I

"RACE" IN THE NAPOLEONIC ERA

The relationship of man to the rest of creation, and of European man to others, was a familiar problem posed afresh to the systematizing Enlightenment mind. This is not the place to reiterate the development of the concept of race in the eighteenth century, except to note that these ideas already involved a good deal of projection, to use Mannoni's language, of European fears about their own dark interiors, and that towards the end of the century they acquired a greater "presence" or centrality in the European mind as a result of informal travel, scientific or scholarly investigation and imperial conquest.[4]

Educated Europeans of the early Enlightenment inherited a view of foreign peoples which was part-fantasy and part-hearsay, little more than an exotic fiction with which to expose the venality of European life, as in Montesquieu's *Persian Letters*, or reportage shaped in such a way as to administer a crude justification for economic penetration and religious conquest, as in Richard Hakluyt or Samuel Purchase. Ironically, however, the hunger for systematic and verifiable knowledge that typifies the mid-century *philosophe* served to reinforce, with a scientific gloss, this Eurocentric perspective. As the fantastic was exchanged for a natural science of plants, animals and foreign peoples, there was an inevitable compulsion to rank not only cultures but also types of people. This in turn encouraged the construction of a system of "races" of men in parallel with the genera and species laid down by Linnaeus for the biological world as a whole. This search for an ordering of Nature by rank no doubt reflects a hierarchical mentality inherent to the aristocratic European tradition.

Rousseau's natural man was an attempt to stand this enterprise on its head by embracing the untutored savage as a model of pre-civilized innocence. It was not, however, a validation of other, alternative, cultures. Rousseau's innocent savage was located within the European psyche itself rather than in the interiors of Africa or the Americas. Moreover the Edenic tradition never really managed to come to grips with inherent ambiguities about the bestial within man himself—a problem which resurfaced in the late eighteenth century in both the evangelical theology of original sin and Burkean conservatism.

Though it is possible to find some continuity of negative stereotyping in European concepts of the dark "Other", towards the turn of the century ideas about racial difference were consolidated and intensified. This trend was no doubt encouraged by the reactionary assault on the political ideas of Rousseau, but it reached its full maturity in the mid-Victorian world of a widely accepted pseudo-scientific racism. There are many sources for such a shift in attitudes, but the extent to which the changes in image and their growing importance in popular culture can be located in the era following the French Revolution suggests that middle-class fears of violent revolutionary "beasts" at home played some role. James Gillray's well-known cartoon of sans-culottes enjoying a meal of dismembered aristocrats brings together precisely these two themes of a bestial and threatening domestic poverty and a cannibalism drawn from the earliest fantasy-pictures of alien savages abroad.

Mary Shelley grew to maturity in a highly charged intellectual and political atmosphere in which revolutionary radicalism was on the defensive. Her parents' close association with the radical cause, her husband's radicalism, her own reading of Rousseau and of *Paradise Lost*, another failed revolution, have been widely commented on and *Frankenstein* persuasively portrayed as, in part, an ambiguous rendering of her father's utopian and universal ideals.[5] If, however, we are to place the novel in the context of the general assault on radical ideas, it may be valuable to bear in mind that the black Jacobins in St Domingue and the parliamentary struggle in England to abolish the slave-trade guaranteed that issues of race played a significant contemporary role in the larger political debate surrounding the capacities and rights of mankind. Nor did a reciprocating awareness of the anti-slavery and the domestic radical movements fade after abolition of the British slave-trade in 1807. In 1814 a proposal was made at the Congress of Vienna to renew the rights of French slave-merchants. Within four weeks some 806 petitions with 1.5 million signatures from towns throughout Britain were sent to parliament opposing it.[6] Negro slavery in the New World provided, if nothing else, a common source of analogy and metaphor in the political polemic aimed at redressing or defending inequality in the Old. Like other radicals, Mary Shelley's parents—William Godwin and Mary Wollstonecraft—at least tangentially addressed questions raised by the West Indian slavery debate in their own writings.

Godwin was concerned to defend the universality of reason in humankind and its operation in the perfecting of governments and human society generally, and in his best-known work, *Political Justice*, he attacked the familiar theory that climate had created types of men with different capacities. Characteristically, however, he obscured his point by admitting some probable effect of climate on character in extreme cases like the Tropics. Here his reliance on Hume led him to confuse racial and national character and further vitiated his object of demonstrating that it was, by and large, governments which shaped the character of their people for good or bad.[7] Though he was, of course, an opponent of slavery and scorned the argument that it was a tolerable institution because the slaves themselves appeared to tolerate it, Godwin nevertheless, in his rambling asides on Negro character, managed to affirm some of the common theories about Negro "differences" which one can find in the pro-slavery literature, as well as among the armchair theorists generally. Specifically he accepted that Negroes reached sexual maturity earlier, had a more passionate temperament than Europeans, and possessed a natural indolence "consequent upon a spontaneous fertility" of the tropical environment. Moreover Godwin, while denying that racial differences posed any absolute barrier to the spread of political liberty, suggested, as many abolitionists did, that instruction and guidance over a lengthy period of time would be necessary to prepare such people for freedom.[8]

If, in the flush of optimism of the early years of the French Revolution, a radical such as Godwin could offer only an ambiguous approach to racial equality—and some radicals like Cobbett had no use for "nigger philanthropy" in any form—conservative polemic often encouraged racial, or at least ethnic, stereotyping in its emotional and intellectual response to utopian radicalism. The French wars, the abortive rebellion in Ireland, the spread of the ideals of the French Revolution to Haiti, and armed resistance to British suzerainty in India served to heighten xenophobia and validate ethnic prejudice as patriotic anti-Jacobinism. In this context the assault on slavery, as well as its vigorous defence, established a discourse that served both to highlight inherent cultural and, increasingly, racial differences between the English and the Other, while at the same time offering allusive and metaphorical ammunition to the enemies of domestic radicalism. Those unsympathetic to claims for "universal" humanitarian and egalitarian rights in Europe had only to wave a hand at the patent folly of enfranchising Jamaican slaves, at Tipu's fanatical followers in India or, for that matter, at "the Hottentot Venus" lasciviously displayed in London in 1810.

The exhibition of this indentured black woman, Saartjie Baartman, to curious crowds in Regency London, the extraordinary interest taken in her physical form by the press, and the way her body was literally disconstructed after death to prove spurious theories about Negro nature,[9] is a reminder of the way in which the cultural prejudices, fears and deep-seated neuroses of the observer may impinge on "science" and literature, and wander from one arena to another. Here the physical "abnormalities" of the South African "Hottentot", hitherto unknown in England, served through popular caricature to reinforce ideas of polygenesis and racial hierarchy, but also, more subtly, to encourage in a reactionary political climate the views of natural inequality generally. When studying even so bookishly inspired a text as *Frankenstein*, it may be well to bear in mind that a writer—and Mary Shelley was perhaps less protected from reality than many young women in her milieu—exists within a popular, as well as an intellectual, culture. A journal recording the books she read indicates possible intellectual sources for Mary Shelley's ideas; other influences are necessarily obscure, but not therefore unimportant. A novel is not only a product of inner psychology and private domestic experience, but also of the wider, enfolding, external environment of shifting values, attitudes and observations which impinged upon the writer.

Free American and West African blacks were not unknown in the England in which Mary Wollstonecraft Godwin grew up, nor were they merely the objects of a distant Caribbean philanthropy. In his *Fables, Ancient and Modern*, published in 1805, William Godwin included a tale, "Washing the Blackamoor White", with the aside that "The other day I stopped involuntarily to look at a negro I passed on the street ... there was nothing brutal or insulting or coarse in his manner".[10] Thousands of mostly destitute Negroes—freed slaves brought to England by their masters, ex-sailors who had manned ships and left them in English ports, as well as those who had fled America—were concentrated in London and the other major ports by the end of the eighteenth century.[11] If the fashion for little black boys in livery, or black footmen as in Godwin's fable, had waned, blacks as beggars and prostitutes, or in the rougher occupations, were relatively common. In 1810 and 1811 a black boxer from America, Thomas Molineaux, almost defeated the legendary English champion Tom Cribb in two widely publicized matches. These fights, attended by thousands, reported in *The Times*, and portrayed in the popular art of cheap prints and caricature,[12] drew the attention of polite society as well as the gaming world. Even the *Annual Register* for 1811 offered a report, with the justification that it "is so characteristic of the taste of the times, and its subject of so much contemporary importance, that we cannot but think it worth recording". An event such as this inevitably roused a sense of national and racial competition in many: "The Black's prowess was regarded by Cribb's friends with a jealousy which excited considerable national prejudice against him ... the laurels of a British champion was in danger of being wrested from him by a Baltimore man of colour". The victorious Cribb was received by his friends "like a Nelson returning from a naval victory".[13]

It was not merely a case of blacks being in the public eye in Britain from time to time. Mary Godwin had certainly also been exposed at home, through both her father's writings and house guests, to the hotly contested issue of the abolition of slavery. It is reasonable to assume that this provided one source of images and buried themes in *Frankenstein*. William Godwin had covered the debates on the slave trade for the Whiggish *New Annual Register* in the 1780s and 1790s. In April 1791 he was actually present in the gallery of the Commons when Wilberforce's motion was defeated.[14] Although he accepted in *Political Justice* that there were racial differences in character as well as body, his sentiments nevertheless lay with the abolitionists, though not with Wilberforce's Tory evangelicalism. Godwin denied that differences of race or gender had any significant effect on an individual's ability to reason or to be educated. In his novel *St Leon* (1799) a prison turnkey is represented as a Negro with "sound understanding and an excellent heart".[15] The political struggle for abolition and the potential of the freed Negro for improvement would have been common subjects of conversation in the home in which Mary Godwin was educated. Dr James Bell, an admirer of Godwin, was introduced to him there in 1799, for example. Bell was determined to go out to Jamaica "to lighten the woes and diminish the horrors of slavery". He died in the island shortly after arrival.[16]

The prominence of the anti-slavery issue in late eighteenth-century European discourse had a direct impact on the characteristic depiction of the negro in Western art. The visual representation of the black shifted from that of an exotic, often in fancy dress, to the naked or semi-clothed victim, an object of pity.[17] While the intention of the evangelical abolitionists may have been to portray the black slave as "a man and a brother", the actual effect of their propaganda—vividly rendered on canvas, medallions and chinaware, in cheap prints and ballad sheets, on mementoes of all kinds—was to reiterate an image of the Other, a special kind of childlike, suffering and degraded being, rarely heroic, that became part of the common coinage of popular culture. Moreover abolitionist propaganda inevitably drew attention to that of the pro-slavery lobby. The apologists of Negro slavery manipulated scientific argument and injected into English popular culture, as well as into European political and intellectual discourse, the paranoid fears, sexual fantasies and, indeed, the whole range of racist stereotypes already current in Jamaican planter society. This served to create misgivings and ambiguities about race which were not unlike the challenge to Painite liberalism posed by the *émigré* descriptions of Jacobin ferocity in Paris.

Finally, while admitting that Mary Shelley's world was suffused with both positive and negative representations of the black man in public discourse, that her father held strong opinions on the subject which, inveterate educator that he was, he would undoubtedly have communicated to his children, and that there was a real presence of the racial Other in the London of her childhood, it is still legitimate to ask whether there is sufficient probability that she absorbed these images in a way that would lead one to expect them to emerge in her first and most important work of fiction.

There is, in fact, proof that Mary Shelley did have recourse, both before and during the writing of *Frankenstein*, to a reservoir of information about the black man in Africa and the West Indies. Turning to the journal which she kept, and in which she meticulously recorded books she and Percy Shelley read, we find some interesting titles. In 1814 they both read the first two large volumes of Mungo Park's relation of the interior of western Africa, an important milestone in European "discovery" of the continent. They read the third volume, containing the narrative of Park's death, in 1816, the year Mary began to write *Frankenstein*.[18] In the winter of 1814–15 they also read a history of the British West Indies by the wealthy merchant-planter, Bryan Edwards.[19] Edwards was a relatively liberal Jamaican, though pro-slavery. His work, which narrated the history of the islands up to the late eighteenth century, dwelt upon differences of colour and caste and the supposed racial characteristics of West Indian slaves from different parts of Africa, as well as the horrors of slave rebellions. Mary Shelley appears to have found the work sufficiently absorbing to spend "all evening" and "all day" engrossed in it.[20] Finally, although her journal suggests that the Shelleys finished reading John Davis's record of his travels through the American South too late (in the summer of 1817, while Murray was considering the *Frankenstein* manuscript) for it to have played a role in the construction of her novel, the themes it treats—musings about the black as natural, Rousseauian man, and the struggle of owners to retrieve fugitive slaves—indicate their continuing interest in the subject of slavery and the Negro race at just the time the novel was being written: "Exposed to such wanton cruelty the negroes frequently run away; they flee into the woods, where they are wet with the rains of heaven, and embrace the rock for want of shelter".[21] It remains to be seen to what extent the evidence of language and themes in the novel indicates a reflection at some level of the contemporary race debate in the creation and fate of Mary Shelley's monster.

II

FRANKENSTEIN

As is well known, *Frankenstein: or, The Modern Prometheus* had its origins at a house party near Geneva in June of 1816 at which the eighteen-year-old Mary Wollstonecraft Godwin (she married Percy Shelley the following December) was challenged to produce a ghost story. The resulting tale was published anonymously in March of 1818, and was surprisingly successful. In the form of a Gothic horror romance it recounts, through the letters of Walton, an Arctic explorer, the tortured history of Victor Frankenstein, the young son of a Genevan magistrate, who, as a Faustian university student, aspired to create life, and whose creation—his monster, fiend or demon— rejected by his creator, flees to the wilderness where he lives rough on nuts and berries. His appearance, however, produces violent revulsion in all who meet him, in spite of the creature's earnest attempts to make friends and do good. Educated vicariously and surreptitiously, he develops a sense of the injustices heaped upon him and turns to vengeance. He first murders Frankenstein's child brother, then causes the judicial murder of an innocent young woman; finally, half-repentant, he tracks down his creator to demand that he create a mate for himself, vowing that they will live apart from mankind. This Frankenstein at first agrees to do, but he betrays his promise after reflecting on the dangers of a race of creatures arising from the union of two such monsters. The enraged creature exacts a further terrible vengeance, first killing Frankenstein's friend Clerval, and then his bride Elizabeth on their bridal bed. The novel concludes with a determined Frankenstein pursuing his creation into the Arctic, only to die before confronting the monster, who mourns his maker and disappears into the northern darkness with a vow of self-immolation.

A reading of this text which attempts to draw out an embedded racial message must begin where racism itself begins, with physiognomy. The monster, it will be seen, is not merely a grotesque, a too-roughly cobbled together simulacrum of a man. He is, first, larger and more powerful than his maker, and, secondly, dark and sinister in appearance. This suggests the standard description of the black man in both the literature of the West Indies and that of West African exploration. Mungo Park's *Travels*, which Mary Shelley had ready to hand, described the Mandingos as "commonly above the middle size, well-shaped, strong, and capable of enduring great labour". A Negro guide who "mounted up the rocks, where indeed no horse could follow him, leaving me to admire his agility" indicates both great strength and, perhaps, the simian dexterity with which the monster eludes Frankenstein in the Alps.[22] The Jamaican Bryan Edwards described the Mandingos as "remarkably tall", while the Eboes were, he averred, a sickly yellow in complexion with eyes that appeared to be "suffused with bile".[23]

By the early nineteenth century, popular racial discourse managed to conflate such descriptions of particular ethnic characteristics into a general image of the Negro body in which repulsive features, brute-like strength and size of limbs featured prominently. Frankenstein's creature, when we first see him, is defined by a set of cliches which might be picked out of such literature. His eyes are "dull yellow" and "watery", hair "a lustrous black" and "ragged", and his black lips contrast with "teeth of pearly whiteness". His skin was "in colour and apparent texture like that of a mummy".[24] Mummies are, of course, ordinarily dark brown or black in colour, a fact which, following the Napoleonic excavations, led to speculation about the racial origin of the ancient Egyptians. There was already a tradition, drawn from classical authors, that the civilization of ancient Thebes had originated in Ethiopia. Count Chasseboeuf de Volney draws on this in his *Ruins*, a book which Mary Shelley knew, and which she used as one of the monster's textbooks in the novel; Volney wrote of "the black complexion of the Sphinx".[25] This is not to say that Shelley intended to create a specifically Negro monster, elsewhere she writes of the monster's yellow skin,[26] but rather that, reaching into childhood fantasy and imagination, she dredged up a bogyman which had been constructed out of a cultural tradition of the threatening "Other"—whether troll or giant, gypsy or Negro—from the dark inner recesses of xenophobic fear and loathing.

This seems to me to be at least as reasonable a reading as the claim that the monster is a feminine/masculine composite which transcends gender.[27] In fact there is very little that is feminine in the monster, a point to which I shall return later. Yet another reading maintains that the alien hideousness of the monster reflects bourgeois fears of an unknown but threatening working class. However, the lineaments of the creature hardly suggest the image of the wan, ground-down and bowed pauper or proletarian labourer, often small in stature and poor in health. Frankenstein's monster is robust and larger than life, ostentatiously rural rather than urban. Of course the monster as industrial worker does not have to be a literal image, but rather the enlarged fear of a collective threat. Nevertheless, at the level of physiognomy at least, a racial reading seems to me to be nearer the mark than a Marxist one.

Beyond size and repulsiveness, the most striking physical attributes of the monster are his ape-like ability to scamper up mountainsides and his endurance of temperatures which European man would find intolerable: "I was more agile", he says, "than they and could subsist upon coarser diet; I bore the extremes of heat and cold with less injury to my frame".[28] This description closely parallels the claims of the apologists for West Indian slavery. The Negro, it was said, had more brute strength than the white man and could stand the heat of the Tropics which would enervate, perhaps kill, a European.[29] One might, without stretching imagination very far, see in Frankenstein's futile chase after his creature in the Alps or the frozen waste of the Arctic a displaced image of the white planter's exhausting and, in Jamaica, often futile search for the runaway slave in the opposite extreme of the Equatorial Tropics.[30] Moreover some apologists for slavery defended a subsistence slave diet of maize and water with the claim that the Negro race did not require the white man's luxuries of meat and drink. This draws on a long European tradition which imagined wild men or natural men of the woods as (like Frankenstein's monster) colossal vegetarians, images which the eighteenth-century naturalists helped to merge with that of more primitive races of men abroad far down the ladder of racial hierarchy. Mungo Park commented on the largely vegetable diet of many Negroes.[31]

Shifting from the image to the story, however, we see that Shelley's monster is no mere ape-man. He has an innate desire for knowledge, a capacity to learn, and feelings of right and wrong. Notwithstanding his hideous appearance, he is a man dreadfully wronged by a society which cannot see the inner man for the outer form. Here one might argue quite plausibly for an abolitionist rendering of the image of the monster as "a man and a brother". However, Shelley's creature is, if not a masculine and feminine composite, a compound of both sides of the slavery debate. He is wild and dangerous, unpredictable and childlike, but at the same time has perhaps been made such by the circumstances of an unjust exclusion, as the creature himself says. Yet the depth of his rage and destructiveness seems to stem from more than environment and frustration; it suggests an inherent bestiality lurking somewhere. How much the monster's excitable character is the result of his unique physiology, and how much of his environment, is an ambiguity which exactly parallels the central conundrum of the anti-slavery debate. Something of this ambiguity might even be said to be buried unconsciously in Godwin's own good-natured telling of the fable about washing the blackamoor, which he intended no doubt as an abolitionist homily that skin colour mattered only to the ignorant. But it would more commonly have been read with another meaning, that the black could no more be educated into whiteness than a leopard could change his spots, that there were basic and ineradicable racial differences for which skin colour was but an outward sign.[32] The story was an old one. In 1776 the Revd Henry Bate's comic opera, "The Blackamoor Wash'd White", was performed at Garrick's Drury Lane Theatre. It contained a song with the lines:

No, you're not an earthly creature
　But death's shadow in disguise!
See him stamp'd on ev'ry feature!
　What a pair of rolling eyes!
　　Don't come nigh me,
　　Let me fly thee,
　Or I faint—I fall—I die!
　　See death yonder!—
　　Now I wonder
Who outruns, the ghost,—or I?[33]

Violently contradictory and unbridled emotions are characteristics which were commonly associated with the Negro. Mungo Park, who was killed by natives in the upper Niger region, related numerous examples of violence—"The Jaloffs (or Yaloffs) are an active, powerful, and warlike race"—and "savagery": "The Negro carried the body [of a deceased boy] by a leg and an arm, and threw it into the pit with a savage indifference, which I had never before seen". Edwards describes the blacks of Jamaica who originated on the Gold Coast, "the genuine and original unmixed Negro", as having a "firmness of body and mind; a ferociousness of disposition; but withall, activity, courage, and a stubbornness ... of soul, which prompts them to enterprises of difficulty and danger; and enables them to meet death, in its most horrible shape, with fortitude or indifference".[34] Many writers, such as John Leyden in 1799, made much not only of the violence of native Africans and slaves, in particular their thirst for revenge, but also their contrasting capacity for gratitude and affection: "The understanding is much less cultivated among the Negroes than among Europeans; but their passions, whether benevolent or malevolent, are proportionately more violent ... Though addicted to hatred and revenge, they are equally susceptible to love, affection, and gratitude".[35] It will be apparent how closely Leyden's choice of description—passionate revenge and loving gratitude—echoes Shelley's own characterization of her monster. It was a common theme which Mungo Park voiced in his observations, for example, of the "Feloops" near the Gambia River: "They are of a gloomy disposition, and are supposed never to forgive an injury ... This fierce and unrelenting disposition is, however, counterbalanced by many good qualities: they display the utmost gratitude and affection toward their benefactors". This combination of vengefulness and affection was in fact a stereotype commonly applied to any savage or primitive race, as when Edwards described the extinct "Caribbees" of the West Indies: "they will be considered rather as beasts of prey, than as human beings", were prone to brood over "past miscarriage" and possessed an "implacable thirst of revenge". "But among themselves they were peaceable, and towards each other faithful, friendly and affectionate."[36]

Mary Shelley's addition of cruel vindictiveness to the portrait of the natural savage accords with a contemporary shifting of attitude from that of Dr Johnson's savage ("a man untaught, uncivilized") to the egregiously cruel as well as ignorant black well established in mid-nineteenth-century opinion.[37] Writing in the 1790s Edwards ascribed a particular cruelty to both the ancient Caribbees (an "unnatural cruelty") and the mulattos and Negroes of his time:

it serves to some degree to lessen the indignation which a good mind necessarily feels at the abuses of power by the Whites, to observe that the Negroes themselves, when invested with command, give full play to their revengeful passions; and exercise all the wantonness of cruelty without restraint or remorse.[38]

In contemporary abolitionist representation it is possible to find positive images of the black as a powerful force for *justifiable* vengeance rather than a mere supplicating child, though this perspective remained somewhat exceptional. In 1811 the abolitionist artist George Dawe exhibited at the British Institution a larger-than-life painting, *A Negro Overpowering a Buffalo*, which depicted a massive black body tensed with brute strength. A few years earlier Henri Fuseli, also an abolitionist, had given the public a towering, elemental and heroic black in his *The Negro Revenged*. If Dawe's message was oblique, Fuseli's was direct, suggested perhaps by lines from Thomas Day's poem "The Dying Negro": "For Afric triumphs!—his avenging rage / No tears can soften, and no blood assuage". In Fuseli's painting a black male, larger than the white woman clinging to him, erect rather than kneeling, calls down the wrath of God on a foundering slave ship.[39] More commonly, however, the image of the black as a destructive force—with a suggestion of irrational bestiality—was drawn from the propaganda of Jamaica's planter class, and was echoed by their parliamentary defenders. For example, in 1796 the *Parliamentary Register*, the *Annual Register* and, presumably, other London publications all gave ample space to Henry Dundas's reply in the House of Commons to humanitarian concerns over the use of bloodhounds to hunt down Negro men, women and children in Jamaica:

The Maroons were accustomed to descend from their fastnesses at midnight, and commit the most dreadful ravages and cruelties upon the wives, children, and property of the inhabitants, burning and destroying every place which they attacked, and murdering all who unfortunately became the objects of their fury.[40]

One might note here the coincidence that Shelley's implacably vengeful monster murders both a woman and a child, and burns the De Lacey cottage to the ground. Such images were common to the literature on the West Indies with which Mary Shelley was recently familiar. She would, for instance, have read Edwards's rather more explicit description of the horrors of a slave rebellion that saw, he claimed, widespread "death and desolation":

> they surrounded the overseer's house about four in the morning, in which eight or ten White people were in bed, every one of whom they butchered in the most savage manner, and literally drank their blood mixed with rum ... [they] then set fire to the buildings and canes. In one morning they murdered between thirty and forty Whites, not sparing even infants at the breast ...[41]

This nightmare Edwards put into verse which, like Fuseli's canvas of 1807, may also echo, if in a more sinister tone, Thomas Day's poem:

> Now, Christian, now, in wild dismay,
> Of Afric's proud revenge the prey,
>   Go roam th'affrighted wood;—
> Transform'd to tigers, fierce and fell,
> Thy race shall prowl with savage yell,
>   And glut their rage for blood![42]

This Gothic image of frenzied blacks drinking the blood of their victims (Frankenstein accuses the monster of being "his own vampire")[43] is a common trope for a depraved and irrational lust for vengeance. It brings together two of the commonly supposed characteristics of the primitive: a manic preoccupation with avenging grievances and cannibalism. The apparent contradiction between the European image of the vegetarian wild man and that of the cannibalistic savage may be related in some way to that other contradiction thought to exist in savage natures between affectionate gratitude and indifferent, casual cruelty. In the late eighteenth century the European tradition of widespread cannibalism among savages abroad, passed down from well-elaborated and largely fanciful sixteenth-century accounts, and lodged in the popular mind by Defoe's *Robinson Crusoe* (recommended by Godwin for the education of children),[44] appeared to receive corroboration in explorers' accounts of the South Pacific and Africa. Bryan Edwards, who believed that cannibalism had been widespread in the West Indies, drew attention to the debate on the extent of the practice in his *History*.[45]

While Mary Shelley's monster cannot actually be charged with cannibalism, the subject is certainly raised, if obliquely, in the novel. William Frankenstein, the child whom the monster strangles, his most horrific crime, charges him at first sight with this savage intention: "Ugly wretch! You wish to eat me and tear me to pieces".[46] The charge is, of course, unjust and part of the prejudice which the creature meets wherever he turns. Though Victor Frankenstein metaphorically associates his monster with vampirism, it is Frankenstein himself who takes on the character of the savage. He is the cannibal who tears "to pieces" both the corpses from which he assembles his creature and the female mate he began to construct. Similarly he also takes on the savage's thirst for vengeance, dedicating himself to revenge the deaths of his brother and bride, in relentless pursuit of his own creation. As Anne Mellor and other critics have noted, Frankenstein and his monster become indistinguishable, "the creator has become his creature".[47]

Dissection in Frankenstein's laboratory is, as with the scientific dismemberment of "the Hottentot Venus", a horror directly mirroring that of savage myth. A racially prejudiced combination of vengeance and cannibalism via dissection (in this case vivisection) already existed in Shakespeare's Shylock, just as a metaphorical cannibalism was, as we have seen, xenophobically associated with the Parisian mob. The Burke and Hare murders later established more firmly in the popular mind the association of cannibalism/dismemberment with godless science. One Victorian edition of *Frankenstein* was published together with a work entitled *London Medical Students*. Ultimately the clandestine and illegal search for human flesh for medical school dissection was conflated with the Frankenstein story itself on stage and in film.

Another aspect of the monster's physical appearance and character is worth emphasizing in any search for a racialized image. A strong tradition, already familiar by the late eighteenth century and insisted upon by racist propagandists for slavery like Edward Long, had it that the Negro was both particularly libidinous and possessed of unusually large genitalia. William Godwin himself had written: "The heat of the climate obliges both sexes [of the Negro] to go half naked. The animal arrives sooner at maturity in hot countries. And both these circumstances produce vigilance and jealousy, causes which inevitably tend to inflame the passions".[48] Edwards related that Negroes were promiscuous and possessed a strong sexual passion, which "is mere animal desire".[49] The threat that white women might be brutalized by over-sexed black men of great strength and size became a cliché of racist writing, ready for appropriation in the creation of Gothic horror and given an extra charge by the recently dramatized and exaggerated stories of the plight of white women in revolutionary Haiti.

Mary Shelley's monster, because of his great strength and unpredictable moods, his alternate plaintive persuasiveness and fiery rage, is suffused with a kind of dangerous male sexuality. In the film *Young*

Frankenstein Mel Brooks equipped his monster with a monstrous "Schlange". Beneath this juvenile satire is a valid, even perceptive, extrapolation from the original. Shelley describes her creation as not only eight feet tall but "proportionably large". Frankenstein's shocked reaction to his first sight of the living creature seems to evoke the image of a great, engorged and threatening phallus: "Great God! His yellow skin scarcely covered the work of muscles and arteries beneath".[50] A similarly threatening masculinity may be suggested in his later awakening to find the monster nakedly towering above him as he lay in his bed.

The murder of Elizabeth, Frankenstein's bride, seems almost certainly to draw, consciously or otherwise, upon the classic threat of the black male. The sharp contrast between the hazel-eyed, auburn-haired, high-browed, fragile white woman and the dark monster was sharp in the 1818 version, but was made much starker in Mary Shelley's revision of 1831. Here we can see the construction of both race and a vulnerable femininity, the "angel in the house", progressing together towards the Victorian age. Elizabeth is described in this third edition as not only of aristocratic, but of stereotypically northern, Teutonic beauty:

> Her hair was the brightest living gold ... her brow was clear and ample, her blue eyes cloudless ... none could behold her without looking on her as of a distinct species, a being heaven-sent, and bearing a celestial stamp in all her features ... Her mother was a German.[51]

It is this master-race maiden whom the monster—her racial negative; dark-haired, low-browed, with watery and yellowed eyes—violently assaults in her bedroom and strangles, just as Othello smothers Desdemona. The scene is emotionally and suggestively that of rape as well as murder, or rather, as murder in lieu of rape.

Finally, the threat of terrible violence which over-sexed "Others" would carry to the whole white race is made explicit in Frankenstein's hesitation to create a mate for his monster:

> Even if they [the monster and his bride-to-be] were to leave Europe [as the monster had suggested] and inhabit the deserts of the new world, yet one of the first results of those sympathies for which the daemon thirsted would be children, and a race of devils would be propagated upon the earth who might make the very existence of man a condition precarious and full of terror. Had I

a right, for my own benefit, to inflict this curse upon everlasting generations?[52]

Two interesting allusions are possible here. First, the idea of the racial Other's exile from Europe to a new Eden, where he would be left free to manage on his own, was already available from the beginning of the Sierra Leone experiment in sending destitute blacks "back to Africa". By the time Mary Shelley was writing, this much-advertised experiment had come to be regarded largely as a failure. More pointedly, there was a strong parallel with the fear of an autonomous "race of devils" in the recent history of Haiti and in highly exaggerated stories about the escaped or freed slave communities of mulattos in the West Indies and the threat they posed to the white planter society, and in particular to its women. Once again this was a fear which the slave-owning class encouraged in their loud protests against humanitarian intervention. The year Shelley began her novel there were reports that rebellious blacks in Barbados flew a flag which portrayed "a black chief, with a white woman, with clasped hands, imploring mercy".[53]

The image of blacks free from the discipline of the white master, in an environment where nature provided unlimited sustenance, breeding like animals at a rate unrestrained by decency or prudence, was already available well before Carlyle's essay on the "Nigger Question". In it lay much of the basis for the prediction of the inevitability of race war which preoccupies so much late nineteenth-century racist literature. *Frankenstein* prefigures this racial Armageddon as much as it does the mad scientist of twentieth-century fiction and film.

III

EDUCATION AND MORAL DILEMMA

The education of Frankenstein's monster occupies an important, indeed central, part of the story, involving a complicated and lengthy sub-plot at the De Lacey cottage. This has drawn the attention of literary critics who see in it more than a mere digression that allows Mary Shelley to parade her grasp of Lockeian ideas on the acquisition of knowledge by sensory association, the monster as *tabula rasa*, but also a sophisticated means of introducing the Rousseauian critique that true instruction must engage the emotions and requires loving contact. It is precisely this, of course, which the monster is denied both by his creator and ultimately by the family from whom he secretly learns language and history. This is a reasonable view which accords well with what we know of Mary Shelley's own reading of both Locke and Rousseau. It should not, however, preclude an examination of the novel as at some level also a comment on sharply focused and pragmatic contemporary issues as well as on earlier educational theory.

The success of Victor Frankenstein's hubristic experiment immediately poses the central problem of the novel, the hinge upon which the moral of the tale turns. This is the dilemma of whether he is willing to acknowledge his responsibility to nurture and educate his creation in the ways of humankind, thus not only making his progeny safe for society but admitting the fact of his paternity and responsibility to both himself and the world at large. This he cannot bring himself to do, and his flight from moral obligation has terrible consequences for all concerned. This ethical problem can be generalized. Can any parent, slave-master, patron or employer escape, without retribution, the moral obligation of providing for the welfare and education of those who are dependent upon him and who have, in some sense at least, been called into being, shaped and perhaps deformed to serve his needs? This is a powerful and demanding issue, which not only hints at a common critique of Rousseau's own notorious avoidance of the obligations of paternity, but directly targets a central, perhaps *the* central, social question of the post-Revolutionary, early-industrial age.

Frankenstein's refusal either to admit responsibility for the creature he has made or to help it achieve full integration into the society of men, coupled with the potential threat of the monster's brute strength, has led some critics to view the story as a metaphor for domestic class relations in the era of early mechanization and Luddism. In such a reading, Frankenstein's refusal to ameliorate the condition of his monster roughly anticipates the coming liberalism of the age of *laissez-faire* and individualism. The monster's later discovery of social injustice through his attempt at self-education comfortably conforms to this interpretation. However, these issues of accountability and paternalism, together with the dangerous self-awareness of a subordinate class, emerge with equal if not greater and more immediate force in nineteenth-century race relations.

Like Frankenstein, the white, gentlemanly abolitionist sought to give reality to an ideal, the potential humanity of the degraded slave. In the eyes of some philanthropists, the slave, like the monster, was indeed a *tabula rasa*, a cultureless creature ready to receive their moral teaching and their theology. In the optimism of the movement, others assumed that the abolition of the institution of slavery alone—in Frankenstein's story, the mere act of creation—would be followed by inevitable improvement, as the liberated black man found his place as a fully responsible, self-improving citizen. By the time Mary Shelley was writing, however, there were already deep misgivings about these expectations. In Sierra Leone the projectors of a free and self-respecting black colony had had to retrench their expectations, impose discipline and withhold self-governance. By the second decade of the century there must have been many, even among the abolitionist camp, who also harboured doubts at least about the immediate consequence of wholesale abolition in the West Indies, and who were ready, emotionally at any rate, to retreat from their own responsibility for any resulting horror. Retreat and denial is of course Frankenstein's first reaction to his own creation. Furthermore leaving the monster to his own devices in the wilderness results in brooding grievance and childlike rage. Already malformed by his creator, he does not rise to full humanity but reverts to the beast, in part because of the prejudice of those he encounters, in part because real self-improvement, without an education involving discipline and a nurturing paternalist connection, was as unlikely for him as—to many—it seemed to prove unlikely for blacks in the West Indies.

Here it will be seen that *Frankenstein* resonates strongly with a great and pressing social concern much in the mind of the upper- and middle-class public. As with Frankenstein's monster, the problem of education in the early nineteenth century had a dual aspect: the advancement, moral well-being and happiness of those to be educated, on the one hand; but also, on the other, the safety of the society to which, to some extent, the new urban citizen of the "dangerous classes" or the freed slave of the plantation was to be admitted.

In Mary Shelley's world, the double issues of responsibility and discipline were sharply debated. The same evangelicals who advocated abolition and missionary activity abroad pressed for Sunday schools and philanthropic instruction at home. The issue of the education of factory children, of women, and of slaves in the West Indies emerged in much the same terms. Where did responsibility lie? What should be taught? What was the (clearly anomalous) social role of an educated black, an educated worker or an educated woman? Clearly the problem facing the rejected monster, how should he educate himself, and the disappointment he experienced on realizing that his efforts at self-tuition were of little use in winning acceptance, closely approximates the issues raised both by abolitionists and domestic educational reformers whether of Benthamite, radical or evangelical persuasion. Behind this lay the frustrations inherent in the formal education of subordinate persons in a society that remained intensely patriarchal, class-bound and colour-prejudiced.

Like race prejudice and class snobbery, the racial and domestic educational issues were inextricably intertwined. The two discourses drew from and reinforced each other; they shared the key questions of appropriateness, responsibility, social control and social danger. The historians of education in this period have neglected the degree to which the "problem" of Negro education—a debate that raged, at least in abolitionist and pro-slavery quarters, from the late eighteenth century until well after the American Civil War—influenced the tenor and substance of the domestic European debate over the educability of the poor and women. Some further consideration of aspects of the novel in this light will therefore be of interest.

In the first place, it is appropriate to recall that the issue of whether black slaves ought to receive any education, enough, at least, to read the edifying homilies of religion, had long been a bone of contention between the Jamaican planters and the humanitarians. Knowledge is power, and the withholding of instruction was a highly symbolic entrenchment of the master–slave relationship. This suggests another debate over whether slaves ought to be baptized into a Christian church, which would bring them into the brotherhood of Christ and pose problems with regard to their disposal as chattels. It is not unduly far-fetched to see some reflection of these issues in Frankenstein's refusal either to instruct or to name his creature. Mary Shelley's monster is not only denied education; he is also denied a Christian name.[54] Frankenstein thus retreated from a commitment to a relationship, an attachment of sentiment and parentage, which was as repugnant to him as it would have been to the white slave-master. The monster's thirst for knowledge is in fact a thirst for deliverance from the condition of "a vagabond and a slave". What little education he could glean from the conversation of the De Laceys (such as a "house-nigger" might pick up from those whom he served) taught him that one such as himself, lacking "unsullied descent" or even a name, was "doomed to waste his powers for the profits of the chosen few!"[55]

It might be thought that the monster's articulateness, his precocious quickness of intellect in learning second-hand from overheard conversation, belies any close comparison with the slave stereotype. Certainly the most brutal stereotype—from, say, the pages of Edward Long—would deny the Negro sufficient intelligence to learn, but liberal opinion, of the kind read by Mary Shelley, held otherwise. Edwards claimed that "he had been surprised by such figurative expressions [from his slaves], and (notwithstanding their ignorance of abstract terms) such pointed sentences, as would have reflected no disgrace on poets and philosophers ... Negroes have minds very capable of observation".[56]

"Observation" is the monster's only means of self-education. Like the Negro slave, he is kept an outsider. In what is clearly a sense of self-recognition, he responds with weeping to the Count de Volney's tragic history of "the helpless fate" of the native inhabitants of America.[57] However, he not only identifies with the sufferers of this racial injustice but, though protesting that "mine shall not be the submission of abject slavery", finally acknowledges to himself his own inferiority and despairs:

> I became fully convinced that I was in reality the monster that I am ... I abhorred myself ... I was the slave, not the master ... I, the miserable and the abandoned, am an abortion, to be spurned at, and kicked, and trampled on ... Your abhorrence cannot equal that with which I regard myself.[58]

His response is at first rebellion, but this turns to despair and, ultimately, to suicide. The monster's "education" has taught him self-contempt just as the little education given the plantation black or freed slave served merely to reinforce his own awareness of inferiority. This mentality conforms to that observed by Edwards of the mulatto in Jamaica, where an official system of racial classification and discrimination "tends to degrade them [freed blacks and mulattos] in their eyes, and in the eyes of the community to which they belong".[59]

It was a commonplace of the literature of slavery that the recently enslaved experienced deep depression and, particularly those from some proud, warlike tribes, were prone to either rebellion or suicide. Edwards remarked on the frequent suicides among the Eboes of West Africa, and elsewhere commented that it was a widely held belief (though one with which he disagreed) that "Negroes consider death not only as a welcome and happy release from the calamities of their condition, but also as a passport to the place of their nativity".[60] The monster's intended self-immolation brings together three cliches of this tradition: the low self-regard of the slave, slave suicide (a form of impotent rebellion) and destruction by fire (the common image of real rebellion).

From overheard conversations and readings the monster also learned the ethnic stereotyping of which he himself, as an alien, ironically was also a victim—of slothful Asiatics, degenerate Romans and *ungrateful*, wicked Turks.[61] Indeed the idea of gratitude, and its opposite, a corrosive sense of resentment, feature strongly throughout the novel. There is the story of the Christian Arab Safie and her Turkish father, who unnaturally rewards his Christian deliverer with treacherous ingratitude. When Justine, a poor relation living as a servant in the Frankenstein household, is unjustly accused of the murder of Frankenstein's brother, the charge of murder was made more horrible in the eyes of the public by the suggestion of "ingratitude" to the Frankenstein family which had protected her. There is also the monster's own repeated assertion that, if he were treated with kindness by someone, he "would bestow every benefit upon him with tears of gratitude" at his acceptance; "my virtues will necessarily arise when I live in communion with an equal", for his heart, the creature says, "was fashioned to be susceptible of love and sympathy".[62] Again, this is a theme that features prominently in the literature with which Mary Shelley was familiar on the African and West Indian black. Edwards, like others, was eager to affirm that, however violent and passionate the black or mulatto might be, there was a counterbalancing tendency to affection. He speaks of "their disinterested gratitude and attachment where favours are shown them"; "if their confidence be once obtained, they manifest as great fidelity, affection, and gratitude as can reasonably be expected from men in a state of slavery".[63]

This projection of gratitude invokes the classic colonizer mentality, evident in the middle-class humanitarian as well as in the paternalist slave-holder. The recipients of liberation, protection or education in the Christian virtues of patience and forbearance are expected to return benevolent condescension with self-abasing thankfulness and loyalty. The cardinal sin in this system is "ingratitude", a failing which Mary Shelley herself at one point calls "blackest ingratitude",[64] and which the Victorians were later quick to ascribe to sepoy troops or Jamaican freed slaves. This discloses the paradox at the centre of the humanitarian, abolitionist enterprise: that while the gift of liberation transforms the slave into a free man, it does so only through the good offices of white, middle- and upper-class patrons, rather than by self-help. In this relationship the idealized black, though a "man and a brother", is inevitably still on his knees as a grateful man and a younger brother.

IV

THE VICTORIAN FRANKENSTEIN

Though Mary Shelley wrote five more novels before her death in 1851, none succeeded with the public nearly as well as *Frankenstein*. Only months after it appeared in the spring of 1818, Thomas Peacock could write to Percy Shelley that *"It seems to be universally known and read"*.[65] The three-volume edition of that year was followed in 1823 by a two-volume version, apparently to take advantage of the popularity of stage adaptations. A cheaper (one-volume) third edition, with revisions and illustrations, was aimed at a yet wider public in 1831, and this was often reprinted.[66] There was in fact either a new edition of the novel or an authorized reprinting in each decade of the century, and two in the 1830s, 1880s and 1890s, in addition to the versions included in collections of horror stories, in pirated (often American) editions, and in foreign translations. A one-shilling pocket edition appeared in 1888.

The successful stage adaptation of 1823 which helped spread and sustain the novel's popularity in fact sparked a number of other dramatizations (at least fourteen in the following three years). Some of these were in fact burlesques, testifying to the work's having achieved a certain place in the popular mind. The first and most successful of the stage adaptations, Richard Brinsley Peake's "Presumption: or, The Fate of Frankenstein", was received with "tremendous enthusiasm" and achieved an "enduring popularity". Thomas Cooke, who made a speciality of weird and villainous roles, made the part of the monster his own, and played it to packed houses for some 350 performances in London and Paris.[67]

On the Victorian stage the Frankenstein story was inevitably altered to fit the melodramatic expectations of audiences of the time. On the one hand, demonic and alchemical elements were emphasized; on the other, songs and dancing were interpolated in some versions, and a comic element was occasionally introduced to lighten the story. Catastrophic storms, the burning of the cottage, and avalanches provided spectacle, while the subtler tones of the novel were sacrificed to a simplified drama of innocence versus demonic terror. Mary Shelley's ambiguities disappeared. Cooke's monster, effectively mimed, lost its articulateness and became the mute beast, tameable only by music. As Steven Forry has recently observed,[68] the monster was "Calibanized", though this is surely only an extension of the densely present, if buried, associations already linking Mary Shelley's monster to the Caliban-like slave. By turning the creature into even more of a caricature, the Victorian stage enhanced its utility as stereotype, as image of the dark "Other". It may be significant, for instance, that both the popularity of a variety of burlesques on the Frankenstein story (still being played as late as the 1880s), as well as the introduction of comic song into even the more serious versions, coincides with the emergence of "Nigger Minstrels" as an enduring entertainment in London music-halls and theatres. In any event the image of the creature swaying to the charms of music at least suggests the caricature of the "singin' and dancin'" Old South slave.

From the 1830s there was another type of association available to public view, one which completes a triangular relationship of images of animal, monster and Negro, in the exhibition of the first large ape-like creatures from Africa at the Regent's Park zoo. Tommy the chimpanzee captivated audiences in 1835, and displayed what seemed to be the learning ability of at least a child. He was followed two years later by a much-publicized orangutan. Many contemporaries, one assumes, responded like Queen Victoria herself, who commented: "He is frightful & painfully and disagreeably human".[69] About the same time Edgar Allen Poe's story *The Murders in the Rue Morgue* (1841) brought to the public what Frankenstein's monster had already suggested, a homicidal simian.[70]

One would like to know more about the performances of the various stage adaptations and whether the available racial and simian associations of the creature were introduced on the stage, as they were in parliamentary debate and magazine caricature. Cooke probably darkened his skin for his performance of the satanic Samiel in an 1824 version of *Die Freischütz* to suggest the darkness of evil. Similarly he, like others after him, used blue greasepaint in his portrayal of the monster,[71] not with the intention of creating a racial villain, but to suggest both the lividity of a corpse and a sinister Otherness. A blue-skinned monster would inevitably, however, have suggested on the one hand an Othello, on the other a "nigger minstrel"— Negro tragedy and Negro farce.

However this may be, the story clearly found its way quickly into popular metaphor and caricature, and such allusions seem to follow, not the publication of the three-volume novel in 1818, but the London stage plays of 1823. In March 1824, for example, in a parliamentary debate over Thomas Fowell Buxton's motion that the children of West Indian slaves be freed on achieving the age of majority, Canning explicitly connected the Frankenstein myth with the dangers of abolition:

> In dealing with the negro, Sir, we must remember that we are dealing with a being possessing the form and strength of a man, but the intellect only of a child. To turn the negro loose in the manhood of his physical strength, in the maturity of his physical passions, but in the infancy of his uninstructed reason, would be to raise up a creature resembling the splendid fiction of a recent romance; the hero of which constructs a human form, with all the thews and sinews of a giant; but being unable to impart to the work of his hands a perception of right and wrong, he finds too late that he has created a more than mortal power of doing mischief and himself recoils from the monster which he has made.[72]

Canning here seized upon three important racial parallels: first, the childishness of monster and Negro slave; secondly, a supposed lack of moral judgement (this reading obviously derives from the stage plays rather than the novel, where the monster has an acute sense of right and wrong); and finally, an implied sexual threat—the "maturity of his physical passions". Coincidentally, the play at this time was accompanied in a double bill at Covent Garden by another called *The West Indian*.[73]

This temptation to use the image of the monster in the portrayal of "uncivilized" and non-white peoples abroad inevitably wandered into domestic politics. As Chris Baldick has noted, Canning was "reclaiming the monster as a Burkean bogy figure", and in this enterprise the dumb, mimed figure of the stage fiend served to better purpose than the articulate reasoner of Mary Shelley's original creation.[74] The monster in caricature was commonly used as a metaphor for radicalism during the Reform agitations of the early 1830s and the mid-1860s, and during the Chartist period. If these were not Negro monsters, they often suggested ethnic prejudice in associating the creature with the Irish working man. "The Irish Frankenstein" in fact became something of a cliché in mid-Victorian humorous magazines, and was used to comment on O'Connell in the 1840s (*Punch*), the Fenians in the 1860s (Matt Morgan in *The Tomahawk*) and the Phoenix Park murders in 1882 (John Tenniel in *Punch*).[75]

This is not to claim, of course, that there must always be a racial or ethnic component in Victorian appropriation of the Frankenstein metaphor. The story worked its way down into popular culture, to become a kind of mythic or iconic element that was drawn up again into serious literature, as in *Middlemarch* where Lydgate's search for the life source in primitive tissues clearly draws from Frankenstein's laboratory.[76] In *Mary Barton* Elizabeth Gaskell compared the uneducated radical working man to "a Frankenstein", in what had possibly become a commonplace allusion. That she received the idea from popular "knowledge" of the Frankenstein story rather than from a direct reading is indicated by the careless way in which she (along with many others) confused Frankenstein with his monster, while the misreading of the monster on the popular stage as an inarticulate child served her desire to represent the working class as child-like.[77] Pip's fear that Magwitch has become his own Frankenstein's monster[78] seems free of racial association as well, though his acute embarrassment over the possibility of public knowledge of the criminal's patronage suggests something of the horror of the discovery of "bad blood", of a "white" having to recognize black relations.

Frankenstein endured in print, on the stage, and as metaphor in a way that belies the weaknesses of its literary construction. Indeed the critical response then and later was slight and mixed, with some praise from a minority of critics and much deprecation of the "immorality" of its apparent message. It is reasonable to assume that it survived partly because of the resonances it evoked and because of its usefulness in reinforcing racial and ethnic prejudice. Seen simply as a somewhat immature and certainly backward-looking exercise in Gothic horror, with a message drawn from reflections on Enlightenment ideas about the perfectibility of man—that is, from the preoccupations of the dated late eighteenth-century radicalism of Godwin—the story's enduring success seems odd. One can attempt to explain it, as with any critical failure and popular success, in terms of the appeal of mere sensationalism to an uncritical public. The rise of the vulgarly educated mass consumer of cheap literature in the nineteenth century offers this answer, but it is not, I think, a sufficient one. Some works which are "in tune" with changes in contemporary mentality achieve a larger-than-life stature, and are "read" by the public in a way not perhaps originally intended. The nineteenth-century development of the Frankenstein story in drama and burlesque reflects this process.

The idea that the story is about science run amok, a critique of the godless, mad professional in the sense that later became standard fare, was one such "reading" not exactly intended in the original but quite quickly developed on the stage.[79] The change from the highly articulate monster of Shelley's creation into the mute horror pursued by villagers, the manufactured zombie with a deformed and criminal brain, is another later interpretation, reflecting perhaps the craniological and neurological concerns of mid-nineteenth-century science, as well as the requirements of stage and film sensationalism.

At a deeper and less obvious level, however, the real explanation for *Frankenstein's* enduring appeal lies in the conjunction of certain readily appropriable images which stirred deep popular anxieties—about revealed religion versus science, the place of women in the masculine world of empire and the professions, the danger of proletarian revolution, or the threat of non-white races. Here it is that the sub-text of racial image and character is important in explaining the attraction of a story which helped formulate a popular emotional response to increasing contact with and threats from non-white cultures abroad. The Indian Mutiny, the Jamaican rebellions of 1831 and 1865, the countless little wars fought by Victoria's armies against Maori, Ashanti, Zulus or Canadian Métis all contributed to the emotional appeal of a text which presented the Other as a rebellious and ungrateful child that owed its very existence to a white male patron. The story loops around and what began as a series of ambiguous images, inspired in part by the noble savage as well as the abolitionist/pro-slavery discourse of the late eighteenth century, plays a role in reifying and entrenching racialist and colonialist values in the nineteenth and twentieth centuries.

V

A CONCLUSION

As developed in this essay, the Frankenstein story has three levels of interest. First, it reveals a deeper kind of signification than is at first apparent. The "Other", the outsider, the racially foreign, is probably buried within the genre of Gothic horror as a whole. Secondly, while in the novel this embedded message reflects contemporary ambiguity or confusion about the racial Other, it entered popular culture at a time of shifting racial and ethnocentric attitudes, and in this context inevitably lent its weight to the construction of sensational (and more firmly pejorative) aspects of "race" in the popular nineteenth-century mind. Finally, the text and its subsequent development reveal inherent linkages between race and the other evolving concepts of class and gender.

A close reading of *Frankenstein* demonstrates how a well-known work of fiction depended in part at least for its inspiration and for its effect on the coded language of contemporary racial prejudice, as well as on a deeply embedded cultural tradition of xenophobia. It is necessary, in consequence, substantially to amend Ann Mellor's judgement that "Mary Shelley created her myth single-handedly. All other myths of the western or eastern worlds, whether of Dracula, Tarzan, Superman or more traditional religious systems, derive from folklore or communal ritual practices". Nor can one entirely accept that the creature should be seen as "a sign detached from a visual or verbal grammar, without diachronic or synchronic context, without precursor or progeny".[80] *Frankenstein* did not spring fully formed from the feminine imagination, but owed much of its language and power to Jamaican and Haitian slave rebellions and to uncertainties over the consequences of abolition. In this context it displaced overtly xenophobic and racial fears to another, imaginary field. A mid-twentieth-century parallel can be found in the way American science-fiction literature and film, for example *The Invasion of the Body Snatchers*, offered a strikingly similar displacement of contemporary fears of Communist subversion and invasion. As a result of the familiarity it achieved with the reading public, on stage and in common discourse, *Frankenstein* attained the status of an icon of popular culture and thus itself became a source, albeit oblique, for the reinforcement of ethnic and racial stereotypes, a reservoir of emotional ammunition which could be deployed against the Other both within Victorian England and beyond.

In some sense the story of *Frankenstein* itself, the construction of the monster, is the fictional equivalent of the simultaneous "construction" of both race and racial prejudice. It is not merely a case of the unknown portrayed as evil. Ironically the monster lives up to the expectations imposed upon him. "By reading his creation as evil", Anne Mellor has observed, "Frankenstein constructs a monster".[81] She sees this as Mary Shelley's own comment on the dangers of romantic imagination. Surely, however, race itself is, in its most emotive sense, a construct of romanticism. Imagination literally gave birth to reality. Prejudice, like the imperialism which is its crudest manifestation, worked to produce the abject degradation and dependency which it expected to find in the Other.

As the nineteenth century progressed, both cultural and scientific racism became ever more widely diffused and achieved an acceptability, almost a consensus, in educated society as well as at deeper levels of popular culture. As a result, what was unconscious or only obliquely hinted at in a work like *Frankenstein* could surface with semantic explicitness in Victorian literature. For instance, there is the problem of "bad blood". In *Wuthering Heights* the savagery of Heathcliff, a "dark-skinned Gypsy" in appearance, "black as Satan", is linked to his darkly suggested origin as a Lascar orphan on the docks in Liverpool, while *Jane Eyre*'s madwoman is a passionate West Indian, with "a goblin appearance ... long dishevelled [black] hair" and a "swelled black face".[82] Moreover what was buried in the Gothic novel often became overt in the late nineteenth-century adventure story. William Harrison Ainsworth's popular *Rookwood* of 1824 produced a repulsive old woman with blackened yellow skin "like an animated mummy" for sensational effect; fifty years later H. Rider Haggard achieved the same less allusively with the withered old Negro witch Gagool in *King Solomon's Mines*. Both recall elements of Godwin's malignant old robber woman in *Caleb Williams*, whose "swarthy" complexion, "the consistency of parchment", "uncommonly vigorous and muscular" arms and "savage ferocity" lend a further racial colouring to her avowed intention to "drink your blood!"[83]

As suggested in the Brontë novels, there is another level of significance in the deployment of racial allusion. This is the way in which it meshes with class and gender. In Heathcliff, threatening masculinity, vindictiveness and sadism are somehow linked to what we have seen to be one of the supposed characteristics of the non-European, a childlike vengefulness and cruelty combined with a strong need for affection. In Charlotte Brontë's Bertha Mason, we encounter perhaps a combination of feminine and racial stereotype, the hysterical, uncontrollably passionate woman and the drunken Jamaican "White" Creole who, in her madness, burns down Rochester's house just as the monster destroys the De Lacey cottage, and commits suicide, just as the monster intends to do. In class terms, moreover, both Heathcliff and the madwoman occupy an uncertain, suspect and barely respectable position as a result of their obscure, non-British origins.

Though I have emphasized the racial aspects of Frankenstein's monster, other critics have pleaded for a class-based and gender-based reading. In fact these issues of class, gender and race are all present and intricately interwoven in the novel. The monster—unnaturally conceived without woman; oversized, over-sexed and physically repulsive; economically and socially marginal—encompasses three confused elements of middle-class nightmare: racial, sexual, and proletarian.

The fifty years that followed the French Revolution saw a hardening of social definition and categorization among the educated classes. This involved the "construction", although not from entirely new materials, of an emerging (and threatening) urban working class, a segregated and subordinated second sex, and racially inferior colonized peoples. This triple evolution, and integration, of attitudes at a deep level of the popular mind was an intimately interconnected response to changing social conditions—to industrialization, the separation of work from family, and the outward expansion of the economy and the state. Each of these prejudices had, of course, a long and distinct history, but they were welded together in the early nineteenth century in a mutually reinforcing tripartite structure that could endure because, like the triangular supports of a geodesic dome, each offered its own resistance to pressure on the others. This strength rested on a common-sense invocation of science, nature, economic necessity and tradition, as well as on shared metaphors appropriate to each area of social, sexual and racial domination. Here, diffuse but heavily charged sources, such as popular romance and sensational theatre, played a clandestine role in confirming the white, English, upper-class male in the empire, the work-place and the home.

NOTES

1. Anonymous English ballad inspired by the contest between the British boxing champion, Tom Cribb, and the Negro challenger, Thomas Molineaux, in 1811: see Peter Fryer, *Staying Power: The History of Black People in Britain* (London, 1984), pp. 447–8.

2. Chris Baldick, *In Frankenstein's Shadow: Myth, Monstrosity and Nineteenth-Century Writing* (Oxford, 1987), p. 5.

3. For the novel as allegory of the class struggle, see Paul O'Flynn, "Production and Reproduction: The Case of Frankenstein", *Literature and History*, ix (1983), pp. 194–213; and, less convincingly, Franco Moretti, *Signs Taken for Wonders: Essays in the Sociology of Literary Forms* (London, 1983), ch. 3, "Dialectic of Fear". For the feminist interpretation, see Ellen Moers, "Female Gothic", in G. Levine and U. C. Knoepflmacher (eds.), *The Endurance of Frankenstein: Essays on Mary Shelley's Novel* (Berkeley, 1979), pp. 77–87; Sandra Gilbert and Susan Gubar, *The Madwoman in the Attic: The Woman Writer in the Nineteenth-Century Literary Imagination* (New Haven, 1979), ch. 7, "Horror's Twin: Mary Shelley's Monstrous Eve"; Mary Poovey, "My Hideous Progeny: Mary Shelley and the Feminization of Romanticism", *P.M.L.A.*, xcv (1980), pp. 332–47; Gayatri Chakravorty Spivak, "Three Women's Texts and a Critique of Imperialism", *Critical Inquiry*, xii (1985), pp. 243–61. Moers argues that the novel is both a dream of awakening sexuality and of the horror of maternity, while Gilbert and Gubar assert that Mary Shelley took the male cultural myth of *Paradise Lost* and rewrote it as a mirror of female experience. Poovey emphasizes the dilemma of the female artist expected to produce literature with a moral, while Spivak offers a deconstructionist perspective of the novel as "a text of nascent feminism" where the binary opposition of male/female is undone in Frankenstein's womb-laboratory.

4. O. Mannoni, *Prospero and Caliban: The Psychology of Colonization*, trans. P. Powesland (London, 1956; 1st pubd. Paris, 1950); Philip D. Curtin, *The Image of Africa: British Ideas and Action, 1780–1850* (London, 1965).

5. See, for example, Burton R. Pollin, "Philosophical and Literary Sources of Frankenstein", *Comparative Literature*, xvii (1965), pp. 97–108; James O'Rourke, "'Nothing More Unnatural': Mary Shelley's Revision of Rousseau", *E.L.H.*, lvi (1989), pp. 543–69; David Marshall, *The Surprising Effects of Sympathy: Marivaux, Diderot, Rousseau and Mary Shelley* (Chicago, 1988); Lee Sterrenberg, "Mary Shelley's Monster: Politics and Psyche in *Frankenstein*", in Levine and Knoepflmacher (eds.), *Endurance of Frankenstein*, pp. 143–71; Christopher Small, *Ariel Like a Harpy: Shelley, Mary and "Frankenstein"* (London, 1972); Anne K. Mellor, *Mary Shelley: Her Life, Her Fiction, Her Monsters* (London, 1989).

6. Fryer, *Staying Power*, pp. 212–13.

7. William Godwin, *Enquiry Concerning Political Justice* (London, 1985; 1st pubd. 1793), pp. 147–53.

8. *Ibid.*, pp. 151–3.

9. Sander L. Gilman, "Black Bodies, White Bodies: Toward an Iconography of Female Sexuality in Late Nineteenth-Century Art, Medicine and Literature", *Critical Inquiry*, xii (1985), pp. 204–42. See also Hugh Honour, *The Image of the Black in Western Art*, iv, pt. 2, *Black Models and White Myths* (Cambridge, Mass., 1989), pp. 47–56.

10. Edward Baldwin [pseudonym for William Godwin], *Fables, Ancient and Modern, Adapted for the Use of Children* (London, 1805), p. 165.

11. Fryer, *Staying Power*, p. 68. Estimates run from 10,000 to 20,000.

12. See Honour, *Black Models and White Myths*, p. 30.

13. *Annual Register ... for the Year 1811* (London, 1812), pp. 110–11.

14. Peter H. Marshall, *William Godwin* (New Haven, 1984), pp. 76, 81.

15. Cited *ibid.*, p. 207.

16. *Ibid.*, p. 234.

17. Hugh Honour, *The Image of the Black in Western Art*, iv, pt. 1, *Slaves and Liberators* (Cambridge, Mass., 1989), pp. 50–7, 62–6.

18. Mungo Park, *Travels in the Interior Districts of Africa: Performed under the Direction and Patronage of the African Association in the Years 1795, 1796 and 1797* (London, 1799); Mungo Park, *The Journal of a Mission to the Interior of Africa, in the Year 1805* (London, 1815); *Mary Shelley's Journal* [ed. Frederick L. Jones] (Norman, Okla., 1947), pp. 32, 71.

19. Bryan Edwards, *The History, Civil and Commercial, of the British Colonies in the West Indies*, 2 vols. (Dublin, 1793).

20. *Mary Shelley's Journal*, p. 34.

21. John Davis, *Travels of Four Years and a Half in the United States of America; During 1798, 1799, 1800, 1801 and 1802* (London, 1803), p. 92. It may also be worth mentioning that, though an apparently obscure and distant "source", *The Arabian Nights' Entertainments* was a childhood reading which the Shelleys continued to dip into when abroad. Black slaves feature in many of the stories, sometimes with a relevant twist, as in that in which "an ugly, tall, black slave" causes a young man to murder his wife: *The Arabian Nights' Entertainments: or, The Thousand and One Nights*, trans. M. Galland, 2 vols. (Liverpool, 1814), i, pp. 178–80 ff. *Mary Shelley's Journal*, p. 47, notes that they read from this in 1815. Godwin recommended it for children: Mellor, *Mary Shelley*, p. 9. Mungo Park claimed that the African stories he had heard bore some resemblance to those of the *Arabian Nights*: Park, *Travels in the Interior Districts of Africa*, i, p. 31.

22. Park, *Travels in the Interior Districts of Africa*, i, pp. 21, 239.

23. Edwards, *History, Civil and Commercial, of the West Indies*, ii, pp. 58, 69.

24. Mary Shelley, *Frankenstein: or, The Modern Prometheus* (London, 1985; hereafter *Frankenstein*), pp. 105, 261. Unless otherwise indicated, all references to *Frankenstein* are to this edition of the 1831 version. This was the edition most commonly available in the nineteenth century; although Mary Shelley made some significant alterations to the 1818 text, they are seldom important for our purposes.

25. Chasseboeuf de Volney, *Ruins: or, A Survey of the Revolutions of Empires* (London, 1795), p. 331. One should also note in this context that Bryan Edwards attempted to associate the West Indian superstition of Obeah with ancient Egyptian sources: Edwards, *History, Civil and Commercial, of the West Indies*, ii, p. 83.

26. Though some writers, as we have seen, drew attention to the yellowish skin and eyes of some Negroes.

27. David E. Musselwhite, *Partings Welded Together: Politics and Desire in the Nineteenth-Century Novel* (London, 1987), p. 60, argues that "the lustrous black hair and pearly white teeth suggest 'feminine' attributes, contrasted with the straight black lips and the prominent musculature, which suggest predominantly 'masculine' traits". See also William Veeder, *Mary Shelley & "Frankenstein": The Fate of Androgyny* (Chicago, 1986).

28. *Frankenstein*, p. 166.

29. A point made by, among many others, John Davis, *Travels in the United States of America*, p. 95.

30. An inversion perhaps suggested to Mary Shelley by her father's discussion of the impact of climate on character: "In their extreme perhaps heat and cold may determine the character of nations, of the negroes for example on the one side, and the Laplanders on the other": Godwin, *Enquiry Concerning Political Justice*, p. 151. It may also be relevant to note that Edwards described the snow-covered mountains of South America in his history

of the West Indies, and the lesser mountains of the islands which "have never yet, that I have heard, been fully explored": Edwards, *History, Civil and Commercial, of the West Indies*, i, p. 20. Davis in the American South alludes to the Alps when in sight of the Blue Ridge Mountains, associating both with escape and melancholy: Davis, *Travels in the United States of America*, p. 376.

31. U. C. Knoepflmacher, "'Face to Face': Of Man-Apes, Monsters and Readers", appendix to Levine and Knoepflmacher (eds.), *Endurance of Frankenstein*, p. 319; Park, *Travels in the Interior Districts of Africa*, i, pp. 279–80.

32. [Godwin], *Fables, Ancient and Modern*, pp. 165–8.

33. Revd Henry Bate [Sir Henry Bate Dudley], *Airs, Ballads, &c in "The Blackamoor Wash'd White"* (London, 1776), pp. 17–18.

34. Park, *Travels in the Interior Districts of Africa*, i, pp. 16, 235; Edwards, *History, Civil and Commercial, of the West Indies*, ii, p. 59.

35. John Leyden, *Historical and Philosophical Sketch of the Discoveries and Settlements of the Europeans in Northern and Western Africa at the Close of the Eighteenth Century* (Edinburgh, 1799), p. 98, quoted in Curtin, *Image of Africa*, p. 223.

36. Park, *Travels in the Interior Districts of Africa*, i, pp. 15–16; Edwards, *History, Civil and Commercial, of the West Indies*, i, pp. 31–6.

37. See Douglas Lorimer, *Colour, Class and the Victorians: English Attitudes to the Negro in the Mid-Nineteenth Century* (Leicester, 1978), p. 147, citing Joseph Hooker [to John Tyndall, 15 Feb. 1867 (Huxley Papers, Imperial College, London)]: "It depends on the definition of the term 'SAVAGE'. Johnson defined savage as 'a man untaught, uncivilized'; in general parlance the world now superadds CRUELTY to the above. Now I hold the Negro in W. Africa and Jamaica is untaught, uncivilized and CRUEL TOO".

38. Edwards, *History, Civil and Commercial, of the West Indies*, i, pp. 33–6, and ii, p. 74.

39. Honour, *Slaves and Liberators*, p. 93; Honour, *Black Models and White Myths*, pp. 25–6.

40. *Parliamentary Register*, xliv (London, 1796), pp. 337ff.

41. Edwards, *History, Civil and Commercial, of the West Indies*, ii, pp. 60–1.

42. Ibid., p. 82.

43. *Frankenstein*, p. 124.

44. Mellor, *Mary Shelley*, p. 9.

45. Edwards, *History, Civil and Commercial, of the West Indies*, i, pp. 29–30, where he attempts to refute Labat's claim that cannibalism had been rare.

46. *Frankenstein*, p. 187.

47. Mellor, *Mary Shelley*, pp. 135–6.

48. Godwin, *Enquiry Concerning Political Justice*, p. 152.

49. Edwards, *History, Civil and Commercial, of the West Indies*, ii, p. 76.

50. *Frankenstein*, p. 105.

51. Ibid., p. 83. For the 1818 description, see Mary Shelley, *Frankenstein* (Berkeley, 1968), p. 31.

52. *Frankenstein*, pp. 210–11.

53. *Annual Register ... for the Year 1816* (London, 1817), p. 77.

54. This was emphasized by the posters advertising the popular stage adaptation of the novel in 1823, where the monster is designated only by "_____".

55. *Frankenstein*, p. 165.

56. Edwards, *History, Civil and Commercial, of the West Indies*, ii, p. 78.

57. *Frankenstein*, p. 165. The De Laceys read Chasseboeuf de Volney's *Ruins*.

58. *Frankenstein*, pp. 159, 262–4.

59. Edwards, *History, Civil and Commercial, of the West Indies*, ii, p. 20.

60. *Ibid.*, pp. 69–70, 80.

61. *Frankenstein*, pp. 164–5, 171.

62. *Ibid.*, pp. 131, 190, 192, 262.

63. Edwards, *History, Civil and Commercial, of the West Indies*, ii, pp. 25, 69–70.

64. *Frankenstein*, p. 131, with reference to public opinion of Justine.

65. Peacock to Shelley, Aug. 1818 (emphasis in original), quoted in Radu Florescu, *In Search of Frankenstein* (London, 1975), p. 155.

66. In 1839, 1849, 1856, 1882 and 1886, not counting unauthorized and American printings of this edition: see *The British Library General Catalogue of Printed Books to 1975*, ccc, p. 382; Donald F. Glut, *The Frankenstein Catalogue* (Jefferson, N.C., 1984).

67. Allardyce Nicoll, *A History of Early Nineteenth-Century Drama, 1800–1850*, 2 vols. (Cambridge, 1930), i, p. 96, and ii, pp. 261, 346, 454; Victor Leathers, *British Entertainers in France* (Toronto, 1954), pp. 55–7; Steven Earl Forry, "Dramatizations of Frankenstein, 1821–1986: A Comprehensive List", *Eng. Lang. Notes*, xxv (1987), pp. 63–79; Steven Earl Forry, "The Hideous Progenies of Richard Brinsley Peake: Frankenstein on the Stage, 1823 to 1826", *Theatre Research International*, xi (1986), pp. 13–31.

68. Steven Earl Forry, *Hideous Progenies: Dramatizations of "Frankenstein" from the 19th Century to the Present* (Philadelphia, 1990), p. 22.

69. Quoted in Wilfrid Blunt, *The Ark in the Park: The Zoo in the Nineteenth Century* (London, 1976), p. 38.

70. For a recent essay on the anthropological treatment of apes, monkeys and humans, and its relationship to the construction of race and gender in the nineteenth and twentieth centuries, see Donna Haraway, *Primate Visions: Gender, Race and Nature in the World of Modern Science* (London, 1990).

71. Forry, *Hideous Progenies*, p. 4.

72. *Hansard*, new ser., x, 16 Mar. 1824, col. 1103.

73. Handbill reproduced in Florescu, *In Search of Frankenstein*, p. 164.

74. Baldick, *In Frankenstein's Shadow*, p. 60.

75. See Forry, *Hideous Progenies*, pp. 43–54; Mary Shelley, *Frankenstein* (London, 1985 edn.), introduction by Maurice Hindle, p. 37; Lee Sterrenberg, "Mary Shelley's Monster: Politics and Psyche in *Frankenstein*", in Levine and Knoepflmacher (eds.), *Endurance of Frankenstein*, p. 166; L. P. Curtis, *Apes and Angels: The Irishman in Victorian Caricature* (Newton Abbot, 1971).

76. George Eliot, *Middlemarch* (London, 1965; 1st pubd. 1871–2), pp. 177–8.

77. Elizabeth Gaskell, *Mary Barton* (London, 1970; 1st pubd. 1848), pp. 219–20. See also Baldick, *In Frankenstein's Shadow*, pp. 86–7.

78. Charles Dickens, *Great Expectations* (London, 1965; 1st pubd. 1861), p. 354.

79. Mellor, *Mary Shelley*, pp. 89–114, I believe, somewhat exaggerates Shelley's intention in this direction, though Shelley did, in attempting to improve the morals of the tale for the edition of 1831, herself shift emphasis to this aspect: see O'Flynn, "Production and Reproduction", p. 201.

80. Mellor, *Mary Shelley*, pp. 38–9, 128.

81. *Ibid.*, p. 136.

82. Emily Brontë, *Wuthering Heights* (London, 1965; 1st pubd. 1847), p. 77; Charlotte Brontë, *Jane Eyre* (London, 1985; 1st pubd. 1847), p. 313.

83. William Harrison Ainsworth, *Rookwood* (London, 1824); H. Rider Haggard, *King Solomon's Mines* (London, 1958; 1st pubd. 1885), p. 121, "the wizened monkey-like figure ... [with a face] made up of a collection of deep yellow wrinkles ... the whole countenance might have been taken for that of a sun-dried corpse"; William Godwin, *Caleb Williams* (London, 1988), p. 222.

MAUREEN NOELLE McLANE

Literate Species:
Populations, "Humanities,"
and Frankenstein

When one is studying man, what can be more exact or more rigorous
than to *recognize human properties in him*?
—Jean-Paul Sartre, *Search for a Method*

I began the creation of a human being.
—Victor Frankenstein

In his 1797 essay, "Of an Early Taste for Reading," William Godwin
announced that "Literature, taken in all its bearings, forms the grand line of
demarcation between the human and the animal kingdoms."[1] Mary Shelley's
Frankenstein, or The Modern Prometheus—boldly dedicated to "WILLIAM
GODWIN, Author of Political Justice, Caleb Williams, &c."—may be read
as a critique of her father's pronouncement.[2] Shelley's corporeally
indeterminate but decidedly literate monster asks us to consider whether
literature—taken in all its bearings—was or is indeed a useful "line of
demarcation between" human and animal. The fate of the monster suggests
that proficiency in "the art of language" (110), as he calls it, may not ensure
one's position as a member of the "human kingdom." Shelley shows us how
a literary education, so crucial to Godwinian perfectibility, presupposes not
merely an educable subject but a human being. Read through Godwin's
dictum, the trajectory of Frankenstein's creation offers a parable of

From *ELH* 63.4 (1996). © 1996 The Johns Hopkins University Press.

pedagogic failure—specifically a failure in the promise of the humanities, in letters as a route to humanization.[3] In assuming language and literature as domains available to him, the monster succumbs to the ruse of the humanities, the belief that "intellectual and literary refinement," in Godwin's terms, might be the route to his humanization. The novel demonstrates, perhaps against itself, that the acquisition of "literary refinement" fails to humanize the problematic body, the ever-unnamed monster. The monster thus introduces and embodies an anthropological problem which literature fails to resolve (within the novel) and yet which literature displays (in the fact of the novel itself). The perfectibility of man meets its violent contradiction in a speaking, reasoning being which men, women, and children throughout Europe are unable or unwilling to recognize as a fellow species-being.

The meaning of "species," like the meaning of the monster, is not self-evident and indeed remains suspended through most of the novel. I will argue that Victor Frankenstein's final deliberations about the monster's future transform and fix the functional meaning of species; moreover, it is Victor's introduction of Malthusian discourse which allows him to arbitrate, in the last instance, the question of the monster's "species." The argument requires that I examine the monster's request for one "of the same species" (140) through the broad contours of the Malthus–Godwin debate, with Malthus representing the principle of population and Godwin the principle of perfectibility. I understand the discourses of population theory and human perfectibility to be part of the same discursive and historical field: Malthus and Godwin appear (in this essay as they did to themselves) as representative antagonists within that field.[4] It was, of course, Godwin's vision of almost unlimited human improvability, and his defense of universal benevolence as the criterion of moral action and political justice, which most irked Malthus. Indeed, it was Godwin's essay "Of Avarice and Profusion" (published in *The Enquirer: Reflections on Education, Manners, and Literature* [1797]), which provoked Malthus to launch his extended attack on Godwinian radicalism, Condordet's theory of mind, and poor relief in his *Essay on the Principle of Population* (1798). Malthus and Godwin maintained their mutually antagonistic positions for several decades; in 1820 Godwin finally published his own *Of Population: An Inquiry concerning the Power of Increase in the Numbers of Mankind, being an answer to Mr. Malthus' Essay on that Subject*. Godwin wrote of his quarrel with Malthus and the surrounding debate, "[such] speculations have now been current for nearly twenty years."[5]

Written toward the end of that twenty-year period, *Frankenstein* should be read in part through the historical specificity of the Malthus–Godwin controversy. During Mary Shelley's lifetime, her father was known publicly as the antagonist of Malthus as well as the author of *Political Justice* and *Caleb Williams*; any discussion of Godwinian "benevolence" would have taken into account its most prominent critic, Malthus, and his cautionary calculus of moral restraint, misery and vice. Certainly Percy Shelley, disciple of Godwin and despiser of Malthus, made the connection between the two, as *A Philosophical View of Reform* demonstrates. Lee Sterrenburg, Ellen Moers, U. C. Knoepflmacher, Anne K. Mellor and Marilyn Butler are only a sampling of the critics who have pointed to Godwin's tremendous influence on his daughter: she was educated by him; she read and reread his works, including *Political Justice*, before and during her writing of *Frankenstein*; she took his novels, particularly *Caleb Williams*, as models for her own novel.[6] Throughout *Frankenstein*, the careful conjunction and repetition of such freighted phrases as "misery," "human benevolence," "selfishness," "justice," and "duty" indicate a careful and conscious crafting of logical and rhetorical argument around the central problem of the Malthus–Godwin controversy: how to imagine the preconditions, possibilities and limits of human happiness.[7] In scene after critical scene, characters in the novel speak their predicaments through a Malthus-Godwin problematic featuring self-love and benevolence, misery and happiness.

Mary Shelley's novel internalizes the broad contours of this debate; moreover, it reveals its anthropological preconditions. Although I hope to restore to the Godwinian readings of *Frankenstein* a Malthusian dimension, I hope not to produce merely another exercise in remedial historicism. The historical specificity of the Malthus–Godwin controversy provides one axis for my reading (and a deferred one, in terms of this essay); the anthropological precondition of that debate provides another axis. The monster is a rupture, a "most astonishing thing" not unlike Burke's French Revolution.[8] All critics agree with Victor that the monster is a problem; how to describe that problem is a further one. He is in the words of Peter Brooks an "aberrant signifier," a disturbingly prolific producer of problems in signification.[9] Yet he is also a bodily problem. The sutures of his body mark a physiological and aesthetic problem; his rhetorical fluency points to a problem of eloquence; he is at various moments and often simultaneously a linguistic, a national, a political, a sexed and a sexual problem. I do not wish prematurely to resolve or categorize the problem of the monster (nor do I think I can); rather, I wish to trace how the monstrous problem emerges in a specific terrain—that of the discursive construction of human being. This aspect of my argument is most heavily inflected by my reading of Michel Foucault, particularly *The Order of Things: An Archaeology of the Human Sciences* and *The Archaeology of Knowledge and The Discourse on Language*. The monster, a product of natural science, becomes a problem for human science; literature fails to resolve that problem for the monster, who discovers himself forever exiled from "the human kingdom." The novel may be read, then, not only as a technophobic allegory, a critique of masculinist presumption, or a Godwinian fable (to cite only a few possibilities) but also as a critique of the anthropological and anthropomorphic foundations of the categories "human" and "humanities."

THE RUPTURE IN THE HUMAN WORLD

The method, the soul of science, designates at first sight any body in nature in such a way that the body in question expresses the name that is proper to it, and that this name recalls all the knowledge that may, in the course of time, have been acquired about the body thus named.
—Linnaeus, *Systema naturae*[10]

if what we saw was an optical delusion, it was the most perfect and wonderful recorded in the history of nature.
—Robert Walton, in *Frankenstein*

What kind of being is the monster? What is this body which desires to humanize itself? Anne Mellor writes that "Mary Shelley saw the creature as potentially monstrous, but she never suggested that he was other than fully human."[11] That he might be "other than fully human" seems to me very much the problem. It is true that Victor Frankenstein's ambition was to create a human being. Possessed of the secret of "the cause of generation and life" (47), the young scientist overcomes his hesitations and begins to work: "I began the creation of a human being" (49). Yet immediately Victor turns from this beginning. The particularity and smallness of the human body frustrate him: "As the minuteness of the parts formed a great hindrance to my speed, I resolved, contrary to my first intention, to make the being of a gigantic stature" (49)—that is, eight feet tall. Within several paragraphs we see Victor raiding charnel houses for bones and body parts; and he further notes, "the dissecting room and the slaughter-house furnished many of my materials." Victor dreams now that "a new species would bless me as its creator and its source" (49).

As this brief summation suggests, Victor's aims undergo an unsteady modulation from a vision of "human being" to a vision of a "new species": the physiologically indeterminate being he creates brings us to the threshold of species-being. That is, Victor's labors ultimately become not an experiment to create a human being but rather an experiment in speciation, an experiment with extremely heterogeneous "materials" (50). Violating the "ideal bounds" (49) of life and death, Victor inadvertently confronts another threshold, the boundary between species. He produces a biological anomaly; moreover, the production of this anomaly threatens his own "human nature," which "turn[s] with loathing from [his] occupation" (50). As soon as the monster convulses into life, Victor defensively remarks on the "un-human features" (52) of the creature, perhaps attempting to establish immediately the difference in species. Victor's revulsion from his creature has been read, among other glosses, as an aesthetic rejection, a disgust with childbirth, and a horror at violating a taboo.[12] Yet we can also see that Victor's concern for his own "human nature" and his specification of the "un-human features" of his creature suggest that human being is the species category in question. The rest of the novel considers whether Victor's response indeed forecasts the monster's final state: will he remain an "inarticulate ... demoniacal corpse" (53), as Victor calls him, or might this creature insert itself within a human community?

Victor's experiment thus implicates human being. This scene is only one of several in which Shelley features the category "human" under critique. The thing originally intended to be a "human being" (49) becomes in fact a threat to "human nature" (50), as Victor sees it. The monster is not decisively human; nor, as his eventual fluency and rationality suggest, is he decisively not human. Victor inadvertently engineers not a human being but the monstrous critique of the very category. The riddle of the monster propels a proliferation of categories, a nominalistic explosion which suggests a taxonomic breakdown: the body in question expresses no name precisely proper to it.

To account for the categorical problem which the monster produces and embodies, it is important to consider the discourses through which the monster speaks (and is spoken), and the modes of being such discourses imply. Victor's ideational and material construction of the monster—the messy work of brain and hand—provides us with at least two routes to the monster's being. Yet the novel offers several other modes of apprehending the monstrous problem, including visual and aural perception, territorial and national forms. These various modes of representation are by no means mutually exclusive. Discourses of human being multiply as the monster forces the rearticulation and reorganization of the content and mode of the "human."

Victor relates the what we might call the conceptual genesis of the monster; in terms of narratological genesis, Robert Walton (the English

mariner, the epistolary framer) introduces the first terms through which to
speak about the monster—distinctions based on form and territory. Walton
proposes the monster as an "optical delusion," a revolution in the "history of
nature" (18). Yet this optical delusion lives and moves and has its being. The
proliferation of discourses around this rupture in natural history attempts to
suture this all-too-corporeal rift in the known and knowable world. Walton
first reports the sighting of "a being which had the shape of a man, but
apparently of gigantic stature" (17); this apparition is soon followed by "a
human being ... He was not, as the other traveller seemed to be, a savage
inhabitant of some undiscovered island, but an European" (18). To Walton,
the first figure, the monster, takes on a gigantic aspect, whereas the second—
soon revealed to be Victor Frankenstein—immediately appears as a fellow
human being, and more precisely, a European. This first encounter
delineates the kind of perceptual oppositions which govern the logic of
territory and species. The most obviously "human beings" in Frankenstein
are inevitably "European," whereas the monster consistently provokes
questions such as Walton's: "is this unknown wast [sic] inhabited by giants, of
which the being we saw is a specimen?" (18). The hailing of Victor as a
European emerges as a differentiation against a savage backdrop. Walton's
very syntax performs the negative construction of European being: Victor
"was not, as the other traveller seemed to be, a savage ... but an European"
(18). Walton's report introduces question of seeming and being, appearance
and essence, which might allow for an ambiguation of his categories. Yet his
very facility with such constructions deserves attention: he provides in
embryo the terms and terrain which the novel will eventually fix and specify
(savage = not European = not human). In such language Walton introduces
one dimension of the anthropological problem of the novel.

Walton's opposition of savage giant and European man soon modulates
into a commentary on linguistic and territorial communities. Walton finds
himself "addressed ... in English, although with a foreign accent": the
European is then identified as a "foreigner" to the English interlocutor.
Walton converses with this figure, who is Victor Frankenstein, "in his native
language which is French" (22). These successive translations and the
becoming-foreign of Victor (to Walton, the de-territorialized Englishman
"at sea," in ice) point to the problematic conjunction of a fantasized unitary
place—Europe—and its multiple linguistic idioms. The European
community includes England and France so far, and will grow to include, as
the novel progresses, Geneva (Victor's native town), Italy (site of Elizabeth
Lavenza's birth), Germany (where Victor attends University), Holland
(where Victor and his friend Henry Clerval tour), the Orkney Isles (where

Victor undertakes the creation of a second female creature), and Ireland (where Henry dies). Yet *Frankenstein* repeatedly suggests that "Europe" may be a phantom, a spectral placeholder beyond and opposed to the clear boundaries of nation and republic, even as "Europeans" appear in contradistinction to savage "giants" (18). Europe exists as a category over and against the strong persistence of "native" lands and languages—note that the "European" Victor is soon denominated a "foreigner" by Robert Walton. The turning of a fellow "human" and "European" into a specifically Genevese French-speaking "foreigner" shows how humans identify each another through increasingly differentiated and estranging categories. The monster strains against and defines the limits of these kinds and levels of classification.

This sighting reads, as David Marshall argues, as a variation on a Rousseauvian topos—"tableaux of primitive man"—that posits an isolated natural man (or post-diluvian man) who would instinctively react with fear whenever he came across another man.[13] "In the beginning" (or after the catastrophe), the hypothesis went, men would not recognize one another as fellow human beings but would rather perceive the other as a giant, as a mortal threat. Common human being was thus imagined as emerging slowly and tortuously, only "après beaucoup d'experiences."[14] Such a fiction asserted there was no automatic sympathetic identification among human beings; sympathy and society were conceived as achieved, not natural, aspects of the human condition. Revising Rousseau and other Enlightenment theorists of the primitive, Mary Shelley locates the primitive tableau in modern Europe. This giant thrives and terrifies not in antiquity but in the contested present of late-eighteenth-century Europe. We can read the gigantism of the creature as Walton's misprision (he is not really a giant but rather appears to be so); yet this gigantism is more than a perceptual error or a trope. Victor tells us later in the novel that he indeed made an extremely large monster, a being "of gigantic stature" (49): Walton is not wrong to identify the monster as such. The monster is not like Rousseau's hypothetical giants; he is not an "optical delusion"; he is quite literally a giant with a specific history, a body whose composition and scale were determined under specific conditions in Victor's workshop. He is theory embodied and made historical.

With its coordination of territorial, cultural and linguistic modes of identification and difference, Walton's sighting introduces the terms by which a human being might know and speak itself—and more relevant to the monster, a discursive range through which an anomaly might humanize itself. When the monster gives the account of his own life, he makes clear that he did not understand himself naturally to be excluded from human fellowship; it is only after he has been rejected as a French-speaking fellow man that he eventually concludes, as his maker seems to have long before, that there can be "no community" (95) between them. It takes the monster several years to learn what all sighted beings "know" about him: that his presence—whether conceived as a "giant ... specimen" (18) or as a "demoniacal corpse" (53)—proves an irremediable rupture in the humanly peopled world. What the monster is forced to learn is that his "birth" remains a breach, and further that literate speech provides no adequate redress for natal alienation.

Natives of the World

In describing the monster as natally alienated, I borrow a term introduced by Werner Sollors in his Harvard lectures on "Literature and Ethnicity in America."[15] This category allows us to trace the relation of knowledge to "nativity" and "natality." Both terms suggest birth, but nativity also connotes the condition of being "native" to a place in addition to having been born. As a made thing, the monster violates natality as a condition of human (and animal) existence; yet his development allows us to see how the newcomer, born or made, forces the society to articulate and redefine its understanding of the "native" and "human"—and the practices proper to humanity— against the anomaly.

One difference between monster and man appears in the different nativities of these figures, and in their relation to exile and emigration. Victor begins his life history with the ringing Rousseauvian statement, "I am by birth a Genevese; my family is one of the most distinguished of that republic" (27). He goes on to describe his father's career as a "public" servant, one who late in life decided to marry, thus "bestowing on the state sons" (27). Victor provides himself with a specific genealogy implicated in the state; he repeatedly asserts his relation to his "native country" (37). Conversely, the monster opens his life story with an assertion of problematic genealogy: "It is with considerable difficulty that I remember the original area of my being: all the events of that period appear confused and indistinct" (97). Unlike every other character in the novel, the monster has no republic, town or nation to call his own. He articulates his beginnings solely in terms of disordered sense perception. As the furiously disappointed monster later tells Victor, "to me, hated and despised, every country must be equally horrible" (135). Unlike Victor, he cannot appeal to familial, political or other territorial categories which would provide him with techniques of authentication and remembrance. For all his claims on Victor as "creator" and "author of his being," he exists as a stateless creature who respects no European boundaries, even as his heterogeneous and formerly dead body violates species boundaries.

The monster is a problem both for himself and for Victor; more specifically, the monster forces what we might call the psychological re-mapping of the native human world. The fact of the monster transforms nativity, even as it transforms human being. If the monster is produced or made as natally alienated, without native place, Victor faces the prospect of becoming natally alienated. He articulates his increasing desperation and guilt as a kind of progressive natal alienation—an exile within Europe, a denaturing of his bonds with Geneva. When he hears of his brother's murder, he heads back to his "native town," finding himself fearful, "dreading a thousand nameless evils" (69). He soon finds "residence within the walls of Geneva very irksome," the "shutting of the gates" at ten the clang of a claustrophobic regime (86). His increasing alienation contrasts with that of his fiancée and father, both of whom offer paeans to the small domestic circle and tranquillity "in our native country" (89). These homages are horribly inappropriate, as Victor realizes: the world has come to Geneva however much his father and Elizabeth think otherwise. It is one of the exquisite ironies of the novel that Victor's first "exile" from home, his going to university in Ingolstadt, was instigated by his father, who thought that Victor "should become acquainted with other customs than those of [his] native country" (37). It is, of course, at Ingolstadt that Victor acquires the means—ideational and technical—of producing his creature. When Victor must later go to England to obtain materials for building his female creature, he parodies his father's logic. He tells his father he wishes "to visit England; but, concealing the true reasons of this request, [he] clothed [his] desires under the guise of wishing to travel and see the world before [he] sat down for life within the walls of [his] native town" (150). Using the language of filiopiety and native allegiance, Victor dissembles his project, appropriates the language of the European tour, and travesties the security of the "walls of the native town" (151).

Victor marks his alienation with the cry, "how much happier that man is who believes his native town to be the world, than he who aspires to become greater than his nature will allow" (48). Even in his disillusion, Victor still attempts to naturalize his alienation and recover his status as a Genevese son. Had he stayed within the bounds of his "nature" (read, his socio-political sphere, his domestic circle, or his pre-technological episteme), he would not have destroyed his belief in his "native town." His lament demonstrates the truth that the native town is not the world, or rather, that the world has come to Geneva. The monster, the living artifact, becomes in fact the figure of the world irremediably transformed.

The monster uses the very same terminology as Victor—"exile," "native" (and, as I will discuss later, "sympathy")—but he circulates in a different species economy. His "emigration" (100), as he calls it, brings him eventually to the De Laceys and to acquaintance with Volney's *Ruins of Empires*. This book constellates his conscious formulation of natal alienation: "Of my creation and creator I was absolutely ignorant; but I knew that I possessed no money, no friends, no kind of property" (115). This "knowledge" brings him only "sorrow," and he exclaims, "Oh, that I had for ever remained in my native wood, nor known nor felt beyond the sensations of hunger, thirst and heat!" (116). Thus the monster, like Victor, expresses the counterfactual wish that he had stayed "native." But however rhetorically parallel their laments, and however similar their respective falls-into-knowledge, there persists between monster and man a crucial rift in modes of being. The monster suffers natal alienation in a register distinct from Victor's revulsion from Geneva. To have "emigrated" from the "native wood" because of hunger is quite another thing than to have found oneself a spiritual "exile" within Europe. The monster experiences a nostalgia for the woods, for nature, for purely sensual being, whereas Victor regrets his exile from a naturalized social state and domestic intimacy. The monster also offers a kind of radical materialism; his fall into consciousness conjoins questions of ontology ("creation") and economy ("money," "property"). In their echoes of the other's predicament, they dramatize the difference of their positions—in terms of the state, the condition of human civilization they embody, and finally in terms of species. They exist on different sides of the human, that is the civilized, propertied, native European, border. It is to cross that border that the monster sets about acquiring a linguistic and ultimately a literary education.

THE SCIENCE OF EDUCATION

The world is much like a school.
        —Godwin, *Essay on Sepulchres*

Just as the monster's being and origin launch a critique of "human being" and "nativity," his intellectual history—"the progress of my intellect" (123) as he calls it—complicates anthropomorphic accounts of mind and educability. That *Frankenstein* concerns itself with the education of its figures (and its readers) is a critical truism: with his exposure to Goethe, Milton, Plutarch, and Volney, the creature receives a highly specified course inflected by concerns both revolutionary and romantic. The monster's political and aesthetic education suggests that he serves as an experimental subject for what Godwin called "the science of education."[16] Mary Shelley's personal pedagogic relations, most notably with Godwin and Shelley, informed her understanding of the complex situations of education. Modelling the monster's reading program on her own in 1815, Shelley furnished her creature's consciousness with the stuff of her own mind. There is now something of a critical consensus about the monster as a figure of the "second sex" (secondary, incomplete, monstrous) and the monster's education as a "sexual education"—its eccentricity both sexed (more like Mary Shelley's, say, than Percy's) and sexual (among the many "lessons" Felix De Lacey inadvertently teaches the monster is that of sexual difference and reproduction).[17] However sexed and vexed, the progress of the monster's intellect implies a theory of improvable mind, which both Mary Wollstonecraft and William Godwin endorsed. As Godwin wrote in "Of the Sources of Genius," in *The Enquirer*, "Give me all the motives that have excited another man, and all the external advantages he had had to boast, and I shall arrive at excellence not inferior to his. This view of the nature of the human mind, is of the utmost importance in the science of education."[18] Shelley's novel may be read as a thought experiment with the anthropomorphic foundations of and limits to Godwin's "science."

Mary Shelley furnished her novel with several routes to and sites of this "science of education": Victor's boyhood schooling in Geneva and university training in "natural philosophy" in Ingolstadt; the monster's eavesdropping on the language and history lessons given in the De Lacey household; Henry Clerval's attaining proficiency in several "oriental" languages (Persian, Arabic, Hebrew).[19] These different educational modes and contents suggest that all knowledges are not equal, nor are they equally obtained. As the work of Anne Mellor, Marilyn Butler and others suggests, science emerges as the most prominent body of knowledge under critique.[20] Mary Shelley's science may be variously described as alchemical "pseudo-science" (in U. C. Knoepflmacher's phrase), as a "serio-comic" version of the vitalist controversy in England (*pace* Marilyn Butler), as a satire on the synthesizing dreams of the *Naturphilosophen*, as a figure for reproduction at the threshold of the "chemical revolution."[21] But however we view the representation of science in the novel, we must concede that it is Victor and not his monster who masters (however unfortunately) this body of knowledge. The monster is a product of natural philosophy, not its student. When he embarks on his own tale of the "progress of [his] intellect" we soon discover that his learning involves not the "science" of "modern chemistry" (or any other natural science) but rather the "godlike science" (107) of "letters" (114).

The word "science" had yet to restrict its range to what we now denominate the physical and social sciences; yet Shelley carefully differentiates among the bodies of knowledge available to and cultivated by the various figures in the novel. Gayatri Spivak has described this apportionment as aligned with "Kant's three-part conception of the human subject," with Henry Clerval (the linguist) embodying practical reason, Elizabeth Lavenza aesthetic judgment, and Victor theoretical reason.[22] This mapping of the subject seems to me inadequate, forsaking as it does the prominence of the monster's own intellectual development. The differential status of "letters" (the monster's material) and of natural philosophy (Victor's domain) illuminates how "the idea of the humanities" increasingly delimited and defined itself against natural science.[23] That is to say, the *agon* of Victor and monster may be read as well as an *agon* between "science" and "the humanities." Indeed, George Levine has called Frankenstein "perhaps the great popular metaphor of the hostility between science and literature."[24] I believe that this "popular metaphor" is no catachresis but rather a recognition of a critical contest within the narrative. Such a reading grossly simplifies the historical conditioning of Shelley's representation of the subjects and techniques of education; I am also choosing to ignore the complications introduced by Robert Walton (the self-described "self-educated" and "illiterate" mariner [13–14]) and Henry Clerval (the oriental linguist whose father, a businessman, asserts that "learning is superfluous in the commerce of ordinary life" [39]). What this simplification allows, however, is an opportunity to explore the novel as a diagnosis of the embodied use and abuse of different knowledges. The novel proposes, in its history of the monster, a remedy for the horrifying body which science has produced—the humanities.

ACQUIRING HUMAN BEING: "HUMANITIES" AS REMEDY

the peculiar dignity of these arts is said to lie in the fact that their cultivation and pursuit differentiates the activities distinctive of man from those of animals.
—R. S. Crane, *The Idea of The Humanities*

I believe that the monster's *bildung* makes explicit the problematic status of "human being" (a species category) and "the humanities" (the cultivation of the "good arts"—as R. S. Crane described it—whether considered as eloquence and reason, *belles lettres*, or the "liberal arts").[25] If the monster appears as the product of scientific experiment fueled by romantic ambition, his attempt to acquire know-how and fellowship through speech and writing represents another effort at producing himself, this time as a speaking and reasoning being. History and literature, supported by a basic literacy, figure as the most sophisticated techniques for the monster's experiment in his own humanization. He tells his maker that he happened upon a cache of books, "written in the language the elements of which I had acquired at the cottage." Among these books are *Paradise Lost*, a volume of *Plutarch's Lives*, and the *Sorrows of Werther* (123). The linguistic, historical, and cultural heterogeneity of the monster's canon is an intriguingly unthought aspect of the novel. How is it possible that all these books should be "written in the language" the monster has acquired? He never speaks of translation, although this is an obvious solution to the difficulty. He makes a point of telling old De Lacey that he "was educated by a French family, and understand[s] that language only" (129). We may understand the monster's assimilation of Milton's English, Plutarch's Latin, and Goethe's German to be a typically "European"—or perhaps Romantically eclecticizing—gesture. And yet, as the monster's assertion of monolingual fluency suggests, the aspirant to human community must speak at least one particular language fluently, must be able to identify his language with a kind of national or at least regional seal—in this case, French.

Several critics have discussed the monster's reading course: the significance of Shelley's choices; the sequence in which the monster reads his books; their political, religious, and aesthetic valences.[26] When considering the anthropomorphic problematic of *Frankenstein*, the content of and expectations generated by such material as *Paradise Lost* (Adamic sonship and prerogative, Satanic exile and heroic despair) seem less significant than the very literacy which such reading presupposes. What is most striking is not what the monster reads and speaks, or even that he reads and speaks, but rather what he thinks such accomplishments should signify: the precondition for his "becoming one among my fellows" (116), as he puts it. Shelley repeatedly emphasizes the function of linguistic mediation in constituting communities. She takes care to provide her Europeans with a linguistic education, Elizabeth and Victor having learned English and Latin. Victor also familiarizes himself with "the easiest Greek" (36) and German (this in addition to his native French). Thus the novel traces a linguistic range for her inhabitants and points to the colonial, commercial, and sexual extension of this range, as in Henry Clerval's orientalism and in the "Arabian" Safie's linguistic Europeanization. Given the novel's elision of "European" and "human," it is not at all surprising that the monster looks to language and to European history and literature as the media for his transformation into a member of the community.

The monster understands language to be a route to human being; he also conceives of language not merely as an oral exchange but also as literate (lettered) speech. In his hovel by the De Laceys, the monster discovers the "science of words or letters" (105). Eventually he recognizes that the De Laceys communicate "by articulate sounds"—a "godlike science" he wishes to learn. There is a particular urgency to the monster's wish: he decides he will remain hidden until he has made himself "master of their language" (109). He expects to use his articulate voice against their perception of his hideous form. His idiosyncratic schooling emphasizes the acquisition of speech and writing, a double linguistic fluency which he acquires almost simultaneously. He becomes both phoneticized and alphabeticized. In this he registers the nineteenth-century turn-to-language, in which scholars increasingly established the study of language as the basis of the human sciences (evidenced in the proliferation of universal grammars, the birth of philology, the development of comparative linguistics). He understands human being to be constituted through a very particular "discourse network," in Friedrich Kittler's terms, in which the learning of language required a "naturalization of the alphabet" and as well as an "oralization" of the alphabet; through such techniques pedagogues attempted to obscure the arbitrariness of what the monster calls the "science of words or letters."[27] The monster's choice of "science" in this last phrase introduces an interesting ambiguity (as does his mention of the "godlike science" of language): he may well be using "science" in its full elasticity, as equivalent to a formal knowledge or method, but he may also register what Kittler describes as the "revolution of the European alphabet"—its oralization through syllabic and spelling methods around 1800 which contributed to "the epistemological shift from a general grammar to the science of language."[28] The problem of phonetics and the alphabet, posed by the monster to himself, suggests that language has been denaturalized, already broken into a particular *combinatoire*. The monster is unable to acquire French by purely oral means; he requires the intervention of a book, of transcription, whose words he then hears Felix reading to Safie. This oral method thus rests on a literate precondition. Whether considered as an art (for example, as part of rhetoric) or as a science (for example, as part of phonetics), language appears as the most basic medium for his humanization.

The monster makes little progress until Safie appears in the De Lacey household. Now the monster realizes there is more than one human language. He notes that, although Safie "appeared to have a language of her own, she was neither understood by, or herself understood, the cottagers" (112). Teaching Safie French out of Volney's *Ruins of Empires*, Felix gives the monster the opportunity to learn both articulate speech and the course of empire, the nature of economics, and conduct of human affairs. As Safie learns French, so does the monster: "the idea instantly occurred to me, that I should make use of the same instruction to the same end" (113). Yet it is important to note that, whereas Safie has "her own" language and is merely acquiring another, the monster is being translated *into* language: he had no language of his own and, unlike a human infant, was unable without administered instruction to "master" (109) their language. Learning the "art of language" (110)—"*their* language" (109; emphasis added)—coincides for him with learning the "science of letters": speaking and alphabetic writing appear to him as two equally alien media which he requires in order to be recognized. Or rather, he requires these techniques as an anticipatory remedy for being visually cognized as anti- or un-human, a monster. Of course, the promise of letters fails the monster, most dramatically when he is beaten out of the De Lacey household. This expulsion from the domestic idyll prompts the monster's declaration of "everlasting war against the species" (133)—that is, the human species, which the monster slowly and inexorably comes to understand as a class of being from which he is excluded.

The final test of the monster's belief in what I am calling the humanities, in acquired *humanitas*, takes place in his encounter with the small brother of Victor Frankenstein. The crux of Mary Shelley's critique of the humanities may be posed as such: is little William "unprejudiced" (138), as the monster hopes? Having come upon the child, the monster deliberates: perhaps the child "had lived too short a time to have imbibed a horror of deformity. If, therefore, I could seize him, and educate him as my companion and friend, I should not be so desolate in this peopled earth" (138). The monster imagines himself as pedagogue to remedy his lack of community. He proposes to himself an experiment in human nature, taking as his subject one still in his "infancy" (138). He approaches the child as a naturally sympathetic being, interpreting the previous horror of all humans to have been a socialized prejudice. But again the monster's experiment fails: the child responds with the instinctive aversion of all other humans and furthermore calls down the juridical wrath of the State in the person of his *paterfamilias*— "Let me go; my papa is a Syndic ... he would punish you." In Louis Althusser's terms, the monster discovers there is no subject before interpellation; the child understands and speaks himself through several ideological state apparatuses—familial, legal—and calls upon them to defend himself against the monster.[29] The language of fairytales and nightmares— "ugly wretch! you wish to eat me, and tear me to pieces" the child cries— segues into the language of the socialized subject, the son who calls out for his papa the Syndic. The monster's faith in education shatters, and he murders the child. The wish to "seize him, and educate him" (139) becomes the act of seizing him for strangling. So ends the monster's "idea" of himself as a pedagogue.

It is striking that the monster's first murder appears as the climax of a pedagogical fantasy. The real question is not why did little William respond so violently to this monster (who is consistently visually aversive to humans), but why did the monster ever consider him educable—or more broadly, why does the monster entertain educational fantasies at all? The monster persists in taking himself as an appropriate object of the liberal arts. He believes the methods and arts available to, for example, Safie, are equally available to him. As he says, relishing his language lessons, "I resolved to make use of the same instructions [given Safie] to the same end" (113). The "end" for Safie is the learning of French in order to be assimilated linguistically and sexually into the Christian, republican, patriarchal domicile; so too the monster aspires, but his aspiration also bears the weight of his desire to humanize himself, to distinguish himself from the animals (as both R. S. Crane and Godwin describe the task of the humanities). In entertaining humanist fantasies, the monster forgets his corporeally and nominally indeterminate status: the community of letters presupposes a human community, and the humanities presuppose humans. The monster presupposes his potential humanity; in this he succumbs to the ruse of the humanities.

RENOUNCING HUMAN BEING: SPECIES REVISING

It is only after the spectacular failure of the monster's education, both in his own training-into-language with the De Laceys, and in his wish to "educate" little William, that the monster admits the anthropological crisis he presents, both for himself and for humans. The monster's tale of his "progress" concludes with his request of Victor:

> I am alone and miserable; man will not associate with me; but one as deformed and horrible as myself would not deny herself to me. My companion must be of the same species, and have the same defects. This being you must create. (140)

The creature's understanding of species takes up, and perhaps parodies, the conceptualization of that term throughout what Michel Foucault terms the Classical period (from the mid-seventeenth to the late-eighteenth century in Western Europe). As both Foucault and François Jacob note, species was defined in this era according to the persistence of the visible structure.[30] For the creature, to be "of the same species" is to look alike, however "deformed and horrible" that might be. Species here seems to follow a logic of appearance. It seems less a scientific category denoting classes of beings which reproduce their like over time than a perceptual-social category which organizes the possibility of contact among beings. Creatures of different species will "not associate" together. Aesthetic revulsion precludes social interaction. This has been repeatedly demonstrated by the visual paranoia the monster induces and the semiological riddle he presents. Yet he is not merely a signifier: he is a body, a potentially reproductive body, as Victor comes to see.

Requesting a female "with whom I can live in the interchange of those sympathies necessary for my being" (140), the monster links the problem of his "being" to the problem of sympathy. As David Marshall has argued, *Frankenstein* may be read as an inquiry into the specular and spectacular logic of sympathy: the monster appears as the very limit of the economy of sympathetic exchange. The monster is of course repeatedly presented as a specular problem; I have argued that the visual distress he induces may be read as well as a figure for the imaginal-conceptual breakdown he embodies. This leads us to the interesting question: is common species being a prerequisite for sympathy, or is sympathy the precondition for what I am calling "common species being"? The question of theoretic priority is ultimately less important than the monster's analysis of the mutual implication of the discourse of sympathy and the construction of human being. The monster acquiesces in the proposition that only beings "of the same species" are capable of sympathizing with each other.[31] His request reflects his experience of sympathy as a specifically *human* specular logic: a body requires a human appearance to stimulate, elicit and participate in human sympathetic reactions. Of course, the monster shows himself capable of sympathizing with humans; yet sighted humans refuse that reciprocity. That blind De Lacey offers an alternative vision of the monster provides not an instance of superior insight (see, the monster really *is* like us) so much as another moment in which blindness calls forth insight. The monster's pleasant discussion with old De Lacey promises an alternative discourse network, a community independent of visual affinity. The sympathetic blindness of old De Lacey allows us to read normal human vision as ideologically blinkered; and yet the visual persists as most powerful mode of understanding the world. Shelley shows us how humans experience sight as transparency; sympathy and its counter, revulsion, occur as if naturally to the sighted. Those with normal and normalizing sight will perceive the anomaly as a threat, as an invasion, and will, like Felix De Lacey, vigorously and righteously resist. She thus displays and critiques the anthropomorphic supports of sympathy. The monster marks the species limit of what Donna Haraway calls, in another context, "primate vision."[32] Both Victor and the monster come to agree: sympathy will not cross the species barrier. Recognizing the primarily specular logic of human sympathy, the monster arrives at a new self-conception. Requesting as he does a being "of the same species," a female who with the "same defects" (140) will presumably violate "human nature" (that is, human appearance) as much as himself, the monster marks his formal and explicit renunciation of human being.

In his turn to Victor for a mate, the monster also marks the narrative convergence of two functions, the critique of the "human" and the critique of the "humanities." The discourse of species confronts the differential power of the disciplines. The well-read and eloquent monster lacks the tools he most needs, the instruments of speciation, the means of production. The monster makes clear the implicit hierarchy of knowledge: the science of "modern chemistry" which led Victor to his first creation stands as a more efficacious knowledge than what the monster hailed as the "science of words or letters" (105). Victor has the solution, the means of production, technical and ideational—the "chemical apparatus" (168), as he calls it, and the university training in natural philosophy. Natural science, not language, literature or consciousness, will provide for the monster the community of two he desires. Implicitly acknowledging the failure of the humanities, of "literature—taken in all its bearings" (as Godwin wrote), the monster also acknowledges his acquiescence in the human—that is, the European—reading of him, which has featured such epithets as "savage," "ogre," and "demoniacal corpse." He defines difference as species difference and no longer looks to linguistic or cultural filiation as a means to override his problematic genealogy and form. Thus his request for another "of the same species."

What I read as the monster's understanding of the stakes of species and sympathy must be contrasted and complemented with Victor's reading of this same request. It is Victor who transforms and fixes the meaningful force of these terms. The category of "species," while obviously a multivalent and potentially vague term, requires a reproductive specificity, as Victor's deliberations illuminate. Just as the "idea" which governs the first making of a creature undergoes several ideational modifications (from creating human to giant to "new species"), so too Victor's conception of his second labor of creation undergoes a kind of imaginative transformation. What was originally latent in the monster's request—reproductive possibility—is made manifest in Victor's panicked thought. Sitting in his laboratory in the Orkneys, Victor considers how his new creature might turn out: "she might become ten thousand times more malignant than her mate" (163), or she might find her fellow creature loathsome and desert him. Even more appalling to Victor is the following possibility:

> Even if they were to leave Europe, and inhabit the deserts of the new world, yet one of the first results of those sympathies for which the demon thirsted would be children, and a race of devils would be propagated upon the earth, who would make the very existence of the species of man a condition precarious and full of terror. Had I a right, for my own benefit, to inflict this curse upon everlasting generations? (163)

Is Victor right to envision an apocalyptic threat to the "very existence of the species of man" (165)? Does Victor suffer from reproductive paranoia? How do we know the creature could reproduce? After all, he is a motley assemblage, and Mary Shelley has done nothing to specify his sexual capacity or organs. He may well be a kind of mule—composite, sterile. Perhaps another way to phrase the problem of the monster's request is this: what does a monster really want? Victor thinks he knows. The monster's request indicates a refutation of Malthus, who in 1798 wrote that, "Life is, generally speaking, a blessing independent of a future state."[33] Victor comes to envision, quite anxiously, the monster's future state in reproductive terms. Victor materializes and sexualizes what the creature has presented in more ambiguous language: the "interchange of sympathies" the creature desires becomes in Victor's imaginings a primarily sexual intercourse. The creature had earlier predicted that, with a mate, his "virtues will necessarily arise when I live in communion with an equal. I shall feel the affections of a sensitive being, and become linked to the chain of existences and events, from which I am now excluded" (143). Certainly this could be read as a series of sexual puns—the monster's phallic virtues rising. We, like Victor, may hear in this the creature's wish to become inserted in the reproductive chain of being, into the time of natural history and generation. In Victor's view, the monster demands a reproductive future, a phylogenic future and not a mere ontogenic existence. The creature aspires to existence *as* a reproductive species being. Only if he can beget like by like will this individual constitute a member of a species. Thus the creature's request for one "of the same species" ironically seeks to make good on Victor's long-dead aspiration, to "create a new species [which] would bless me as its creator and source" (49).

In contriving this second experiment Mary Shelley transforms the problem of monstrous life: Victor shows his Malthusian hand and gropes his way to the principle of population, a principle through which he finally excuses his frenzied dismemberment of the half-finished female "thing" (64). What the monster proposes as a solution, a species companion, becomes in Victor's prospectus the route to a further and more horrifying problem, that of species competition. The work of speciation, so troubling in the first experiment, now introduces the further threat of reproductive populations. The contest between Victor and monster, at first an agonistic doubling of individuals, becomes in this second experiment a world-historical contest between imagined populations—the "whole human race" versus "a race of devils" (163). Victor's thought follows and parodies the inexorable logic of the principle of population. He cannot imagine his creatures *not* reproducing: this is the most striking thing about his reflection. In this second experiment and its truncation, Victor shows himself to be an adept not of Paracelsus nor even of Humphry Davy but rather of Malthus, who wrote, regarding progress in human society, that "in reasoning upon this subject, it is evident that we ought to consider chiefly the mass of mankind and not individual instances."[34] From the moment Victor imagines the children of his creatures—monsters as "mass" and not "individual instance"—he introduces a Malthusian calculus in which species "struggle for existence."[35] Whereas the monster newly conceives of himself as an other species being, Victor comes to conceive of him and his potential mate as Malthusian bodies, progenitors of a "mass." Victor is obviously not a doctrinal Malthusian; he does not dabble in the particulars of geometric versus arithmetic growth (increase of people versus increase in means of subsistence); he is a Malthusian inasmuch as he is a population theorist, an imaginer of mass bodies competitively peopling the globe.

In these last pages, Shelley makes clear what has been suspended throughout the novel. The self-cultivation of the problematic body, the assumption of consciousness by the monster—these achievements in the Godwinian "science of education" count for little when the monster is considered as a mass being, a specimen of a potential population. The introduction of the Malthusian problematic thus supports Victor in the contest over the meaning of species difference. That Shelley may be satirizing the Malthusian position—Victor is no reliable narrator, and his thoughts are frequently disordered—does not erode my point: thinking species difference in reproductive terms involves Victor in a Malthusian calculus, and this calculus leads to Victor's thwarting of the monster's aspirations.

Securing the World for Human Being: Towards a Malthusian Humanitarianism

Victor is not just a Malthusian; he is a humanist Malthusian. The emergence of a Malthusian calculus in *Frankenstein* propels the final revaluation of the category "human." Both monster and Victor circulate the category "human" in this final contest. In his request for a mate, the monster convincingly presents his request for a partner as his last and greatest attempt at humanizing himself. Describing how he will live as a peaceful vegetarian with his mate in South America, the creature says, "The picture I present you is peaceful and human, and you must feel that you could deny it only in the wantonness of power and cruelty" (142). At the very moment he renounces human being, the monster demonstrates his fluency in anthropologic: clearly his literary education has taught him how to speak human being if not to inhabit it. Indeed, the monster identifies the relentless anthropomorphic prejudice of Victor's thought; as he says to Victor, "you would not call it murder, if you could ... destroy my frame, the work of your own hands" (141). He is even willing to acquiesce in the naturalization of this lethal anthropomorphism: he wants his own mate precisely because he recognizes that "the human senses are insurmountable barriers to our union" (141).

The monster shows himself to be a canny theorist of human being, a theorist from the outside; Victor persists in the muddy and ultimately murderous thought of the natively and naïvely human being. Even as the monster promises to "quit the neighborhood of man, and dwell, as it may chance, in the most savage of places" (143), Victor questions whether he will truly be able to "fly from the habitations of man." "How can you," he asks the monster, "who long for the love and sympathy of man, persevere in this exile?" (142). Victor persists in conjuring the romance of humanization, the appealing exchange of "sympathy" among men, at the very moment the monster has imagined for himself and his mate a future as "monsters, cut off from all the world" (142)—from Europe. Victor finally accedes to the request on one condition—that the monster promise "to quit Europe for ever, and every other place in the neighborhood of man, as soon as I shall deliver into your hands a female who will accompany you in your exile" (144). It is striking that "the vast wilds of South America" do not register, for either

Victor or the monster, as among the "neighborhood[s] of man." Both Victor and monster imagine this emigration to the New World as an exile from Europe (the ambiguous geographic territory) and from human being (the contested category of being). The monster's prospective exile from Europe thus defines his status as de-territorialized non-human body and reminds us of that early equation established in Walton's account of his first sighting: "Man" = European.

Victor's Malthusian deliberations lead him, then, to re-think not only the problem of anomaly (monstrous individual becomes monstrous population) but also to re-configure the humanly habitable world. Victor asks the monster "to quit Europe forever"—a dream of forced deportation and species isolation (and a bleak parody of forced emigration throughout Europe). He seeks to ensure that the savage within Europe will exile himself from Europe. Yet, as suggested earlier, the very idea of "Europe" appears as a linguistic and juridical phantom to which human citizens appeal only in a crisis of differentiation. The world no longer offers a secure place for the "exile" of undesirables. The world has contracted to a contest: as Victor foresees, the world is already potentially populated. The problem of exile and emigration—formerly described in terms of individual movement (Victor's exile from Geneva, the monster's "emigration" from the "native wood")—acquires world-historical importance when considered as a movement of potential populations. There is no safely policed or policeable border; the monster who invades Geneva cannot be confined to the "vast wilds of South America." Monsters will mate, monsters will people (as it were) the globe, monsters will eventually threaten the "existence of the species of man" (161).

Now that the monster appears not as a local but rather as a global threat to humanity, Victor can no longer persist in his second experiment in speciation. His final deliberations suggest a transvaluation of the category human, since he is simultaneously capable of envisioning the female monster as a future "thinking and reasoning animal" and as a threat to the "whole human race" (163). Victor clearly resolves the contradiction of the monster: he decisively dissociates literacy and rationality from human being. Contrary to Godwin's belief, thinking and reasoning will not, indeed must not, carry a creature across the border from animal (or "creature") to human. Confronted by the monstrous contradiction to human being, Victor must dissociate human being from certain capacities and sympathies thought native to it. The culmination of his work on the female shows the violence required to secure such a resolution. Victor looks on the work of his hands: "The remains of the half-finished creature, whom I had destroyed, lay scattered on the floor, and I almost felt as if I had mangled the living flesh of a human being" (167). Almost. As the monster had predicted, Victor "would not call it murder" if he destroyed "the work of [his] own hands" (141).

Victor's aborting of the monster-mate becomes, as he reflects, an exercise in humanitarianism. His increasingly biological interpretation of "species" and of the monster's future state provides Victor with the humanist alibi:

> During these last days I have been occupied in examining my past conduct; nor do I find it blameable. In a fit of enthusiastic madness I created a rational creature, and was bound towards him, to assure, as far as was in my power, his happiness and well-being. This was my duty; but there was another still paramount to that. My duties towards my fellow creatures had greater claims to my attention, because they included a greater proportion of happiness or misery. Urged by this view, I refused, and I did right in refusing, to create a companion for the first creature. (214)

Victor's declaration of human conscientiousness invokes and revises a utilitarian calculus: Godwinian concerns about "duty," "happiness," and universal benevolence confront the species barrier. The "duties towards [his] fellow creatures" trump the duties toward created living non-human beings. Indeed, by 1831 Shelley had revised the phrase "fellow creatures" to "beings of my own species," further reminding us that one's "own species" has come to stand, for Victor, as a reified category for human fellowship conceived over and against this monstrous alternative.

By tearing up the female, Victor begins to repair the rent in the humanly habitable world. His heightened species-consciousness allows him a partial recovery of natality, not as a native Genevese but as a "human." In "exile," having left Geneva to create the second monster, he comes to see himself as the species-being *par excellence*. To invoke Marx, "Man is a species being, not only because in practice and in theory he adopts the species as his object (his own as well as those of other things), but—and this is only another way of expressing it—but also because he treats himself as the actual, living species."[36] Taking his species, "the whole human race," as his object, Victor acquires, or rather produces, a distinctive consciousness of human species being, which allows him to remember the destroyed female thing with a clear conscience. Victor's refusal to complete the monster-mate does, at least for him, mark his re-entry into the human social body, one which is now imagined as persisting through time, unto "everlasting generations" (165). In a roundabout and perverse way, Victor does traffic in a human reproductive economy, if only in his capacity to imagine future human generations under threat. Indeed, the dismembered female, recollected in tranquillity, embodies the culmination of Victor's conscientious foresight, his carefully defended Malthusian humanitarianism. From a purely human perspective, Victor's violence appears as a true demonstration of Malthusian philanthropy.

What we might call ideological biologization of species difference—first by the monster (who wants one "of the same species") and then by Victor (who refers to "his [the monster's] own species")—fixes the asymmetry between monster and man. In Victor's turn to population he demonstrates the motivation of a discursive shift: he is no innocent, ingenuous, or disinterested speculator but rather a human being who imagines his "species" under threat and acts accordingly. Victor's Malthusian panic ensures that the conflict of monster and man will be imagined as a species or race conflict. Clearly this progression can be read as an allegory of the colonial enterprise, or of the racial consciousness of English romanticism, or as a representation of the unruly proletariat. Yet, in a more localized reading, we can also see how biologization, the nominalization of a corporeal and social problem as a species difference, succeeds (that is, follows) and supports the failure both of humanism and the humanities. It is Victor—the human being, the natural philosopher, the population theorist—who emerges dominant, both in terms of species competition and in the utility of his education. The course of the novel suggests that the principle of population, of species competition in a world become suddenly too small, trumps the principle of benevolence. Considered as such, the novel undermines not only Godwin's faith in the "science of education" but indeed the very anthropological foundations of *Political Justice*. One could say, in fact, that in *Frankenstein*, Malthus triumphs over Godwin: the "perfectibility of man" announced by Godwin and ridiculed by Malthus appears in the novel as a perfectibility for European species men only. In the ideological contest between "benevolence" (the Godwinian principle) and "misery" (the Malthusian check), benevolence extends only to the limits of one's own species being, a status represented in the novel as constituted through various local apparatuses—familial, political, educational, yet with a biological, anthropological determination in the last instance. The monster's misery is, in the end, no business of Victor's and indeed must be resisted with the newly discovered language of human-all-too-human fellowship. Victor's experiments have demonstrated, however ironically, the truth of Malthus' dictum: "an experiment with the human race is not like an experiment upon inanimate objects."[37] Neither human nor inanimate, the monster persists as a challenge to those who would build communities of affinity, to those who wish to redeem the promise of the humanities.

NOTES

I would like to thank James Chandler, Françoise Meltzer, Janel Mueller, Victoria Olwell, Robert Richards, Erik Salovaara and Mary Lass Stewart, each of whom read or heard this paper in various incarnations and offered incisive comments.

1. William Godwin, "Of an Early Taste for Reading," in *The Enquirer: Reflections on Education, Manners, and Literature in a series of essays*, 1st ed. (London: G. G. and J. Robinson, 1797), 31.
2. Mary Shelley, *Frankenstein; or, the Modern Prometheus, The 1818 Text*, ed. James Rieger (Chicago: Univ. of Chicago Press, 1974, 1982), 5. All quotations from the novel will hereafter be cited parenthetically in the text by page. Throughout the essay I will refer to Mary Wollstonecraft Godwin Shelley as "Mary Shelley" or "Shelley," though she was still Mary Godwin when she wrote *Frankenstein*.
3. William Godwin, *The Enquirer*, x: "The cause of political reform, and the cause of intellectual and literary refinement, are inseparably connected."
4. Frances Ferguson's essay, "Malthus, Godwin, and the Spirit of Solitude," in *Literature and the Body: Essays on Populations and Persons*, ed. Elaine Scarry (Baltimore: Johns Hopkins Univ. Press, 1988), first stimulated my thinking about *Frankenstein* in the context of the Malthus–Godwin debate. Ferguson delineates a "Romantic political economy" and offers a feminist critique of the logic of scarcity and its implications for consciousness; she notes that, in Malthus's *Essay*, concern about "the pressure of too many bodies registers the felt pressure of too many consciousnesses" (106). Also important for its incisive reconsideration of Malthusian bodies and political economy is Catherine Gallagher's "The Body Versus the Social Body in the Works of Thomas Malthus and Henry Mayhew," in *The Making of the Modern Body: Sexuality and Society in the Nineteenth Century*, ed. Catherine Gallagher and Thomas Laqueur (Berkeley: Univ of California Press, 1987).
5. Godwin, *Of Population* ... (1820; New York: Augustus M. Kelley, Reprints of Economics Classics, 1964), iii.
6. See "The Shelleys' Reading List," in *The Journals of Mary Shelley 1814–1844*, ed. Paula R. Feldman and Diana Scott-Kilvert, 2 vols. (Oxford: Clarendon Press, 1987), 2:649. Shelley records reading, among other works, Godwin's *Essay on Sepulchres* (1809) on 22 October 1814; *Fleetwood; or, the New Man of Feeling* in 1815; *An Enquiry concerning ... Political Justice* (1793) in 1814 and 1817. *The Enquirer* is listed with a "?" as having been read in 1817.
7. Elizabeth Lavenza's faith in "human benevolence" (81) is shattered when she thinks Justine killed her brother; the monster contrasts his natural "benevolence" (137) with his "miserable life in the woods" (138); his "insupportable misery" impels his declaration of "everlasting war against the species" (133); rejected from fellowship, he bitterly derides the "eternal justice of man" (96). For his part, Victor weighs "justice" and "selfishness": Victor considers the claims of "justice due both to him and my fellow-creatures" (144); he worries that creating a female "would be an act of the most atrocious selfishness" (168). Other examples of such phrases, and their crucial deployment, abound.

8. Edmund Burke, *Reflections on the Revolution in France*, ed. L. G. Mitchell (New York: Oxford Univ. Press, 1993), 10.

9. Peter Brooks, "'Godlike Science'/Unhallowed Arts: Language, Nature, and Monstrosity," in *The Endurance of Frankenstein*, ed. George Levine and U. C. Knoepflmacher (Berkeley: Univ. of California Press, 1979), 213.

10. Quoted in Michel Foucault, *The Order of Things: An Archaeology of the Human Sciences* (New York: Vintage Books, 1973), 159.

11. Anne K. Mellor, *Mary Shelley: Her Life, Her Fiction, Her Monsters* (New York: Routledge, 1989). 63.

12. See Fred Botting for a reading of the monster as a critique of aesthetic totality and as a figure of the uncanny: *Making Monstrous: Frankenstein, Criticism, Theory* (Manchester: Manchester Univ. Press, 1991). The 1974 collection of essays in *The Endurance of Frankenstein*, a watershed in *Frankenstein* criticism and in the rehabilitation of Mary Shelley the writer, contains several essays highlighting gender, family, and biography: Ellen Moers's "Female Gothic" and U. C. Knoepflmacher's "Thoughts on the Aggression of Daughters" differently discuss the novel's fascination with and horror of childbirth. See also Mellor's analysis of Victor's gendering of nature and his "usurping [of] the female" (chapter 6) in *Mary Shelley: Her Life, Her Fiction, Her Monsters*.

13. See Marshall's chapter "*Frankenstein*, or Rousseau's Monster: Sympathy and Speculative Eyes," in *The Surprising Effects of Sympathy* (Chicago: Univ. of Chicago, 1988). Alan Bewell details several Enlightenment "hypothetical histories," including Condillac's and Rousseau's, which he terms the fiction of "the primitive encounter"; he brilliantly traces the impact of such eighteenth-century anthropological fictions on Wordsworth's poetry. See his chapter "First Encounters of the Primitive Kind," in *Wordsworth and the Enlightenment: Nature, Man, and Society in the Experimental Poetry* (New Haven: Yale Univ. Press, 1989).

14. Jean-Jacques Rousseau, *Essai sur l'origine des langues*, quoted in Marshall, 205.

15. I have not been able to locate this term in Sollors's *Beyond Ethnicity* or *Consent and Descent in American Culture*. The lecture series mentioned above took place in 1987 at Harvard.

16. Godwin, "Of the Sources of Genius," in *The Enquirer*, 14.

17. See Mellor, chapter 10, for one of the more recent discussion of scenes of "sexual education" in Shelley's works and life; also relevant are David Marshall, *The Surprising Effects of Sympathy*, and Alan Richardson, "From *Emile* to *Frankenstein*: The Education of Monsters," in *Literature, Education, and Romanticism: Reading as Social Practice, 1780–1832* (New York: Cambridge Univ. Press, 1994).

18. Godwin, *The Enquirer*, 14.

19. "Natural philosophy" is, as Mary Shelley well knew, an Anglicization of the *Naturphilosophie* typically associated with the German tradition of philosophical science— a tradition with which Coleridge, for one, was well acquainted. Victor is a philosophical scientist in the German tradition, not an English empiricist. Historians of science such as Trevor H. Levere note that the *naturphilosophie* tradition, a kind of "romantic science," persisted in England alongside the more empirically, analytically oriented work of the mainstream thinkers (see Levere, *Poetry Realized in Nature: Samuel Taylor Coleridge and Early Nineteenth-Century Science* [New York: Cambridge Univ. Press, 1981]). Coleridge believed, in fact, that men like Humphry Davy could unite the claims of empirical and philosophical "science." As the work (and reception) of Davy and Erasmus Darwin

suggests, the lines between the more romantic natural philosophy and the empirical tradition of induction, analysis, and experiment were not always easily distinguishable in England. Levere's discussion of "national styles of science" and his account of the Lawrence-Abernethy debate is especially relevant to *Frankenstein*. Shelley's interest in the "principle of life" and its manipulation may be read as a displacement of the "vitalist controversy" in England to a Bavarian locale, Ingolstadt, which was associated with the conspiratorial Illuminatists.

20. For a discussion of Shelley's familiarity with the work of Erasmus Darwin, Humphry Davy, and Luigi Galvani, see Mellor, chapter 5. Marilyn Butler's new introduction to the Oxford World Classic edition of *Frankenstein* (1818 text; New York: Oxford Univ. Press, 1994) situates the novel in terms of the "schism in the life-sciences between strict materialists and those willing to share a vocabulary with the religious" (xviii), with Shelley on the side of the materialist skeptic and radical scientist William Lawrence. In his debate with John Abernethy, Lawrence satirized those who proposed the existence of a "life-principle" independent of organization (xviii); it is this very principle which Victor claims to discover and manipulate. Butler sees Mary Shelley as more of a Peacockian satirist—a "serio-comic" novelist (xxi)—than I do, but her exploration of the "comic analogy" (xxi) of the novel provides a useful antidote to a large body of perhaps over-serious critical discussions of the novel as a polemic against masculinist science and technophilic hubris.

21. For the characterization of the novel's science as "pseudo-science," see U. C. Knoepflmacher, in *The Endurance of Frankenstein*, 317. Butler considers Shelley's representation "detached and serio-comic" (xxi). Thomas Kuhn dates the "chemical revolution" to Lavoisier's discovery of the "oxygen theory of combustion" in the 1770s (*The Structure of Scientific Revolutions*, 2nd edition, enlarged [Chicago: Univ. of Chicago Press, 1970], 56). It was in fact the chemical threshold and its relation to life that most fascinated and troubled Shelley's contemporaries Erasmus Darwin and Coleridge. Coleridge's extended essay, *Hints toward the Formation of a More Comprehensive Theory of Life* (1816; revised through the mid-1820s, published in 1848), is in part an attack on those who would look to chemistry to provide an explanation of life. Coleridge asks, "How ... could men of strong minds and sound judgments have attempted to penetrate by the clue of chemical experiment the secret recesses, the sacred adyta of organic life, without being aware that chemistry must needs be at its extreme limits? ... the failure of its enterprises, will become the means of defining its absolute boundary" (*Theory of Life*, ed. Seth B. Watson, M.D. [London: John Churchill, 1848], 32).

22. Gayatri Chakravorty Spivak, "Three Women's Texts and a Critique of Imperialism," in *'Race,' Writing and Difference*, ed. Henry Louis Gates, Jr. (Chicago: Univ. of Chicago Press, 1986), 275.

23. R. S. Crane, "Shifting Definitions and Evaluations," in *The Idea of the Humanities and Other Essays Critical and Historical*, 2 vols. (Chicago: Univ of Chicago Press, 1967), 1:155.

24. George Levine, "Introduction," in *One Culture: Essays in Science and Literature*, ed. Levine with Alan Rauch (Madison: Univ. of Wisconsin Press, 1987), 9.

25. In "Shifting Definitions and Evaluations," R. S. Crane traces the historical emergence, development, and interpenetration of such concepts as "humanity" and "the humanities." The humanities have encompassed different subjects in different periods (Quintilian's rhetoric, the "good arts" commended by the grammarian Aulus Gellius, the

medieval trivium and quadrivium, Matthew Arnold's "culture"). Regardless of subject content, however, it is the humanities, as Crane notes, which traditionally offered the means of cultivating "*humanitas*": educators in antiquity assumed that the men who pursued the "good arts" "are most humanized" (23).

26. See Anne McWhir, "Teaching the Monster to Read: Mary Shelley, Education, and *Frankenstein*," in *The Educational Legacy of Romanticism*, ed. John Willinsky (Waterloo, Ontario: Wilfrid Laurier Univ. Press, 1990), for a wonderful discussion of the monster as ideologically trapped by his education, which provides him "intellectual parents" and "a sense of self only to discover that he has no right to exist" (74). See also Alan Richardson's "From *Emile* to *Frankenstein*; The Education of Monsters."

27. Friedrich A. Kittler, "The Mother's Mouth," in *Discourse Networks, 1800/1900*, trans. Michael Metteer with Chris Cullens (Stanford: Stanford Univ. Press, 1990), 29, 32. See especially the section entitled, "Learning to Read in 1800." In my turn to Kittler I elide several differences, including Kittler's focus on German discourse networks, his emphasis on the mother as the new state-created pedagogue, the role of the new grammars and the phonetic method circa 1800. Clearly the monster has no mediating mother; moreover he learns not from grammars but from an auralized/oralized written history. Yet his encounter with the "science of letters" (114) suggests that his experience of language is always already alphabeticized; the monster's labor (and Safie's) also highlights the differing and simultaneous functions of Felix's pedagogy—the monster seeks to enter human being by accessing what seems to the residents of the cabin a closed discourse network. That the monster succeeds in acquiring words, letters, eloquence, consciousness demonstrates the monstrous productivity of Felix's pedagogic machine.

28. Kittler, 32.

29. I am of course alluding to Althusser's "Ideology and Ideological State Apparatuses (Notes towards an Investigation)," in *Lenin and Philosophy and other essays*, trans. Ben Brewster (New York: Monthly Review Press, 1971). See in particular the section, "Ideology Interpellates Individuals as Subjects" (170–77). Little William and the monster engage in a complex and asymmetrical "hailing" of each other. In the course of their encounter, the monster addresses the frightened William as "Child" and then as "boy"; the child, struggling violently, calls the creature "monster," "ugly wretch," and "ogre." The lethal outcome of this double interpellation baldly dramatizes Althusser's implication that "recognitions" entail violence, ideological and otherwise. As if to confirm Althusser's observation that becoming-a-subject requires subjecting oneself, we see in *Frankenstein* that the young child is fully capable of interpellating himself and does so vociferously. Althusser's essay also allows us to read Walton's earlier hailing of the "savage ... giant" and the "European" (18) as ideological and not simply "optical" (18) events.

30. In the section "Species" in the chapter, "The Visible Structure," Jacob writes, "Throughout the Classical period, it was primarily by their visible structure that living beings were known and investigated" (*The Logic of Life: A History of Heredity*, trans. Betty E. Spillman [Princeton: Princeton Univ. Press, 1973], 44). Foucault asserts, in his chapter called "Classifying": "Natural history is nothing more than the nomination of the visible" (*The Order of Things*, 132).

31. Marshall brilliantly conjoins the problem of species and the "failure of sympathy" (195); in many ways his reading of the monster's request and Victor's response coincides with my own. He constellates Shelley's critique of the species-sympathy problem through Godwin, Wollstonecraft, and Rousseau. As he notes, Shelley's "story about the denial of

sympathy, fellow feeling, and fellow creatures seems to draw upon Wollstonecraft's critique of the ideology of sexual difference" (199).

32. Donna J. Haraway, *Primate Visions: Gender, Race, and Nature in the World of Modern Science* (New York: Routledge, 1989). Haraway's insistence that vision and perspective be embodied and theorized as such, as well as her call for "situated knowledges," has obvious implications for my reading of *Frankenstein*. See especially the section, "The Persistence of Vision," in "Situated Knowledges: The Science Question in Feminism and the Privilege of Partial Perspective," *Simians, Cyborgs, and Women: The Reinvention of Nature* (New York: Routledge, 1991).

33. Thomas Robert Malthus, *An Essay on the Principle of Population* (1798), ed. Philip Appleman (New York: Norton, 1976), 128.

34. Malthus, 122.

35. Malthus, 29. Malthus introduces the "struggle for existence" in a review of the "savage or hunter state." We should read Malthus as much as Rousseau as a theorist of primitive encounters.

36. Karl Marx, *Economic and Philosophic Manuscripts of 1844*, in *The Marx-Engels Reader*, ed. Robert Tucker, 2nd ed. (New York: Norton, 1978), 75.

37. Malthus, 94.

DENISE GIGANTE

Facing the Ugly:
The Case of Frankenstein

He approached; his countenance bespoke bitter anguish, combined with
disdain and malignity, while its unearthly ugliness rendered it almost too
horrible for human eyes.[1]
　　　　　　　—Mary Wollstonecraft Shelley, *Frankenstein*

I. THE *VIA NEGATIVA* OF UGLINESS

Whatever else can—and has—been said about Victor Frankenstein's
monster, one thing cannot be denied: the creature is exceedingly ugly. But in
what does this ugliness consist? Such a question is deceptively simple; any
recourse to aesthetic theory is bound to come up empty. Traditional
categories from the eighteenth century—the sublime, the beautiful, the
picturesque—exclude the ugly, and though the grotesque (particularly
prominent later in the nineteenth century) may at first seem related, it is
never specifically invoked in *Frankenstein* and must not be confused with the
ugly. While the etymological heritage of the grotesque combines both the
comic and the horrific, the ugly lacks comic effect.[2] In fact, aesthetically
speaking, the ugly simply lacks. If it is mentioned at all, it is treated as a
negative form of the beautiful: either as a lack of beauty in general or as a gap
in the beautiful object.[3] Hume, for example, speaks of "defects" or
"blemishes" in the beautiful object in his essay "Of the Standard of Taste"

From *ELH* 67 (2000). © 2000 by The Johns Hopkins University Press.

(1757).[4] Because the ugly is assumed to be everything the beautiful is not, it emerges as a mere tautology. In *A Philosophical Enquiry into the Origin of our Ideas of the Sublime and Beautiful* (1757), Burke sums up the Enlightenment point of view: "It may appear like a sort of repetition ... to insist here upon the nature of *Ugliness*."[5] Although Burke's binary of the sublime and the beautiful does not assert an antithesis between these two aesthetic modes, it adopts a bifurcated approach that Kant will later take up in *The Critique of Judgement* (1790).[6] For while Kant's third *Critique* transforms Burke's empiricist aesthetics substantially, it does not deviate from his basic assumption about the ugly, that it is a shadow form of the beautiful, its silent, invisible partner.

This *via negativa* of aesthetic theory, however, will not suffice as a hermeneutic mode to account for the positive ugliness of Mary Shelley's Creature. If the ugly object lacks beauty, the Creature, as the aesthetic object of Frankenstein's "unhallowed arts" (1831; *F*, 339), functions more actively than lack. He not only fails to please, he emphatically displeases. And in his relation to the subject, Victor Frankenstein, he manifests precisely the opposite of lack: excess. In a recent psychological foray into the uncharted field of the ugly, Mark Cousins proposes a model of ugliness as excess, which Slavoj Žižek develops in his discussion of "Ugly *Jouissance*" and which will be useful to us here:

> Contrary to the standard idealist argument that conceives ugliness as the defective mode of beauty, as its distortion, one should assert the ontological primacy of ugliness: it is beauty that is a kind of defense against the Ugly in its repulsive existence—or, rather, against existence *tout court*, since ... what is ugly is ultimately the brutal fact of existence (of the real) as such.[7]

Unlike the ghostly figments populating the *Fantasmagoriana* which Shelley originally set out to emulate on the shores of Lake Leman, Frankenstein's Creature is only *too* real. He is, like the blood and guts oozing from the fissures in his skin, an excess of existence, exceeding representation, and hence appearing to others as a chaotic spillage from his own representational shell.[8] While this portrayal might seem analogous to that of the Kantian sublime object, in which the representation of the thing [*Vorstellung*] in empirical form can never adequately present the Thing itself [*Ding an sich*], we must be careful to distinguish the ugly from the sublime object in order to explore a category not sufficiently accounted for by aesthetic discourse.

For as this essay will show, ugliness in *Frankenstein* is less of an aesthetic experience than a question of survival. Regardless of how we choose to map Victor Frankenstein onto his socio-historical grid, his subject position is radically threatened by the intrusive reality of his Creature. It is important to remember that the Creature's ugliness did not bother Victor (or anyone else for that matter) before he came to life: "he was ugly then; but when those muscles and joints were rendered capable of motion ..." (*F*, 87). As we shall see, he insists on himself, on the very stuff of his existence, which Victor's socially (in Lacanian terms, symbolically) constructed identity must, by definition, repress. Although one might point to Victor's difficulty in laying his hands on the Creature toward the end of the novel as evidence to the contrary, that is, as evidence of the Creature's insubstantiality, that difficulty has more to do with Victor's failure to get in touch with his own existence (the "real" Victor) than with any lack of materiality on the part of the Creature himself.[9] Once we confront him, as Victor does, in the raw ugliness of his own existence, we discover that he symbolizes nothing but the unsymbolized: the repressed ugliness at the heart of an elaborate symbolic network that is threatened the moment he bursts on the scene, exposing to view his radically uninscribed existence.

If we are to employ the Freudian vocabulary of repression, however, we must be careful to distinguish the ugly from the uncanny [*unheimlich*] object, which Freud discusses in similar terms as "*everything that ought to have remained ... hidden and secret and has become visible*," and which thus constitutes a return of the repressed in the subject.[10] Like the ugly, the uncanny occupies a "remote region" of aesthetics that has been theoretically neglected:

> The subject of the "uncanny" ... undoubtedly belongs to all that is terrible—to all that arouses dread and creeping horror; it is equally certain, too, that the word is not always used in a clearly definable sense, so that it tends to coincide with whatever excites dread. Yet we may expect that it implies some intrinsic quality which justifies the use of a special name. One is curious to know what this peculiar quality is which allows us to distinguish as "uncanny" certain things within the boundaries of what is "fearful."[11]

Both the uncanny and the ugly fall under the rubric of the fearful; the crucial distinction between them is that while something may be uncanny for one person and yet not so for another, the ugly is universally offensive.

The uncanny finds its being in whatever object serves to trigger an intrusion of repressed childhood complexes into the mind of the subject; hence nothing is intrinsically uncanny. The Creature's ugliness, on the other hand, constitutes a return of the repressed not linked to any particular childhood fixation. Instead the Creature appears as a return of what is universally repressed, or what Freud's precursor, F. W. J. Schelling, considers the horror at the core of all existence. Our concern, consequently, is not with the specific subject of psychoanalysis so much as with ugliness itself. The task will be to discover how Shelley extracts the Creature from the crack opened up by the ugly in eighteenth-century aesthetic theory in order to posit him as that aesthetic impossibility: the positive manifestation of ugliness.

Much critical debate surrounding *Frankenstein* has focused on the discourse of political monstrosity and how it relates to Victor's "miserable monster" (*F*, 87). Fred Botting, for example, surveys the context of political monstrosity from Hobbes to Burke and concludes that monstrosity represents "a complex and changing resistance to established authority."[12] Like the monstrous, the ugly resists, but what it resists is not established authority so much as the aestheticization that enables that very authority. Accordingly, this essay shall address not monstrosity per se so much as the ugliness that precedes and predetermines that monstrosity. Indeed I must agree with Harold Bloom that "a beautiful 'monster,' even a passable one, would not have been a 'monster.'"[13] But what is it about the ugly that aesthetic theory cannot face and that inevitably translates into the socio-political discourse of monstrosity?

In his *Reflections on the Revolution in France*, Burke maintains the need for "pleasing illusions" and "superadded ideas" to beautify or "cover the defects of our naked shivering nature."[14] Mandeville states the case more plainly earlier in the century when he writes that "all Men endeavour to hide themselves, their Ugly Nakedness, from each other ... wrapping up the true Motives of their Hearts in the Specious Cloke of Sociableness."[15] As Victor's experience during the 1790s (when the novel is set) demonstrates, direct exposure of the raw, unaestheticized stuff of humanity (its "Ugly Nakedness") threatens not only the subject itself, but the entire system of symbolic representation, the disruption of which would constitute the "horrible and disgustful situation" (*R*, 90) that Burke describes as monstrous:

> Everything seems out of nature in this strange chaos of levity
> and ferocity, and of all sorts of crimes jumbled together with

all sorts of follies. In viewing *this monstrous tragicomic scene*, the most opposite passions necessarily succeed and sometimes mix with each other in the mind. (*R*, 11; my emphasis)

What Burke fears is the irruption of the repressed social real through the skin of "pleasing illusions" that contain—and sustain—society. Any fissures in the "system of manners" become infections, "mental blotches and running sores" that inevitably infect the social body with the "contagion of their ill example" (*R*, 88, 116). Significantly, these particular "running sores" spring from the aristocracy, the luxurious if "miserable great" (*R*, 116), for it is not only the lower orders that constitute a threat to society: it is whatever threatens to disrupt order as such, to undo those very distinctions.[16]

Cousins draws upon this notion of "contagion," proposing that the ugly object appears as "an invasive contaminating life stripped of all signification," one that "gorges on meaning" as it engulfs the subject with its own lack of meaning, its excessive *in*coherence.[17] In fact, in *Frankenstein*, the term "ugly" emerges at the precise point when the speaking subject is about to be consumed by such incoherence. Descending the Mer de Glace after a traumatic encounter with the Creature, for example, Victor describes the wind "as if it were a dull ugly siroc on its way to consume [him]" (*F*, 176). While the sirocco is as invisible as wind and hence cannot, strictly speaking, qualify as ugly, his pathetic fallacy is apt. For as the "contaminating life" of the Creature shills out from his overstretched skin to pursue Victor physically and psychologically, it threatens to "consume" him and the entire symbolic order in which he is implicated. Thus while it is couched in admittedly boyish terms, William Frankenstein's fatal encounter with the Creature—"monster! ugly wretch! you wish to eat me, and tear me to pieces" (*F*, 169)—contains a fundamental insight into the nature of ugliness itself: the ugly is that which threatens to consume and disorder the subject. William cries, "Let me go, or I will tell my papa" (*F*, 169), and it is appropriate that his defense should be a psychological appeal to the Name of the Father, the site of symbolic authority that guarantees the young Frankenstein his ground of meaning in the face of consuming chaos. That the Creature is ready to gorge on that meaning we may infer from his desperate plea, "Child, what is the meaning of this?" (*F*, 169), which he utters as he draws the boy forcibly toward him, wrenching his hands away from his eyes. Like the aesthetic category of the ugly itself, the Creature cannot be faced.

II. THE BURKEAN ANTI-DEFINITION

Since our purpose, however, is to face the ugly, not as inversion or lack but as positive fact, we must first develop it in the darkroom of late eighteenth-century aesthetic theory. Burke's definition of ugliness is brief and divides into three parts. The first states negatively that the ugly is that which the beautiful is not: "I imagine [ugliness] to be in all respects the opposite to those qualities which we have laid down for the constituents of beauty" (E, 119). To consider the Creature according to Burkean aesthetics, therefore, we must view him in reverse through the lens of the beautiful as the aesthetic object of Victor's artistic fashioning. Indeed Victor prefers to regard himself not as a scientist so much as "an artist occupied by his favourite employment" (F, 85), selecting disparate harts for their beauty rather than choosing an entire body to reanimate. In a passage reminiscent of Mary Shelley's original "reverie" (1831; F, 364), in which she first envisioned the Creature, he describes the scene of creation:

> ... by the glimmer of the half-extinguished light, I saw the dull yellow eye of the creature open; it breathed hard, and a convulsive motion agitated its limbs.
>
> How can I describe my emotions at this catastrophe, or how delineate the wretch whom with such infinite pains and care I had endeavoured to form? His limbs were in proportion, and I had selected his features as beautiful. Beautiful!—Great God! His yellow skin scarcely covered the work of muscles and arteries beneath; his hair was of a lustrous black, and flowing; his teeth of a pearly whiteness; but these luxuriances only formed a more horrid contrast with his watery eyes, that seemed almost of the same colour as the dun white sockets in which they were set, his shrivelled complexion, and straight black lips. (F, 85–86)

Victor's description takes the form of what might be called an "anti-blazon," whereby individual features, such as the Creature's hair "of a lustrous black, and flowing" and "his teeth of a pearly whiteness," are sutured together with other unsightly features (his "work of muscles and arteries," his "straight black lips") that radically disrupt aesthetic representation. As cracks and fissures emerge in the representation, the visceral reality of the Creature leaks through to destroy all fantasy. Despite the fact that Victor specifically chose each feature for its beauty ("I had selected his features as beautiful"), the combined form cannot aesthetically contain its own existence.

Here Victor's creative method resembles that which Mary Wollstonecraft ascribes to the sculptors of Greek antiquity: "beautiful limbs and features were selected from various bodies to form an harmonious whole ... It was not, however, the mechanical selection of limbs and features; but the ebullition of an heated fancy that burst forth."[18] While in the case of the Greek statue, the sculptor's "heated fancy" manages to contain the hodgepodge of individually selected limbs and features, Victor "went to it in cold blood" (*F*, 191). As a result, what "burst forth" was not his vision so much as the brute fact of the Creature himself. Coleridge would have condemned this "mechanical selection of limbs and features" as a "mechanical art," one inherently unable to transform the artist's materials into a harmonious whole.[19] Following Francis Hutcheson, who earlier in the eighteenth century had asserted "the universal Agreement of Mankind in their sense of Beauty from Uniformity amidst variety," Coleridge defined beauty as "*multëity in Unity*."[20] "The BEAUTIFUL," he writes, "is that in which the many, still seen as many, becomes *one*."[21] If the Creature is not to be seen as a mere mechanistic collection of limbs, he must inspire his viewer with the imaginative power necessary to unite his various anatomical components into the totality of a human *being*. Otherwise, like the "mechanistic philosophy" that Burke complains would "confound all sorts of citizens ... into one homogenous mass" (*R*, 216), the creation of an individual from anatomical parts, or a social body from parts that are themselves individuals, can be a futile—if not perilous—endeavor.[22]

What immediately disrupts Victor's imaginative effort to unite his Creature's various components into a single totality is the "dull yellow eye of the creature." It dominates his thoughts, doubling from a single "yellow eye" to two "watery eyes" as he struggles to contain it in representation.[23] He notices with disgust how the eyeballs are lost in the murkiness, the "dun white" of their surrounding sockets, and he even doubts "if eyes they may be called" (*F*, 87). Yellow, watery, and dun, the Creature's eyes are antithetical to the beautiful eye that Burke claims has "so great a share in the beauty of the animal creation" (*E*, 118). In the section directly before "UGLINESS," entitled "The EYE," he writes:

> I think then, that the beauty of the eye consists, first, in its *clearness*; ... none are pleased with an eye, whose water (to use that term) is dull and muddy. We are pleased with the eye in this view, on the principle upon which we like diamonds, clear water, glass, and such like transparent substances. (*E*, 118)

By focusing on the ideal of transparency, Burke draws attention away from the materiality of the eye itself. While a clear eye serves as a proverbial window into the soul, the Creature's eye is little more than a reminder of its own existence: a lump of vile jelly attached to the skull. With reference to the "depthless eyes" of Shelley's Creature, Žižek writes: "The nontransparent, 'depthless' eye blocks out our access to the 'soul,' to the infinite abyss of the 'person,' thus turning it into a soulless monster: not simply a nonsubjective machine, but rather an uncanny subject that has not yet been submitted to the process of 'subjectivization' which confers upon it the depth of 'personality.'"[24] Leaving aside for a moment Žižek's use of the word "uncanny," his insight is grounded in the Burkean aesthetic theory that serves as context for *Frankenstein*.

As a mere reminder of its own existence, the Creature's "depthless" eye serves as the prototype for various hideous progeny, including the "dead grey eye" of Polidori's vampire, another creature to emerge from the same evening at Villa Diodati:

> ... some attributed [their fear] to the dead grey eye, which, fixing upon the object's face, did not seem to penetrate, and at one glance to pierce through to the inward workings of the heart; but fell upon the cheek with a leaden ray that weighed upon the skin it could not pass.[25]

If the vampire is opposite to the Creature in that he constitutes an excess of representation over existence, his eye is also opposite to the Creature's eye. While the latter prevents the viewer from penetrating through to the Creature's soul, the vampire's "dead grey eye" cannot penetrate through to the "heart" or soul of his viewer. Both eyes are monstrous, and may be considered opposite sides of the same coin: a facial blob that blocks or clogs imaginative representation. Viewed in these terms, Milton's insistence that despite his blindness his eyes had remained "as clear and bright, without a cloud, as the eyes of men who see most keenly" may indicate more than aesthetic vanity.[26] What is at stake is his subjectivity as such, a transcendence over his own physical existence in the eyes of the world. Thus the invocation (rather, lamentation) to the "heav'nly Muse" in the third book of *Paradise Lost*—"these eyes, that roll in vain / To find thy piercing ray, and find no dawn; / So thick a drop serene has quencht thir Orbs"—makes a point of referring to his blindness as one that has not clouded his eyes (the "drop serene" being the Latin medical term for blindness that does not affect the appearance of the eye).[27] Elsewhere this point becomes central to Milton's defense against the charge of being "A monster, dreadful, ugly, huge, deprived of sight."[28]

Unlike the "dull yellow" or "dead grey" eye, the beautiful eye diverts attention from the substance of the eye itself. Burke writes that "the eye affects, as it is expressive of some qualities of the mind, and its principal power generally arises from this" (*E*, 118–19). In direct contrast to the Creature's ugly eye, therefore, stands Victor's description of the "fair" Elizabeth: "Her brow was clear and ... her blue eyes cloudless ... none could behold her without looking on her as of a distinct species, a being heaven-sent, and bearing a celestial stamp in all her features" (1831; *F*, 323).[29] Victor's fantasy takes possession of him here and suggests a three-dimensionality of the human being, rather than of the brow or the eye itself. As a result, the mere fact of her head, the physical stuff of it, is repressed. Indeed his representation contains her materiality to such a degree that she becomes completely etherealized: she is "heaven-sent" and bears a celestial "stamp." Whereas the "unearthly creature" is classed beneath the "superior beauty of man" (*F*, 192), Elizabeth is elevated above it as "a distinct species"—presumably one unencumbered by those "real" bodily functions that Wollstonecraft for one considered "so very disgusting."[30] Like the fair Elizabeth the "wondrously fair" Safie exhibits an "animated eye" and "countenance of angelic beauty and expression" (*F*, 144). While an animated eye conveys the animating mind behind, a static eye only increases the chance that the viewer's gaze will come to light on the horrific substance of the eye itself. As Burke observes, "the motion of the eye contributes to its beauty, by continually shifting its direction" (*E*, 118). One look in the "dull yellow" eye of the Creature is enough to reveal the horror of his full-blown existence and demolish all "pleasing illusions."

In addition to the transparent eye, Burke considers smoothness to be a "very considerable part of the effect of beauty ... indeed the most considerable" (*E*, 114). He argues that if we "take any beautiful object, and give it a broken and rugged surface ... however well formed it may be in other respects, it pleases no longer" (*E*, 114). Cousins and Žižek both implicitly follow Burke in emphasizing the "broken" surface as a contributing effect of the ugly: "The shock of ugliness occurs when the surface is actually cut, opened up, so that the direct insight into the actual depth of the skinless flesh dispells the spiritual, immaterial pseudodepth."[31] In this sense, Victor's observation that the Creature's "yellow skin scarcely covered the work of muscles and arteries beneath" may be seen as metonymic for his ugliness in general. While a smooth skin provides an imaginary screen for the subject to project his or her fantasy of the transcendent human being inside the object of perception, the "shrivelled complexion" of Frankenstein's Creature radically disrupts any effort to elevate him above the "filthy mass" (*F*, 174) of his flesh.[32]

In *Gulliver's Travels* (1726), another one of the many books Mary Shelley was reading during the genesis of *Frankenstein*, Swift illustrates a similar phenomenon. When Lemuel Gulliver views the enormous, naked bodies of the women of Brobdingnag, their skin is magnified to such giant proportions that it loses its ability to function as a fantasmatic screen: it is too close and insists on its own reality.[33] As the real, subcutaneous existence of the women bursts traumatically through Gulliver's fantasy of them, they strike him as terribly ugly:

> they would strip themselves to the Skin ... their naked Bodies; which, I am sure, to me was very far from being a tempting Sight, or from giving me any other Motions than those of Horror and Disgust. Their Skins appeared so coarse and uneven, so variously coloured when I saw them near, with a Mole here and there as broad as a Trencher, and Hairs hanging from it thicker than Pack-threads; to say nothing further concerning the rest of their Persons.[34]

The hairs protruding through the skin of the Brobdingnagian women, like the veins and arteries protruding through the skin of the Creature, reach out to Gulliver as tentacles from an alien (because repressed) zone of existence and choke him with disgust.[35] The reality of their naked bodies serves as a foil to the etherealized Elizabeth, whose skin displays no cutaneous incoherence but is completely of a piece. While the "celestial stamp" on all her features testifies to her wholeness as a created product, the Creature's skin struggles unsuccessfully to conceal the raw physicality of his gigantic (though not quite Brobdingnagian) stature. The stitches we can only assume are holding him together (a visual image impressed upon us by screen versions of *Frankenstein*) expose the mechanics of his creation and produce an effect opposite to that of Elizabeth's mystified "stamp."

In the second part of his (anti-)definition of the ugly, Burke states that "though ugliness be the opposite to beauty, it is not the opposite to proportion and fitness. For it is possible that a thing may be very ugly with any proportions, and with a perfect fitness to any uses" (*E*, 119). Certainly, the Creature is not "opposite to proportion." Despite the fact that Victor's eyes "start[ed] from their sockets" at the sight of him, Victor makes clear that the Creature's "limbs were in proportion" and that, in accordance with his eight-foot stature, his figure was designed "proportionably large" (*F*, 82–86). As Burke explains, it is not ugliness but "deformity" that is opposed to proportion: "*deformity* is opposed ... to the *compleat, common form*" (*E*, 102; emphasis in the original). One must keep in mind that Burke is working from an aesthetic tradition that he feels has been unsystematic in its use of terms and inexact in mapping the terrain of the non-beautiful. Even the Creature refers to the "deformity of [his] figure," despite the fact that, though large, he is not technically deformed (*F*, 141). When he sees himself in a transparent pool for the first time, he laments "the fatal effects of this miserable deformity" (*F*, 142). Yet as his creator seems to know better than himself, deformity is a distinct category not to be confused (literally, fused together) with the ugly.

If the Creature is not "opposite to proportion," neither is he opposite to "fitness." Like the monkey, whom Burke claims may be physically fit and still qualify as ugly, "he is admirabl[y] calculated for running, leaping, grappling, and climbing: and yet there are few animals which seem to have less beauty in the eyes of all mankind" (*E*, 105). The Creature, too, is fit—or *too* fit. His superhuman ability to overcome natural adversity, far from inspiring admiration, horrifies his persecuted maker: "he had followed me in my travels; he had loitered in forests, hid himself in caves, or taken refuge in wide and desert heaths" (*F*, 193). In short, just as the Creature is opposed to those qualities that constitute beauty (a clear eye, beautiful skin, and so forth), he is not opposed to those qualities (proportion and fitness) that are not opposed to ugliness. (I have allowed the convoluted syntax of the previous sentence to stand in order to emphasize the difficulty of discussing the ugly in terms of aesthetic discourse.)

In the final third of his section on "UGLINESS," Burke separates the ugly from the sublime: "Ugliness I imagine likewise to be consistent enough with an idea of the sublime. But I would by no means insinuate that ugliness of itself is a sublime idea, unless united with such qualities as excite a strong terror" (*E*, 119). While the beautiful object is calculated to excite pleasure and the sublime object pain, the paradox is that sublime pain in turn leads to pleasure: "When danger or pain press too nearly, they are incapable of giving any delight, and are simply terrible; but at certain distances, and with certain modifications, they may be and they are delightful, as we every day experience" (*E*, 39–40). Although it would be somewhat reductive (and in the terms Burke sets forth, inaccurate) to do so, it can be tempting to read the Creature as an object of sublimity. Victor complains that the monster has consumed all his thoughts and "swallowed up every habit of [his] nature" (*F*, 84), and such obsession with the object is typical of the sublime. Burke could almost be describing Victor when he writes that in the experience of sublimity "the mind is so entirely filled with its object, that it cannot entertain any other, nor by consequence reason on that object which employs it" (*E*, 57). As Victor himself relates, "The form of the monster on whom I had bestowed existence was for ever before my eyes, and I raved incessantly concerning him" (*F*, 91). Not only does Victor experience several rounds of the "terror" associated with sublimity, but he takes perverse delight in pursuing his Creature on a homicidal chase to the ends of the earth, the very landscapes identified with the Burkean sublime.

However the principal factor of sublime experience—being elevated from terror to a comprehension of greatness—is absent from Victor's experience. Instead, he becomes psychologically debased after every encounter with the Creature: a "miserable wretch" (*F*, 227) like the Creature himself. Instead of attaining an awareness of his subjective capacity, he grows feverish and weak, descending into the chaotic jumble of sensations from which he had originally emerged as a subject. As he loses control over his own existence, he tries fruitlessly to run from it, begging his father, for example: "take me where I may forget myself, my existence" (*F*, 209). After another particularly feverish night on the Orkney Islands, he remarks: "when I awoke, I again felt as if I belonged to a race of human beings like myself" (*F*, 196). Like his younger brother William, who seeks refuge in the Name of the Father, Victor seizes upon the symbolic order to make sense of his own ugly existence.

III. THE KANTIAN APORIA

If Burke theorizes the ugly object in reverse, stating methodically what the ugly is *not*, Kant effectively obliterates it. He swerves from Burke's empiricist aesthetics by dismissing the "real existence" of the object: "All one wants to know is whether the mere representation of the object is to my liking, no matter how indifferent I may be to the real existence of the object of this representation."[36] As a result, the site of aesthetic experience shifts from the physiological subject, the "work of muscles and arteries" that register sensation, to the subject's fleshed-out representation of the object. An aesthetic judgment must represent "the accord, in a given intuition, of the faculty of presentation, or the imagination, with the *faculty of concepts* that belongs to understanding or reason, in the sense of the former assisting the latter" (*C*, 90; emphasis in the original). With regard to the human figure, for example, the ideal of beauty is related to the idea of good (*C*, 79–80). If beauty entails the idea of good, and if ugliness is the implied opposite of beauty, then it would seem that the ugly entails the idea of evil.

Such a proposition has a long literary heritage. In *Paradise Lost*, the term "ugly" first appears with Sin herself, who is described as being "uglier" than the "Night-Hag" (*PL*, 2.662); later the devils are transformed into "a crowd / Of ugly Serpents" (*PL*, 10.538–39), and this juxtaposition of "ugly" with the morally repulsive Sin and serpent is reinforced in Adam's prophetic vision of evil: "O sight / Of terror, foul and ugly to behold" (*PL*, 11.463–64). In *Pamela* (1740), to take another example from Shelley's reading list at this time, Richardson's heroine protests: "It is impossible I should love him; for his vices all *ugly him all over*, as I may say."[37] Percy Shelley has the "Spirit of the Earth" describe women as the "ugliest of all things evil, / Though fair" in *Prometheus Unbound* (1819), and in a *Reflector* essay several years earlier, Charles Lamb satirizes the long-standing connection: "How ugly a person looks upon whose reputation some awkward aspersion hangs, and how suddenly his countenance clears up with his character."[38] The Creature himself is called a "devil" (*F*, 104) and a "daemon" (*F*, 112) before he ever has a chance to speak for himself. Nevertheless, in strictly aesthetic terms, according to Kant this approach will not do. The concept of good must be distilled from the ideal of "pure" beauty since "an estimate formed according to such a standard can never be purely aesthetic" (*C*, 80). It would follow that the concept of evil must likewise be distilled from the ideal of pure ugliness, but (and one may readily anticipate the problem) while we can distill the good from the ideal of beauty, there is no aesthetic ideal of the ugly from which to distill evil or anything else.

The object finds its being in the realm of the imaginative ideal for Kant, and if there is no ideal of the ugly, in what manner can the ugly object be said to exist? Kant says it does not. He avoids his own theoretical aporia by claiming that the ugliness that cannot be denied in nature must be represented within given aesthetic categories, namely the beautiful or the sublime, for to present the ugly qua ugly would make the viewer turn away in disgust—and hence obviate all aesthetic judgment:

> The Furies, diseases, devastations of war, and the like, can (as evils) be very beautifully described, nay even represented in pictures. One kind of ugliness alone is incapable of being represented conformably to nature without destroying all aesthetic delight, and consequently artistic beauty, namely, that which excites disgust. For, as in this strange sensation, which depends purely on the imagination, the object is represented as

insisting, as it were, upon our enjoying it, while we still set our
face against it ... (C, 173–74)

What we discern in the passage above is that the ugly is that which disgusts;
and it disgusts because it "insists." Whether we pursue this "insistence" back
to its Latin root *sistere* (to stand still) or the German "insist" [*bestehen*] to its
root, *stehen* (to stand), we find that what "insists" is that which "stands" in the
way. The ugly is offensively obtrusive in standing between the subject and its
representation of the object. It stands in for itself, as it were, refusing to
budge, and thus stripping the subject of imaginative capacity. Freud argues
that reality is that which stands in the way of desire, and in this sense what
we find insisting is "real existence" as such. It stands in the way of the
subject's quest for the elusive *Ding-an-Sich*, the thing the subject can never
attain, and thus must incessantly desire, by presenting itself as an unwanted
Ding. It obtrudes itself through the noumenal gap in the object, clogging it,
and hence closing the subject off from its own imaginative capacity.

While the subject is seeking the phantasmal *Ding-an-Sich*, in other
words, the ugly stands in the way, like Blake's "opake blackening fiend," to
turn the subject back on its own opacity.[39] Unlike the ugly, the beautiful
object can be imaginatively comprehended. And even the sublime object,
though it inspires a representation of limitlessness, can still be
comprehended as an object: it causes "a representation of limitlessness, yet
with a superadded thought of its totality" (C, 90). In both kinds of Kantian
sublimity, the dynamic and the mathematical, the mind attains an awareness
of its own capacity, its ability to "fit over" sublimity itself with its own "superadded thought." We may call nature sublime, but what we really mean is that
we can contain it, that it is our mind, rather than nature, that expands toward
the infinite. But if the sublime object is not truly "limitless," then, we might
posit the ugly, or that which cannot be contained as an object, as a more
radical antithesis to the beautiful. For if beauty is a transparency, in the sense
that it is nothing distinct from the feeling of the subject, and if ugliness is its
radical antithesis, then what emerges is an anti-transparency, an opacity or
material abhorrence that leaks through representation to disorder the mind
of the subject. We may imagine beauty as a form causing delight, but the ugly
stops us in our tracks as something we can't even imagine.

Since Kantian aesthetics are founded upon the repression of the object
by the subject such that the subject can always "fit over," and thus prove itself
more extensive than, the object, that which the subject suddenly fails to
contain in representation appears as a traumatic excess—a sudden intrusion
of what should not be there. In Kant's case, that excess is "real existence" as

such. In this sense the ugly constitutes a "return of the repressed" more radical than the *Unheimlich*, for it does not merely threaten to unsettle the subject; it threatens to destroy it [*zu Grunde zu richten*]. Thus unlike the "creeping horror" that overtakes the Freudian subject of the uncanny, the response to the ugly is immediate. Victor abruptly flees his newborn Creature in "horror and disgust" (*F*, 86), and the Creature's first public appearance is proleptic of those that follow: "[The shepherd] turned on hearing a noise; and, perceiving me, shrieked loudly, and, quitting the hut, ran across the fields with a speed of which his debilitated form hardly appeared capable" (*F*, 133–34). Adorno has suggested that by repressing what Kant calls "real existence" the beautiful object only manages to preserve the fear of it: "Terror itself peers out of the eyes of beauty as the coercion that emanates from form."[40] His insight may go some way toward explaining why, when "real existence" finally does break out in the mode of the ugly, a violent reaction should be axiomatic.

In his advertisement to his 1809 exhibition, Blake illustrates the typically kneejerk response to the ugly. There the "Ugly Man" appears as one of the three "Antient Britons" who escaped from the last battle of King Arthur against the Romans:

> The most Beautiful, the Roman Warriors trembled before and
>   worshipped:
> The most Strong, they melted before him and dissolved in his
>   presence:
> The most Ugly they fled with outcries and contortion of their
>   Limbs.[41]

At the sight of the Ugly Man, the warriors exhibit no uncanny "creeping horror" but violently contort their limbs and cry out. Blake explicitly describes him as "one approaching to the beast in features and form, his forehead small, without frontals; his jaws large; ... and every thing tending toward what is truly Ugly, the incapability of intellect."[42] While the Ugly Man serves Blake's particular purposes as a figure of Urizenic reason, he is bestial in that he has not undergone the process of subjectifying his existence. He demonstrates the same incapacity to elevate himself over himself and achieve coherence in the eyes of his viewer that is characteristic of the ugly.

Along similar lines, Coleridge, quoting Plotinus, asserts that in confronting beauty, "the soul speaks of it as if it understood it, recognizes and welcomes it and as it were adapts itself to it. But when it encounters the ugly it shrinks back and rejects it and turns away from it and is out of time and alienated from it."[43] The soul shrinks back from the lack of harmony it finds threatening to its oven coherence; what it cannot comprehend it rejects. The Creature is alienated from everyone he confronts precisely because his ugliness prevents those he meets from seeing past his "real existence" to the greater sum of his being—or from imaginatively representing him at all. Indeed the one person (old man De Lacey) who forms an opinion of the Creature as an integrated being is blind—and hence unable to process his ugliness. By refusing that such ugliness can aesthetically exist, aesthetic theory itself turns away, shrinking back, rejecting, and (in Kant's terms) setting its face against it.

IV. THE BIRTH OF THE UGLY IN *FRANKENSTEIN*

If the groundwork of aesthetic theory yields no better understanding of ugliness than its very resistance to aestheticization, we might attempt a dialectical transposition of the problem into its own solution. We might, in other words, conclude that such resistance itself, and the threat it poses to the very survival of the subject qua subject, is what defines the ugly. If the aesthetic can be considered the only mode of transcendence left in a highly rational, empirical age, then the deaestheticizing ugly comes fraught with all the horror of not just primal but final chaos, of apocalyptic destruction. From the outset, Victor attempts to fortify himself against such destruction by identifying his place within a larger network of national, political, and family ties:

> I AM by birth a Genovese; and my family is one of the most distinguished of that republic. My ancestors had been for many years counsellors and syndics; and my father had filled several public situations with honour and reputation. (*F*, 63)

By parceling out his subjective content into the various links that comprise his chain of existence, Victor cloaks himself in the "pleasing illusions" of symbolic identity. As he consecutively elides "family" and "republic," "ancestors" and "counsellors," "father" and "public situations," his genetic encoding fuses with the social, and his patrilinear and largely patriotic conception of his origins serves to distance him from the reality of the "birth" itself.

The Creature, on the other hand, whose birth is quite literally patrilinear, plunges directly into the "strange chaos" (to borrow Burke's expression) of that birth:

> IT is with considerable difficulty that I remember the original aera of my being: all the events of that period appear confused and indistinct. A strange multiplicity of sensations seized me, and I saw, felt, heard, and smelt, at the same time; and it was, indeed, a long time before I learned to distinguish between the operations of my various senses. (*F*, 130)

While Victor's narrative commences under the pretense of absolute clarity ("I am ..."), the Creature emphasizes the murkiness of memory, the "considerable difficulty" of remembering a past that is "confused and indistinct": a primal, amniotic sea of sensation.[44] Yet the mere fact that he tries to remember those origins distinguishes him from his maker, who evades such messiness by describing a self that is a social, and largely familial, construction: "My mother's tender caresses, and my father's smile of benevolent pleasure while regarding me, are my first recollections" (1831; *F*, 322). While Victor's description illustrates the Lacanian parental gaze, or the constitution of the subject as a "thing to be looked at," his own horrified parental gaze—abruptly turned away at the very instant the Creature is about to confirm himself as a subject and return the gaze in the form of the infantile "grin" that "wrinkled his cheeks" (*F*, 87)—parodies this formative moment.

Because the Creature cannot grasp hold of any symbolic connections in reconstructing his past, he gropes blindly for the source of his "real" being. He tries to remember the original era ("aera") of that being as if it were a thing, an "aura" hovering about him as a sign of his integration into the world at large. His indistinct aera resembles the "eyry of freedom" that Mary Shelley associates with her own earliest memories in the 1831 introduction to *Frankenstein* (*F*, 361). As an alternate form of "aerie" or nest, the "eyry" of freedom may be seen as a realm of embryonic "aeration," an original "aera" of being. And like the jumble of referents that hover around "aera," the "strange multiplicity of sensations" that the Creature recalls as his earliest memories reflects the "strange chaos," the monstrous Burkean disorder "of levity and ferocity, and of all sorts of crimes jumbled together" at the core of the social order. Revealingly, Adorno locates the origin of ugliness in the transition from the archaic to the post-archaic: "The concept of the ugly may well have originated in the separation of art from its archaic phase: It marks the permanent return of the archaic."[45] That same transition from the archaic-chaotic to a post-archaic, symbolic order is one the Creature cannot seem to accomplish for himself. He remains stuck, striving for subjective completion in the fermenting crack of the ugly.

Unable to affirm himself as a subject, the Creature thus commences his own autobiographical narrative by inverting Victor's declarative "I am" into the pathetically interrogative "Who was I? What was I?"[46] He despairs of "brother, sister, and all the various relationships which bind one human being to another in mutual bonds," and then demands: "where were my friends and relations? No father had watched my infant days, no mother had blessed me with smiles and caresses; ... I had never yet seen a being resembling me, or who claimed any intercourse with me. What was I?" (*F*, 149). Throughout the novel, he continues to complain of his isolation—"No sympathy may I ever find" (*F*, 244), "I am quite alone" (*F*, 245), etc.—and the fact that he cannot identify his position in the signifying "chain of existence and events" (*F*, 174). This is a version of the same chain Byron, writing at the same time, has Manfred label "the chain of human ties."[47] Both are derived from the chain of phenomenal reality that Burke refers to in his aesthetic inquiry as the "great chain of causes, which linking one to another ... can never be unravelled by any industry of ours" (*E*, 129).[48] And it is this very "chain of existence," from which the Creature is excluded, that keeps the other characters in the novel in existence—paradoxically, by repressing their "real existence."

After Victor's father, for instance, loses his wife, his son William, and his adoptive daughters Justine and Elizabeth to death, and his other son Victor to what he assumes must be madness, his "springs of existence" suddenly give way and he dies in Victor's arms (1831; *F*, 356).[49] Elizabeth repeatedly reminds Victor of his own implication in the sustaining "chain of existence and events": "We all ... depend upon you; and if you are miserable, what must be our feelings?" (*F*, 181). Yet as we know from his own self-portrayal, Victor needs no reminding of his position in this intersubjective symbolic. He informs Clerval that without social connections "we are unfashioned creatures, but half made up" (1831; *F*, 320). With the deaths of his mother, brother, sister(s), and father, Victor himself becomes increasingly "unmade-up." His family skin becomes fissured, and he is driven to renounce the national identity so important to his sense of self. "My first resolution was to quit Geneva for ever" (*F*, 225). As Frances Ferguson suggests, the skin of all symbolic identity in *Frankenstein* ("the skin of inclusiveness") is inevitably overstretched.[50]

Ultimately, the same may be said for *Frankenstein*. Shelley's novel has been traditionally criticized as uneven, a chaotic intertextual jumble. In a review of *The Frankenstein Notebooks*, Stuart Curran speaks of "the depth of the intertextuality in *Frankenstein*" and comes to the defense of Shelley's authorship: "the entire machinery of this novel, from its knowledge of contemporary chemistry in the early chapters to its elaborate and ongoing play against *Paradise Lost* was the project of Mary Shelley."[51] His use of the term "machinery" is propitious, for it harks back to the Frankensteinian creative process: a method of production mechanical to the degree that it cannot contain its own reality. Although Shelley struggles to contain her "very hideous ... idea" (1831; *F*, 360) in narrative frame after frame, the Creature himself will not be restrained by his textual "skin," but instead breaks forth as one of the most enduring figures of the Romantic period. He takes on a life of his own, proliferating wildly and engendering an ever-increasing number of dramatic and cinematic adaptations, "hideous progeny" of the original "hideous progeny" (1831; *F*, 365).[52]

As he slips out of her text, he slips out of her control, and Shelley finds herself surprised, for example, at the theatrical success of Richard Brinsley Peake's *Presumption: or the Fate of Frankenstein*, which opened at the English Opera House on 28 July 1823. The Creature remained nameless in that original production, and Shelley was immensely pleased that in the list of *dramatis personae* there was a blank space for the name of the Creature: "this nameless mode of naming the u[n]namable is rather good."[53] Her comment offers itself up to a facile deconstruction that were perhaps best handed over to Derrida for proper treatment. In his analysis of the Kantian *Häßlichkeit* [ugliness], Derrida writes: "The disgusting X cannot even announce itself as a *sensible* object without immediately being caught up in a teleological hierarchy. It is therefore in-sensible and un-intelligible, irrepresentable and unnamable, the absolute other of the system."[54] In later enactments, this seeming aesthetic impossibility—the unrepresentable, unnamable positive manifestation of ugliness—takes over the identity of his creator and comes to be known as "Frankenstein." Less than a month after Peak's adaptation, for example, the Royal Court Theatre in London produced *Frankenstein; or, The Demon of Switzerland*, where in a slippery switching of subtitles, "The Demon of Switzerland" replaces "The Modern Prometheus." The "or," then, becomes a pivotal transition, a vanishing mediator between "Frankenstein" and "Demon," with the latter threatening to engulf the former. Finally, as the Creature breaks out through the various pores (that is, the —'s and or's) in the text, he takes over the text itself, becoming, in effect, *Frankenstein*. The fact that it is common, if not *de rigueur*, for audiences to equate the Creature himself with Frankenstein (and consequently, *Frankenstein*) confirms the premise that no matter how one may attempt to contain it, the ugly ultimately bursts forth to consume whatever it confronts: in this case, Mary Shelley.

NOTES

I am grateful to Christopher Rovee, Susan Wolfson, and Sarah Churchwell for critical attention to this essay. I would also like to thank David L. Clark and those who attended an earlier version of the paper at the 1997 NASSR conference in Hamilton, Ontario, as well as Slavoj Žižek, who provided the "vital spark."

1. Mary Wollstonecraft Shelley, *Frankenstein; or, The Modern Prometheus: The 1818 Version*, ed. D. L. Macdonald and Kathleen Scherf (Peterborough, Ontario: Broadview Press, 1996), 127. Hereafter cited parenthetically in the text and abbreviated *F*. The 1831 introduction and 1831 textual variants included as appendices to the Broadview edition are also cited parenthetically and abbreviated 1831; *F*.

2. While the term "ugly" derives from the Old Norse *ugglig* (causing fear or discomfort), the "grotesque" descends from the fantastical hybrid forms painted in "grottoes" of ancient Roman buildings. Most accounts of the grotesque from the time of John Ruskin stress its hybrid (comic/horrific) nature: Wolfgang Kayser focuses on the demonic aspect of the grotesque in *The Grotesque in Art and Literature* (trans. Ulrich Weisstein [New York: Columbia Univ. Press, 1957]); Mikhail Bakhtin, on the other hand, embraces its low or comic aspect in *Rabelais and his World* (trans. Hélène Iswolsky [Cambridge: MIT Press, 1968]); Philip Thomson discusses the tension between the comic and the terrifying in *The Grotesque* (London: Methuen, 1972); Arthur Clayborough speaks of the grotesque as ugliness born again through humor (*The Grotesque in English Literature* [Oxford: Clarendon Press, 1965]); Geoffrey Galt Harpham examines grotesque contradiction (*On the Grotesque: Strategies of Contradiction in Art and Literature* [Princeton: Princeton Univ. Press, 1982]); to name a few.

3. The negative modality of the ugly was first recognized by Hegel's disciple Karl Rosenkranz, in his *Aesthetik des Hässlichen* (1853). Hegel himself conceives of beauty as a dynamic category in tension with its spectral other, the ugly. Yet because Hegel's *Aesthetics* (1823–28) postdates the development of the ugly in *Frankenstein*, this essay will focus on the late eighteenth-century aesthetic theory of Burke and Kant.

4. David Hume, "Of the Standard of Taste" (1757), in *Selected Essays*, ed. Stephen Copley and Andrew Edgar (Oxford: Oxford Univ. Press, 1993), 138 and following.

5. Edmund Burke, *A Philosophical Enquiry into the Origin of our Ideas of the Sublime and Beautiful* (1757), ed. James T. Boulton (Notre Dame: Univ. of Notre Dame Press, 1958), 119. Hereafter cited parenthetically in the text and abbreviated *E*.

6. As Samuel H. Monk has pointed out, this binary of the sublime and the beautiful departs from the earlier binary of the "non-beautiful" and the beautiful, which the aesthetic theory of the first half of the century had employed: "Hume, it will be recalled, had taken pain and pleasure as the effects of the ugly and the beautiful, and it may be said that in general this was the point of view of the first half of the century" (Monk, *The Sublime: A Study of Critical Theories in XVIII-Century England* [Ann Arbor: Univ. of Michigan Press, 1960], 91). I use the term "non-beautiful" since Hume does not concern himself with "the ugly"; rather, he claims that "the sentiments of men often differ with regard to beauty and *deformity* of all kinds" (Hume, 134; my emphasis). The distinction between ugliness and deformity is one Burke himself emphasizes in his *Philosophical Enquiry*, as we shall see.

7. *The Abyss of Freedom / Ages of the World: An essay by Slavoj Žižek with the text of Schelling's* Die Weltalter, trans. Judith Norman (Ann Arbor: Univ. of Michigan Press,

1997), 21. Compare to Mark Cousins, "The Ugly" (2 parts), *AA Files* 28 (1994): 61–64 and *AA Files* 29 (1995): 3–6.

8. Žižek remarks on a similar phenomenon in science fiction film, where the ugly often appears as an "excess of stuff that penetrates through the pores in the surface, from science fiction aliens whose liquid materiality overwhelms their surface ... to the films of David Lynch where (exemplarily in *Dune*) the raw flesh beneath the surface threatens to emerge" (*Abyss of Freedom*, 22).

9. Technically, one need not shy away from this spectral aspect of the Creature since, as both Cousins and Žižek suggest, spectrality itself is a form of excess; it is the antithesis to ugliness in the form of ghosts, vampires, and other phantasms, who provide an excess of representation over existence. Victor himself refers to the Creature as a vampire: "my own vampire, my own spirit let loose from the grave" (*F*, 105). One might further recall his origins in *Fantasmagoriana, ou Recueil d'Histories d'Apparitions de Spectres, Revenans, Fantomes, etc.*, the volume that inspired the guests at Villa Diodati (including Mary and Percy Shelley, John Polidori, and Byron) to try their hand at an original ghost story. When the Creature does present himself, however, it is always as an excess of existence.

10. Freud here relies upon Schelling's definition, which he selects from the complex etymology of the *Unheimlich* in "The Uncanny" (1919, in *The Collected Papers of Sigmund Freud*, ed. Philip Rieff, 10 vols. [New York: Collier, 1963], 10:27; emphasis in the original).

11. Freud, 19 ("remote region"; "The subject of").

12. Fred Botting, "*Frankenstein*'s French Revolutions: the Dangerous Necessity of Monsters," in *Making Monstrous: Frankenstein, Criticism, Theory*, ed. Botting (Manchester: Manchester Univ. Press, 1991), 139. James A. W. Heffernan worries the question of monstrosity with regard to film in "Looking at the Monster: *Frankenstein* and Film" (*Critical Inquiry* 24 [1997]: 133–58); he writes that film makers "compel us to face—more frankly and forthrightly than critics of the novel usually do—the problem of the creature's appearance ... What makes Victor's composition of such beautiful features monstrous?" (142–43). See also Chris Baldrick's Foucaultian reading of monstrosity as a social vice in "The Politics of Monstrosity," *New Casebooks: Frankenstein*, ed. Botting (Macmillan: Houndsmills, 1995), 48–68; Peter Brooks's Lacanian-Derridean "Godlike Science / Unhallowed Arts: Language, Nature, and Monstrosity," in *The Endurance of* Frankenstein: *Essays on Mary Shelley's Novel*, ed. George Levine and U. C. Knoepflmacher (Berkeley: Univ. of California Press, 1979), 205–20; as well as Brooks's "What Is a Monster? (According to *Frankenstein*)," in his *Body Work: Objects of Desire in Modern Narrative* (Cambridge: Harvard Univ. Press, 1993), 199–220. According to Brooks, the Creature's monstrosity results from his failure to enter the signifying chain of language and achieve meaning as a transcendental signified. Our inquiry is concerned with the ugliness that predetermines (rather than the monstrosity that results from) his inability to enter the greater signifying chain of society at large.

13. Harold Bloom, "Introduction" to Mary Shelley's *Frankenstein* (New York: Penguin, 1965), 65.

14. Burke, *Reflections on the Revolution in France* (1790), ed. Thomas H. D. Mahoney (Indianapolis: Bobbs-Merrill, 1955), 87. Hereafter cited parenthetically in the text by page number and abbreviated *R*.

15. Bernard Mandeville, *The Fable of the Bees: or, Private Vices, Publick Benefits* (1714), ed. F. B. Kaye, 2 vols. (Oxford: Clarendon Press, 1924), 1:234–35.

16. Adorno makes a similar claim for different political ends, namely that the disruption of the social order is a *positive* effect of ugliness. For him, the ugly represents the socially repressed (in the sense of oppressed), and he argues that in order to avoid deteriorating into a vacuous plaything, art must assert the ugliness of the social real against the ideological status quo of the beautiful ideal. Ugliness thus acquires a social dimension that Burke would acknowledge, but condemn. See Theodor Adorno, "The Ugly, the Beautiful, and Technique," in *Aesthetic Theory*, 2d ed., ed. Greta Adorno and Rolf Tiedeman, trans. Robert Hullot-Kentor (Minneapolis: Univ. of Minnesota Press, 1996), 45–61. One also finds the socio-political disruptive potential of the ugly in the aesthetic theory of Kant: the ugly threatens the community of feeling subjects united in the intersubjective realm of the imaginative ideal.

17. Cousins, "The Ugly" (part 1), 62.

18. Mary Wollstonecraft, *A Vindication of the Rights of Woman*, 2d ed. (1792), ed. Carol H. Poston (New York: W. W. Norton & Company, 1988), 171. Mary Shelley was studying her mother's volume during the genesis of *Frankenstein* (*The Journals of Mary Shelley, 1814–1844*, ed. Paula R. Feldman and Diana Scott-Kilvert, 2 vols. [Oxford: Clarendon Press, 1987], 1:149). Henceforth I will ground this discussion of *Frankenstein* by filtering most cross-textual references through the *Journals*.

19. Samuel Taylor Coleridge, *Biographia Literaria or Biographical Sketches of My Literary Life and Opinions* (1817), ed. George Watson (London: J. M. Dent, 1975), 218; compare to Mary Shelley, *Journals*, 1:102.

20. Francis Hutcheson, *Inquiry into the Original of Our Ideas of Beauty and Virtue* (London: J. Darby, 1725), 11; Coleridge, "On the PRINCIPLES of GENIAL CRITICISM concerning the FINE ARTS, especially those of STATUARY and PAINTING. Essay III" (1814), in *The Collected Works of Samuel Taylor Coleridge*, ed. H. J. Jackson and J. R. de J. Jackson, 14 vols. (Princeton: Princeton Univ. Press, 1969–98), 11.1:369 (emphasis in the original).

21. Coleridge, "Principles," 371; emphasis in the original.

22. Victor's method of selecting the most beautiful parts and suturing them together parallels another "mechanistic" process in vogue during the late-eighteenth and early-nineteenth centuries: the mode of anthologizing beauties. Volumes of "Beauties" were produced from recycled parts, which could be culled either from a single poetic corpus or from several corpora (as in the case of *The Beauties of Milton, Thomson, and Young* [1783]) to form a composite textual body in the Frankensteinian mode. Whether this process of clipping and culling and stitching together calls more attention to the individual beauties or to the fissures in the overall product, it is not my purpose to discover. Suffice it to note that if Victor had textual precedent for his artistic method of selecting anatomical beauties, he faced the added challenge of animating them into something greater than the sum of their parts.

23. The qualities of "yellowness" and "wateriness" are also prominent in Shelley's portrait of the Creature as he first appeared to her "with yellow, watery, but speculative eyes" in the 1831 introduction (*F*, 365).

24. Žižek, *Tarrying with the Negative: Kant, Hegel, and the Critique of Ideology* (Durham: Duke Univ. Press, 1993), 240 n.

25. John William Polidori, *The Vampyre* (1819; Oxford: Woodstock Books, 1990), 27–28.

26. John Milton, "Second Defense of the English People" (1654), in *Complete Prose Works of John Milton*, ed. Don M. Wolfe, 8 vols. (New Haven: Yale Univ. Press, 1953–82), 4.1:583.

27. Milton, *Paradise Lost* (1674), in *Complete Poems and Major Prose*, ed. Meritt Y. Hughes (New York: Odyssey Press, 1957), 3.22–25. Compare to Mary Shelley, *Journals*, 1:146–47. *Paradise Lost* is hereafter cited parenthetically in the text by book and line numbers and abbreviated *PL*.

28. Milton, "Second Defense," 582. He adds: "Ugly I have never been thought by anyone, to my knowledge, who has laid eyes on me. Whether I am handsome or not, I am less concerned" (582–83).

29. This 1831 description dwells longer on Elizabeth's physical appearance (vs. her mind and manners) than the 1818 edition. Yet since the two versions do not conflict in any way that is relevant here, I will draw upon them both.

30. Wollstonecraft, 128. The Creature's status as a distinct (subhuman) species recalls the downtrodden Jemima from Wollstonecraft's unfinished novel *Maria*, who complains that she was "treated like a creature of another species": "I was ... hunted from family to family, [I] belonged to nobody—and nobody cared for me. I was despised from my birth, and denied the chance of obtaining a footing for myself in society" (*Maria; or the Wrongs of Woman* [1798; New York: W. W. Norton, 1975], 38–40). Although Jemima ultimately earns a place within society, the Creature's ugliness blocks all of his efforts to become "linked to the chain of existence and events, from which [he is] excluded" (*F*, 174).

31. Žižek, *Abyss of Freedom*, 22. Compare to Cousins, "The Ugly" (part 2), 4.

32. Notably, Milton's other major defense against the charge of being ugly is that of his smooth skin: "Nor is it true that either my body or my skin is shriveled" ("Second Defense," 583).

33. Along similar lines, Burke identifies smallness as a quality of the beautiful: "A great beautiful thing, is a manner of expression scarcely ever used; but that of a great ugly thing, is very common" (*E*, 113).

34. Jonathan Swift, *Gulliver's Travels* (1726), 2d ed., ed. Robert A. Greenberg (New York: W. W. Norton & Company, 1970), 95. Compare to Mary Shelley, *Journals*, 1:145.

35. This scene might be read against the Lacanian thesis that "a minimum of 'idealization,' of the interposition of fantasmatic frame [*sic*] by means of which the subject assumes a distance vis-à-vis the Real, is constitutive of our sense of reality—'reality' occurs insofar as it is not (it does not come) 'too close'" (Žižek, *Abyss of Freedom*, 23).

36. Immanuel Kant, *The Critique of Judgement* (1790), trans. James Creed Meredith (Oxford: Clarendon Press, 1952), 43. Hereafter cited parenthetically in the text and abbreviated *C*.

37. Samuel Richardson, *Pamela; or Virtue Rewarded* (1740; New York: W. W. Norton, 1958), 206; emphasis in the original. Compare to Mary Shelley, *Journals*, 1:146–47.

38. Percy Shelley, *Prometheus Unbound* (1819), 3.4.46–47, in *Shelley's Poetry and Prose*, ed. Donald H. Reiman and Sharon B. Powers (New York: W. W. Norton, 1977), 190; Charles Lamb, "On the Danger of Confounding Moral with Personal Deformity" (1811), in *The Works of Charles and Mary Lamb*, ed. E.V. Lucas, 6 vols. (London: Methuen, 1903), 1:64–65.

39. William Blake, *Jerusalem* (1818), 7.8, in *The Complete Poetry and Prose of William Blake*, ed. David V. Erdman (New York: Anchor, 1988), 149.

40. Adorno, 51.

41. Blake, *Descriptive Catalogue* (1809), in *The Complete Poetry & Prose*, 526.

42. Blake, *Descriptive Catalogue*, 544–45.

43. Coleridge, "Principles," 383 n. In similar terms, Kierkegaard writes of Socrates, who "spoke about *loving the ugly*": "What then is meant by *the beautiful? The beautiful* is the immediate and direct object of immediate love, the choice of inclination and of passion. Surely there is no need to command that one shall love the beautiful. But the ugly! This is not anything to offer to inclination and passion, which turn away and say, 'Is that anything to love!'" (Soren Kierkegaard, *Works of Love* [1847], trans. Howard V. Hong and Edna H. Hong [Princeton: Princeton Univ. Press, 1995], 373).

44. This must not be confounded with the "monstrous birth" described in Ellen Moers's seminal essay "Female Gothic," in her *Literary Women* (New York: Doubleday, 1976), 90–110. For even the most monstrous human birth yields a creature who is always already inscribed into a family, a citizenship, a language, and a gender.

45. Adorno, 47.

46. Compare with Adam's more hopeful wonderment in *Paradise Lost* (8.270–71).

47. Lord Byron, *Manfred, A Dramatic Poem*, 2.2.102, in *The Complete Poetical Works*, ed. Jerome J. McGann, 7 vols. (Oxford: Clarendon Press, 1980–81), 4:73.

48. An internalized version of the signifying chain appears later in the novel, when Victor claims: "I know not by what chain of thought the idea presented itself" (*F*, 206).

49. In the 1818 text his death results from an "apoplectic fit," which is a more scientific way of saying that "the springs of existence gave way" (*F*, 222).

50. Frances Ferguson, *Solitude and the Sublime: Romanticism and the Aesthetics of Individuation* (New York: Routledge, 1992), 109–10.

51. Stuart Curran, Review of *The Frankenstein Notebooks*, ed. Charles E. Robinson, 2 vols., in *The Wordsworth Circle* 27 (1996): 211.

52. Albert J. Lavalley lists thirty-one film and stage productions of *Frankenstein* between 1823 and 1975 ("The Stage and Film Children of *Frankenstein*: A Survey," in *The Endurance of Frankenstein*, 286–89). Compare to Heffernan, 133–58.

53. Mary Shelley to Leigh Hunt, 9–11 September 1823, in *The Letters of Mary Wollstonecraft Shelley*, ed. Betty T. Bennett, 3 vols. (Baltimore: The Johns Hopkins Univ. Press, 1980), 1:378.

54. Jacques Derrida, "Economimesis," trans. R. Klein, *Diacritics* 11 (1981): 22; emphasis in the original.

CYNTHIA PON

"Passages" in Mary Shelley's Frankenstein: Toward a Feminist Figure of Humanity?[1]

In this paper I wish to draw upon several ideas of "passages" in Mary Shelley's *Frankenstein*, to compare masculine and female creation in terms of conventions, ideals and practices. The question I would like to raise is whether Mary Shelley's work as a woman writer opens the way to a feminist figure of humanity such as argued for in Donna Haraway's essay, "Ecce Homo, Ain't [Ar'n't] I a Woman, and Inappropriate/d Others: The Human in a Post-Humanist Landscape." Much is at stake in the creation of a new figure of humanity, Haraway declaims. The humanist landscape that has given birth to individual rights and destiny, the flowering of civilization, scientific discoveries on land, at sea, in space, including atomic space, has also produced a history of suffering and annihilation, of physical as well as psychological enslavement, and dismemberment. A humanity developed at the expense of those who were considered less human or non-human. Until very recently, those who suffer, who do not own their own identity or property, are assumed to be voiceless, incoherent, capable at best of being represented by those who command the master-trope, the master-language (such as Shakespeare's Caliban). Haraway, however, maintains a different premise by focusing on discourses of suffering—discourses that are constituted differently by those who have been dismembered or displaced.[2] Second, Haraway warns that historical narratives, gendered masculine and

From *Modern Language Studies*, Vol. 30, No. 2 (Autumn, 2000). © 2000 by *Modern Language Studies*.

dubbed modernist, are in crisis. One risks entrapment or annihilation, not just of select groups, but more, by reproducing established figures of a seriously curtailed humanity. Third, and here is how the warning can turn into hope: the "disarticulated bodies of history" can serve as "figures of possible connection and accountability."

This paper will follow Haraway's cue and explore a critique based on gender in Mary Shelley's *Frankenstein*. Mary Shelley seems to occupy a dubious place in feminist projects. In her essay, Haraway studies the examples of Jesus and Sojourner Truth as trickster figures who bear the signs of "a broken and suffering humanity," yet whose power derives from generating a multiple discourse, "signifying—in ambiguity, contradiction, stolen symbolism, and unending chains of noninnocent translation—a possible hope" (p. 87). Mary Shelley's text shares some of these ambivalent and multiplying features. The story, written in the gothic tradition, and narrated by three male personae, is replete with physical and psychological violence. Shelley presents herself in the preface as a highly diffident writer; yet she is read, more recently, as the monstrous autobiographical woman writer by feminist critics such as Barbara Johnson and Anne Mellor.[3] Her "hideous progeny," perhaps the most successful popular icon since the nineteenth century, continues to regenerate in contemporary cultures, with multiple implications. Could it be that Mary Shelley's disputed standing as a feminist (contrary to her famous lineage) masks the birth of a new feminist figure? Haraway points out: "Humanity's face has been the face of man. Feminist humanity must have another shape, other gestures ... Feminist figures of humanity ... must somehow both resist representation, resist literal figuration, and still erupt in powerful new tropes, new figures of speech, new turns of historical possibility." But before we examine the birth of something unnatural, something not representable in Mary Shelley's discourse, let us retrace some masculine ideas of "passages" in *Frankenstein*.

MASCULINE CREATION

The novel begins with a literal passage. The first narrator, Walton, writes in a letter to his sister: "you cannot contest the inestimable benefit which I shall confer on all mankind to the last generation, by discovering a passage near the pole to these countries" (p. 12). Walton is following his childhood dream, inspired by "all the voyages ... of discovery [that] composed the *whole*" of his uncle's library (my emphasis). By his own admission, his education had been partial. Driven by a single vision, he had toiled, braved, suffered: "I commenced by inuring my body to hardship ... I voluntarily endured cold, famine, thirst and want of sleep" (p. 13). He asked rhetorically: "do I not deserve to accomplish some great purpose. My life might have been passed in ease and luxury, but I preferred glory" (p. 13). This theme of the masculine quest, endured at great pains, and justifiable by the promise of glory is as old as the *Odyssey*. But unlike the epic, Mary Shelley does not offer us the diversion of endless adventures. In her novel, heroic quest is presented almost in naked parody. The artistry lies not in the embroidery of adventurous details. But more like Penelope's art, each tale by the potential hero gets undone. I will return to this female art a little later.

In Walton's case, nothing much happens until his sighting of the creature and Frankenstein, when his narration gives way to the transcribing of Frankenstein's tale. Walton's high-seas discourse is self-absorbed and rather boring. "I have no friend," Walton complains. He discounts his shipmates who are professionally adept and upright in character, but who are not his social equal. "I have no one near me, gentle yet courageous, possessed of a cultivated as well as of a capacious mind, whose tastes are like my own" (p 15). The qualities that Walton lists as criteria for friendship, as Raymond Williams and others remind us, are keywords of an established, privileged order.[4] The discourse of masculine humanity, intent on "conquer[ing] all fear of danger or death" (p. 12), is monologic. Walton's story is told in the form of letters addressed to his sister, but we do not hear of any letter in return: "I may receive your letters (though the chance is very doubtful)," he writes (p. 18). There is no recorded place for the writings of Margaret Saville (initial, M.S.) in the voyage of discovery. With no true interlocutor, this singular, heroic discourse dwindles into melodrama: "Remember me with affection, should you never hear from me again" (p. 18). Masculine discourse is tired of its own company, but is capable of loving only the heroic image of himself. Walton is overjoyed when he finally encounters someone like himself—a quester, and someone from his own class and race. He describes the human wreckage that he saved from the Arctic sea: "He was not, as the other traveller seemed to be, a savage inhabitant of some undiscovered island, but an European" (p. 21). Masculine humanity "has a generic face, a universal shape," Haraway points out. From the beginning of Mary Shelley's novel, masculine humanity only recognizes its own image on the basis of gender, class and race. The female, the socially inferior, and the non-European—these are excluded from the ideal and practice of generic humanity. Writing at the beginning of a century that was to launch successive modernist quests, Mary Shelley's gaze is directed backward—she recalls a history of genocide and enslavement that resulted from insatiable quests:

"if no man allowed any pursuit whatsoever to interfere with the tranquility of his domestic affections, Greece had not been enslaved; Caesar would have spared his country; America would have been discovered more gradually; and the empires of Mexico and Peru had not been destroyed." (p. 51)

Critics have cautioned about the ideological control behind the privileging of a domestic discourse, or discourse of sensibility in this period. The lauding of domestic virtues can signify backlash, political accommodation; and in some cases, sympathy for the enslaved or unfortunate "other" may mask an assumption of cultural superiority over the oppressed.[5] But Mary Shelley's text, written at the crossroads of the European humanist project (post-Enlightenment faith in human infrastructures, reactions to French-revolution hope and excess, the inauguration of the age of imperialism), uniquely combines both posthumanist and retrospective visions. From this ambiguous position, it poses the critical question: what constitutes humanity? By unravelling heroic discourses, her text causes us to look at the underside of progress, to reintegrate the voices of those who have been dismembered or displaced.

Passage, in the interest of exploration and trade, becomes much more ambitious in the case of Frankenstein, the primary narrator in the story. He announced: "Life and death appear to me ideal bounds, which I should first break through, and pour a torrent of light into our dark world" (p. 49). The passage that Frankenstein seeks would lead to the generation of a new species, in this case, salvaged and resuscitated from the dead. It would challenge humanity, understood in its mortal condition. It would *not, however, give rise to a new figure of humanity*. For the creature was created to resemble, to reflect glory on his creator. Frankenstein's interest in the scientific breakthrough is ultimately self-congratulatory: "A new species would bless me as its creator and source" (p. 49). It is science for the scientist's sake, an ego-trip. Like Walton, Frankenstein's quest takes him away from human society, from family and friends. His lone research in charnel houses and in his workshop was void of ethical considerations. He too had only one goal: "I was surprised that among so many men of genius ... that I alone should be reserved to discover so astonishing a secret" (p. 47). He would steal not only the thunder of his fellow scientists, and of God the creator. But significantly, as in Walton's narrative, there is no room for the female. The quest that would break the code of life and death, that would create a new species, is strictly masculine. "No father could claim the gratitude of his child so completely" (p. 49), he boasts, for there is no other parent. His quest bypasses the female (as successive female figures are killed in the story).

Masculine creation in the novel is preoccupied with, and justified by "originality"—to "tread a land never before *imprinted,*" says Walton (p. 12, in other words, also never before put in print). In Mary Shelley's story, creation takes on multiple senses, from scientific quest to reproduction of species, and creative writing. In each case, Mary Shelley describes the doomed trajectory of masculine creation that displaces the female, and that is premised on self-reflection. Twice, the 1818 and 1831 prefaces refer to the competitive genesis of the story. Mary Shelley, her husband, Percy, and their friends, Byron and Polidori, entered into a friendly competition to each write a ghost story. "The illustrious poets also, annoyed by the platitude of prose, speedily relinquished their uncongenial task" (1831 preface). Masculine creation, personified here by the two dazzling poets, Percy Shelley and Lord Byron, had little patience for the uncongenial task of raising their own children (according to biographical sources), or of completing the present project. The 1818 preface records: "My two friends left me on a journey among the Alps, and lost ... all memory of their ghostly visions. The following tale is the only one that has been completed." Masculine humanity once more sets off on a venture, while Mary Shelley, the only woman in the creative circle, and pregnant for the third time, labors to complete her project—we are told—in awe and anguish. Could the anguish be in part a recognition of the unequal task of parenting traditionally assigned to women? A task that parallels the overseeing of a literary progeny? As we shall see later, the disparity between masculine and female creation is repeated once more in the lifelong projects of Percy and Mary Shelley. In the novel, the author of the new species, the father who dispenses with the role of the mother, likewise fails to complete his task. Frankenstein is repulsed when the ghostly vision he entertained comes to life: "now that I had finished, the beauty of the dream vanished, and breathless horror and disgust filled my heart. Unable to endure the aspect of the being I had created, I rushed out of the room" (p. 53). This paradigm of creation has significant repercussions.

In the novel, masculine humanity that has usurped the role of the female, and that has ruled the female outside the scope of accomplishment, can only produce something monstrous. The creature, we are told, has skin that "scarcely covered the work of muscles and arteries beneath ... his watery eyes ... seemed almost of the same color as the dun white sockets in which they were set" (p. 52). But there is something even more monstrous than the creature's appearance. Frankenstein has set about reproducing the ideal human figure. The creature's "limbs were in proportion;" he "had selected his features as beautiful" (p. 52). The problem is, this ideal figure bears little in relation to reality. The whitest teeth, the most lustrous hair—perfect body parts are gathered, but without regard to how the parts would fit together into a composite, living whole. Universal shape (a pertinent example is the twentieth-century decolonizing pens that construct new geopolitical entities, displace mass populations, and sow seeds of future discord, as in Palestine, India and Pakistan, central African nations, whose people suffer from generations of violence) fails to take into consideration the particular, the historical, as well as interactions of the multiple. Frankenstein's creative vision does not tolerate, nor does it stand the test of what may challenge the "original," drawing-board conception. In Haraway's words, the ideal construction of masculine humanity does not allow for the "self-critical practice of 'difference'" (p. 87). This practice of difference is by nature more complex, more unpredictable and messy. It means entering into relations with another in ways that exceed the limits of our knowledge, that may put into question previously accepted notions of identity or security (who we think we are, and who we think are our "enemies"). Twentieth-century history alone is full of examples of monstrosities (holocaust, genocides, discrimination) when we fail to develop the "self-critical practice of difference," when self-identical exclusion of differences becomes the order of the day.

Frankenstein's creature is literally created from the dead. Metaphorically, Mary Shelley makes an even stronger point about the social forces that lead to death. We have seen in Walton's example how he could recognize and love only an image of himself, his own class, gender and race. In the case of the creature, difference from the "universal shape" is rejected finally because it violates the ideal, self-reflecting image of Frankenstein. To suppress the "untoward," the "unseemly" means that certain groups are deemed "improper," less worthy, and are legislated out of existence, in some cases, physically exterminated. More than a series of gratuitous violence as befits the gothic genre, in the novel, the violence of exclusion begets further violence. Abandoned by his creator-father, and repulsed wherever he turns, the creature is said to learn "the barbarity of man" (p. 109). Father and son, reproducing a partial humanity, come to share the same disorder of self-loathing and destruction. Mary Shelley, whose parents, Godwin and Wollstonecraft, were staunch believers in educational reforms, is careful to point out how education has the power to humanize or dehumanize the subject. The books the creature reads teach him about sensibility; they allow him to articulate his inclinations toward love and community. Injustices and repulsion by others prompt him to unlearn all this. He learns instead the language of solipsism and revenge. The creature recounts: "I am solitary and detested" (p. 136); "increase of knowledge only discovered to me more clearly what a wretched outcast I was" (p. 137); "[my creator] had abandoned me, and in the bitterness of my heart, I cursed him" (p. 137). Similarly, we see Frankenstein embark on a path of alienation and despair:

> "often, I say, I was tempted to plunge into the silent lake ... Remorse extinguished every hope ... My abhorrence of this fiend cannot be conceived ... I ardently wished to extinguish that life which I had so thoughtlessly bestowed." (pp. 92–3)

In sum, the narratives of Walton, Frankenstein and the creature unravel as monstrous self-reproduction of pain, deprivation and mutual/mass destruction. Haraway calls this "entrapment in the stories of established disorders." Walton and Frankenstein recognize themselves in each other, in the cold, sterile Arctic. Frankenstein and the creature, likewise, become reflections of each other. They pursue each other in order to kill each other. The two become indistinguishable.[6] The creature acts out what Frankenstein has done symbolically—the elimination of female figures as well as those who sustain life.

FEMALE CREATION

The destruction of one character stands out in this story, because of its incomplete status, and Frankenstein correctly perceives it to be a threat to the "established disorder." I refer to the female creature that is aborted in the novel. Frankenstein has yielded to the creature's request to create for him a mate. Halfway into the process, Frankenstein changed his mind: "I thought with a sensation of madness on my promise of creating another like to him, and, trembling with passion, tore to pieces the thing on which I was engaged" (p. 179). We have an inkling of this thing that was not finished, not represented, when Frankenstein speculated: "she, who in all probability was to become a thinking and reasoning animal, might refuse to comply with a pact made before her creation" (p. 178).

The female creature was destroyed; but the novel, *Frankenstein*, was completed. I wish, therefore, to explore female creation in terms of the work of a woman writer. I do so by looking at several passages in Mary Shelley's writing.

In her introduction to the 1831 edition of *Frankenstein*, Mary Shelley conveys a sense of her ambiguity about writing: "It is true I am very averse to bringing myself forward in print." Recalling her childhood writing, she calls herself "a close imitator." She further refers to the conversations that took place between Percy and Byron in the summer of 1816, in which she was a "nearly silent listener." But at the same time, she lays exclusive claim to her authorship of *Frankenstein*: "I certainly did not owe the suggestion of one incident, nor scarcely of one train of feeling, to my husband, and yet but for his incitement, it would never have taken the form in which it was presented to the world. From this declaration, I must except the preface. As far as I can recollect, it was entirely written by him" (p. 251). Contemporary scholarship reveals that Percy Shelley did in fact play an important role in changing the language of Mary Shelley's novel, substituting more complex diction, and more specific terminology in place of Mary's more unadorned, simple phrasing.[7] Self-effacing, deferential, yet at the same time assertive—recent critics have advanced different reasons for Mary Shelley's ambivalent posture.[8] I will focus on how this ambiguity articulates a practice of creation very different from the concept of "originality" played out in the novel.

Walton's presumption to find a passage to the East, to "tread a land never before imprinted" (with echoes of the "discovery" of America) is contravened by Mary Shelley who points to examples of imperialist tragedies. In the 1831 introduction, perhaps with unconscious irony, she actually borrows a creation-metaphor from the East: "The Hindoos give the world an elephant to support it, but they make the elephant stand upon a tortoise."[9] Absolute originality, according to the Hindu tradition, is a myth. She backs up this idea of nonoriginal creation with her famous definition: "Invention, it must be humbly admitted, does not consist in creating out of void, but out of chaos ... it can give form to dark, shapeless substances, but cannot bring into being the substance itself." In comparison with the male creators in her life and fiction (Percy who aspires to images of light, who suffers from the ideal and its disillusionment; and Frankenstein who rejects his own unnameable creature out of fear), Mary Shelley is much more accepting of the dark, "chaos" and difference. She refers to her early novel with affection as "my hideous progeny." We have noted in the earlier section how she unravels the narratives that are based on self-identity, "originality" and suppression of the "other." In the larger context of her works, we notice that her boundaries of creation are also more diffused. The creator of the novel, *Frankenstein*, owes her work to other people's interventions and collaboration. Conversely, a good part of Shelley's career is devoted to creating the works of her late husband.

I turn now to two prefaces that Mary Shelley did write—the prefaces to *Posthumous Poems of Percy Shelley*, published in 1824, and to the *Second Collected Edition of Percy Shelley*, published in 1839. Mary Shelley declares in these passages her admiration and love for Percy, and her commitment to preserving his work. I quote from the 1824 preface: "his fearless enthusiasm in the cause which he considered the most sacred upon earth, the moral and physical state of mankind, was the chief reason why he, like other illustrious reformers, was pursued by hatred and calumny ... His life was spent in the contemplation of nature, in arduous study, or in acts of kindness and affection. He was an elegant scholar and a profound metaphysician." The prefaces also reveal how these collected works came into being: "*The Triumph of Life* was his last work, and was left in so unfinished a state that I *arranged* it in its present form with great difficulty. All his poems which are scattered in periodical works are *collected* in this volume ... Many of the Miscellaneous Poems, written on the spur of the occasion, and never retouched, I found among his manuscript books, and have carefully copied ... I frankly own that I have been more actuated by the fear lest any monument of his genius should escape me than the wish of presenting nothing but what was complete to the fastidious reader." In the preface to the *Second Collected Edition* (1839), she describes her motivation: "I hasten to fulfil an important duty,—that of giving the productions of a sublime genius to the world ... In the *notes appended* to the poems I have endeavoured to narrate the origin and history of each. The loss of nearly all letters and papers which refer to his early life renders the execution more imperfect than it would otherwise have been. I have, however, the liveliest recollection of all that was done and said during the period of my knowing him ... In other respects I am indeed incompetent: but I feel the importance of the task, and regard it as my most sacred duty" (my emphases). What these prefaces summarized was the laborious, virtually impossible task of copying and recreating the work of Percy Shelley, impossible because of the fragmentary, draft-conditions of many of his pieces; if the drafts were confusing to Mary, they would be virtually indecipherable to others; she alone was capable of compiling and "originating" the work of Percy, which subsequent editors were able to carry on. (On a related note, Mary Shelley's father, Godwin, also bequeathed to his daughter the task of editing his life's works. But Mary could not, or would not complete this other task.) These passages reveal a practice of female creation that differs sharply from the masculine creation depicted in the early novel. We saw Frankenstein and Walton back away when they saw what they had imprinted, when they realized what terrible mess they had got themselves into; in contrast, Mary Shelley stuck through her project for 17 years.

TOWARD A FEMINIST FIGURE OF HUMANITY?

I began this paper by raising the question: whether Mary Shelley's work as a woman writer opens the way to a feminist figure of humanity? I wish to essay an answer by drawing several analogies, beginning with the character of Penelope in the *Odyssey*. Traditionally both Mary Shelley and Penelope are seen as figures of domesticity, while their husband sail off in search of original "passages." Does Penelope represent female power (as figured by her constancy, her ability to survive, and preserve the household for 20 years)? or is she a passive figure who plays her prescribed role in patriarchal discourse? A significant clue, I think, lies in Penelope's art. Her double act of weaving and unweaving holds the violent suitors at bay. And she is devious enough to coax gifts from them to replenish the dwindling estate. By virtue of her art, Penelope is able to play an active role in shaping her own destiny amidst predominantly masculine discourses.[10] In a strikingly similar way, Mary Shelley's art also consists of weaving and unweaving. As we see in her early novel, one by one she unravels the heroic discourses—the masculine shroud that betokens suffering and destruction; her later work, on the other hand, is a careful weaving of unreadable fragments and scattered pieces of her husband's works into a coherent, redeeming corpus.[11] In these two of her most important works, Mary Shelley reveals a different kind of creation that stresses not originality, but that strangely originates. The Frankenstein story is vital to this day (giving rise to multiple cultural expressions, morphing to fit into cultural debates on ethics, technology, politics, etc.). And but for her labors to present Percy Shelley's writings to the world, the histories of Romanticism and radical reformism would have been writ-ten in a very different way.[12]

Haraway has suggested that "feminist figures of humanity ... must somehow both resist representation, resist literal figuration, and still erupt in powerful new tropes, new figures of speech, new turns of historical possibility." I recall next the female creature who was destroyed and dismembered in the novel, and who therefore resisted representation. I have cited earlier Frankenstein's reason for destroying the female creature. For the female writer who questions and unravels masculine discourses, the non-representation of the female creature also carries important implications. Had the female creature been completed, she would have been made to order according to the desire of the male creature. I quote the male creature's request to Frankenstein: "I demand a creature of another sex, but as hideous as myself ... It is true, we shall be monsters, cut off from all the world; but on that account, we shall be more attached to one another;" "my companion will be of the same nature as myself, and will be content with the same fare" (p. 153–4). (She was to be his reflection, much as the male creature was to reflect Frankenstein ideally.) It is possible to see Mary Shelley writing this passage with prior texts in mind, possibly with irony—for among the books the creature has read is Milton's *Paradise Lost*, and through it, the prior creation story, Genesis. In one thread of the prior story, Eve was created from the side of Adam ("flesh of thy flesh," "he / Whose image thou art," *Paradise Lost*, book four, 441, 471–2). In Milton's text, the mother of human race was presented as follows: "Her unadorned golden tresses wore / Disheveled, but in wanton ringlets waved / As the vine curls her tendrils, which *implied / Subjection*, but required with *gentle sway*," book four, ll. 305–8, my emphasis). But Frankenstein's creature ought to know that in the earlier story—what turned the world upside down, was that the female creature was not content with the same fare. The rest is *history* (including the history of misogyny). If women had been for the most part misrepresented in history as subordinate, or inferior to men, or polarized as either the extolled figure of virtue or the cause of temptation, how do women break through these images that are based primarily on masculine self-idealization? In what sense may Mary Shelley's text articulate a new woman figure?

Out of the dismemberment of the female creature, something "unnatural" came into being—Mary Shelley the artist, who likewise resists representation. Critics have speculated on Mary Shelley's guilt for not living up to Percy's figure of the ideal woman.[13] Neither does she live up to the Romantic icon of an unworldly poet, nor for that matter, to images of a feminist writer. Who is Mary Shelley? In the chapter, "A Multiplicity of Marys," for instance, Fred Botting examines the many biographical as well as literary relations that could have engendered Frankenstein. One of the perennial questions that critics ask is: which Mary Shelley wrote this novel? The daughter of the two foremost radical reformers? A member of the Shelley circle? (And what is her status, her role in this infamous circle?) Or is it a writer who has taken on a more conservative outlook, when she reedits the novel in the 1830s?[14] These questions yield multiple and elusive answers. A brief resume of Mary Shelley may include: a woman artist, a mother, struggling to support herself and her child, who undertakes diverse assignments—writing for popular magazines and annuals, such as *Keepsake*, translations, several volumes of *Lives of the most Eminent Literary and Scientific Men*; Mary the scrivener, editor, besides a novelist and short-story writer ...

Each category, each title potentially lends new shades, new complexities to this nineteenth-century figure who seems at once conformist and radical. I would argue that more so than her husband, she is much closer to the composite figure that Raymond Williams depicts: the Romantic artist who in everyday terms is deeply aware of, and plays a direct role in the ideological and material struggles in the early nineteenth century.[15] She wrote in a letter to the publisher, Edward Moxon: "and don't despise me if I say I wish to write for I want money sadly." Still other evidence documents Shelley as a shrewd businesswoman, negotiating contracts, fighting for copyrights as editor of her husband's poetry. Far from retiring, she gained influence in literary, intellectual circles; and used it to champion causes and friends. Her miscellaneous literary output, written out of a variety of resources, genres and motives, speaks of chaos and variable achievement. Yet, from the violence of her decentering (some would call it a lack of focus, identity and coherence), she effects the possibility of connection (with her deceased husband through creat/editing his body of work; by supporting herself, her son and a few relatives in need; and against all odds, forging a sympathetic reading public, by reinventing herself and Percy). The unrepresentable woman artist, like the female creature in the novel, is inconclusive. For this reason, she continues to divide and to be relevant.[16]

Finally, I wish to draw a quick reference to Sojourner Truth who is Haraway's example of the "disarticulated bodies of history." Haraway reminds us that Sojourner Truth's question, "arn't I a woman?" has "more power for feminist theory 150 years later than any number of affirmative and declarative sentences" (p. 92). Sojourner Truth's discourse, which is a discourse of suffering, derives its power from the "radical dis-membering and dis-placing of ... names and ... bodies" (Haraway, pp. 88). I quote from her speech:

> "I have plowed and planted, and gathered into barns, and no man could head me—and arn't I a woman? I could work as much and eat as much as a man (when I could get it), and bear de lash as well—and arn't I a woman? I have borne thirteen chilern, and seen 'em mos' all sold off into slavery, and when I cried out with a mother's grief, none but Jesus heard—and arn't I a woman?"

The power of Sojourner Truth's question is borne out of/by experiences of utter dehumanization (not unlike Frankenstein's creatures who are made of human scraps, yet whose power Frankenstein fears). As Haraway points out, this truth is errant, wandering. It refuses to stay put. It exceeds the prescribed place and boundaries drawn according to "universal shape," that are subsequently allotted to those who do not fit the "universal." Examples of such restrictions abound, from exploitative labor to cycles of poverty, from race-targeted immigration quotas to internment camps. The unsettling power of Truth's question is echoed nearly a century later by another black writer, Langston Hughes, whose poem, "What happens to a dream deferred?" further inspires Lorraine Hansberry's provocative play, *A Raisin in the Sun*.

> What happens to a dream deferred?
> Does it dry up
> Like a raisin in the sun?
> Or fester like a sore—
> And then run?
> Does it stink like rotten meat?
> Or crust and sugar over—
> Like a syrupy sweet?
> Maybe it just sags
> Like a heavy load.
> Or does it explode?

Sojourner Truth's speech carries the explosive power, the moral force of those who have been deprived of their humanity (from basic survival to matters of dreams and aspirations, as the works of Hughes and Hansberry illustrate). It is the discourse of the unrepresented, in a legal, economic and political sense. Her speech calls attention to three areas where women have traditionally been held in a position of disadvantage—in conditions of work, livelihood, and motherhood. From slavery to today's sweatshops, and even in higher education, women have to work as hard as men but generally receive less remuneration. Particularly in developing countries where resources are scarce, women often are the ones who are made to sacrifice in nutrition, education, and sometimes, where female infanticide is practised, the opportunity of life itself. The other gross violation involves the dehumanization of women as sexual objects. Pertinent to Sojourner Truth's experience, Haraway cites Hazel Carby, that in the New World, specifically in the United States: "black women were not constituted as 'woman,' as white women were. Instead black women were constituted simultaneously racially and sexually—as marked female (animal, sexualized, and without rights), but not as woman (human, potential wife, conduit for the name of the father)" (pp. 93–4). Motherhood therefore confers Sojourner Truth no rights over her children. She was merely a vehicle of reproduction, of capital gains. On the subject of rights, Haraway points out that, for women of color today, "reproductive rights" go far beyond white women's contests of conception, pregnancy, abortion, and birth, but "hinge on comprehensive control of children—for example, their freedom from destruction through lynching, imprisonment, infant mortality, forced pregnancy, drug addiction, drug wars, and military wars" (p. 95). The dismembering and displacing of women and their family, both physically and as social subjects, trace back to social-economic disparity. Sojourner Truth argues: "if my cup won't hold but a pint and yourn holds a quart, would'nt ye be mean not to let me have my half-measure full?" Her question still echoes today in conditions of domestic and global inequities. According to the United Nations Human Development Report 1998, two-thirds of the world's population, about 4.4 billion people, live in developing countries. Of that 4.4 billion, one-quarter lacks adequate housing, one-fifth is not educated past the fifth grade; one-fifth is undernourished. Slowly, on the level of practice, some changes are taking place. There have been more attempts, for example, in the last two decades, among relief and development organizations, to channel resources to women who, as "figures of possible connection and accountability," demonstrate a better record of effecting fundamental social change such as in nutrition, education and sustainable economy.

On still another level, Sojourner Truth's speech marks the discourse of the unrepresented (in response, as it were, to Haraway's call for feminist figures of humanity that must "both resist representation, resist literal figuration, and still erupt in powerful new tropes"). Sojourner Truth's "arn't I a woman?" is more than a rhetorical question. It does not presuppose an answer. Rather, it has the power to disrupt the categorizing of women—whether it be the male physician's challenge of her sex based on biological essentialism, or the myth of the self-identical woman (read "white women" and women of developed countries). Haraway quotes Trinh Minh-ha: "If feminism is set forth as a demystifying force, then it will have to question thoroughly the belief in its own identity" (p. 93). Sojourner Truth refuses to subscribe to a definition of "womanhood" based on sex. She refuses to be elided into the category of the "undifferentiated" woman.

Haraway's point that there are significant differences between the non-freedom of white woman and the enslaved African woman is well taken. She reminds us that "free women in ... white patriarchy were exchanged in a system that oppressed them, but white women inherited black women and men" (p. 94). She cites Hortense Spillers: "free men and women inherited their name from the father, who in turn had rights in his minor children and wife that they did not have in themselves, but he did not own them in the full sense of alienable property. Unfree men and women inherited their condition from their mother ... Slave mothers could not transmit a name; they could not be wives; they were outside the system of marriage exchange" (p. 94).[17] Mary Shelley, writing in a condition of want as widow of Percy Shelley, and mother of the later Sir Percy Florence Shelley, is very different from Sojourner Truth, whose life experience included being traded, raped, forced into union with another slave, and who saw most of her children sold. But on a discursive level, both women speak powerfully about hope and change. Like the dismembered female creature that figures an *unrepresentable* female artist, the "disarticulated bodies of history" can offer "figures of possible connection and accountability." Haraway says of Sojourner Truth: "This decidedly *unwomanly Truth* has a chance to refigure a nongeneric, nonoriginal humanity after the breakup of the discourses of European humanism" (p. 96, my emphasis). Out of a history of enslavement, displacement and dehumanization, Sojourner Truth spoke with power about being human, the condition of slaves, the condition of women, the definition of women's work, the ability of women to make a living. The account of the 1851 women's rights meeting in Akron, Ohio, for instance, recorded that during intermission, and before her powerful rebuttal, Sojourner Truth was busy selling "The Life of Sojourner Truth."

Perhaps from very different circumstances, Mary Shelley is attempting a similar project. This juvenile writer, with terrible anxiety, who unravels self-identical heroic discourses in *Frankenstein*, who later salvages the literary remains of her husband, and who cobbles a living by taking on miscellaneous literary tasks, is an artist of disarticulation. Her nongeneric, nonoriginal "passages" may not aspire to her own immortality, but they constitute a writing of difference that "[p]refigure[s] a nongeneric, nonoriginal humanity after the breakup of the discourses of European humanism." Her discourse of dismemberment offers new turns of possibility, after the breakup of reflexive ideals that power European humanism—a practice of connection and accountability that creates and sustains new life.

Notes

1. I thank my colleague, Sandy Sterner, for reading and commenting on this paper.

2. The discourses of suffering follow a different principle of organization or articulation. In "Caliban and Ariel Write Back" (*Shakespeare Survey*, 48, pp. 155–62), Jonathan Bate analyses the collapsing of historical moments, the oral, musical, classical and vernacular amalgamation of sources, sounds and rhythms in Edward Braithwaite's compositions. In Aimé Cesaire's *A Tempest*, Caliban speaks a rich, highly charged poetry

evocative of sex, violence and indigenous culture. Compare this with the primitive and infantile rendering of Caliban in Shakespeare's *The Tempest*.

3. See "My Monster/My Self" in Barbara Johnson's *A World of Difference* (Baltimore: Johns Hopkins University Press, 1987), and Anne Mellor's *Mary Shelley: Her Life, Her Fiction, Her Monsters* (New York: Routledge, 1989), as well as Mellor's Introduction to the Enriched Classics edition of *Frankenstein* (edited by A. Mellor & T. Reyes, New York: Washington Square Press, 1995).

4. See also Terry Eagleton on the criteria of Enlightenment discourses in *The Function of Criticism* (London: Verso, 1984).

5. For analyses of changing discourses of feminism, domesticity and sensibility, see e.g., Stuart Curran's "Women readers, women writers" in *The Cambridge Companion to British Romanticism*, (Cambridge: Cambridge University Press, 1993, pp. 177–95) and Anne Mellor's "'Am I Not a Woman, and a Sister?': Slavery, Romanticism, and Gender" in *Romanticism, Race, and Imperial Culture, 1780–1834* (Bloomington: Indiana University Press, 1996, pp. 311–329).

6. In "The Politics of Monstrosity" (*Frankenstein*. Ed. Fred Botting. New York: St. Martin's Press, 1995), Chris Baldick reads the novel in terms of revolution debates in the 1790s—did the monstrosity of the *ancien regime* beget the monstrosity of revolutionary excesses?

7. See Mellor, "Choosing a Text of Frankenstein to Teach," in *Approaches to Teaching Shelley's Frankenstein*, ed. S. Behrendt (New York: MLA, 1990).

8. In *The Proper Lady and the Woman Writer*, e.g., Mary Poovey suggests that Shelley, bowing to conventional prejudice, is keen to adopt a self-deprecating and domestic position; yet writing is at the same time important to her as a means of self-definition. Put in social-economic terms, Shelley has to thrive, compete as a woman writer, without, however, alienating a generally conservative, bourgeois reading public, especially a growing class of women readers. On the significance of the changing class of female readers (from the elite Bluestockings in the 1750s and '60s, to bourgeois circles in this period), see Curran, "Women readers, women writers."

9. Cf. Atlas in the Greek myth, who carries the entire weight of the world on his shoulders, as punishment.

10. For example, in grief, she interrupted the bard's singing of the heroic exploits of the Trojan war, including those of her husband; second, she subverted the plundering suitors who sought to win her hand, and thereby the kingdom of Ithaca; third, she raised her son, Telemachus, to early manhood, and while she submitted to him who by law inherited the authority of her missing husband, the young master still showed signs of deference to his mother.

11. According to Susan Wolfson, Mary Shelley was instrumental in favorably altering Percy's reputation, from someone who had been branded as "radical," "heretical" and "immoral" to an "ideal humanist," a "misunderstood" poet. Through editorial presentations and sympathetic interpretations, she was successful in gaining sympathy for Percy among significant Victorian poets, critics and readers. See Wolfson's extensively researched "Editorial privilege: Mary Shelley and Percy Shelley's Audiences" in *The Other Mary Shelley: Beyond Frankenstein*. Eds. A. Fish, A. Mellor and E. Schor (New York: Oxford University Press, 1993).

12. For some reflections on Percy Shelley's influence on nineteenth- and twentieth-century political reforms, see e.g., Bouthaina Shabaan's "Shelley and the Chartists," *Meena*

Alexander's "Shelley's India: Territory and Text, Some Problems of Decolonization;" and Alan Weinberg's "Shelley's Humane Concern and the Demise of Apartheid," collected in *Shelley: Poet and Legislator of the World*. Eds. B. Bennett & S. Curran. Baltimore and London: The Johns Hopkins University Press, 1996.

13. Susan Wolfson argues that, in reaction to this guilt, Mary sets out to position herself as Percy's "privileged reader," through the editing and annotating of his works. As the volumes sculpt an image of an unworldly and frequently misunderstood poet, Mary Shelley becomes the mediator of his poetry through her prose, in addition, using to advantage her own reputation as a prose-writer.

14. Fred Botting, *Making Monstrous*. Manchester: Manchester University Press, 1991.

15. See Raymond Williams's "The Romantic Artist" in *Romanticism: Points of View*. Ed. R. Gleckner and G. Enscoe (Detroit: Wayne State University Press, 1974). 269–85. Mary Shelley's persistent efforts to reshape Percy's public persona, and make available his collected works, contribute to the ideological and political developments in Britain in the decades after his death.

16. In "From Avant-Garde to Vanguardism," Gary Kelly compares Percy's *Laon and Cythna* and Mary's *Frankenstein*. He traces the ebb and flow of British cultural revolution from the 1790s to the 1830s, and argues that Percy's poetic-political reform becomes isolated vanguardism, whereas Mary "succeeded in reaching the 'large field of production' ... to become part of the modern cultural mythology." *Shelley: Poet and Legislator of the World*, pp. 73–87.

17. Cf. Gayatri Spivak reads the English lady (Margaret Saville) and the unnameable monster as both (escaping) outside the frame of the text. I quote from "Three Women's Texts and a Critique of Imperialism": "It is satisfying for a postcolonial reader to consider this a noble resolution for a nineteenth-century English novel" (in *"Race," Writing, and Difference*. Ed. H. L. Gates, Jr. Chicago: Chicago University Press, 1985, 1986. p. 278). Historically, slavery in England itself was abolished in 1772. But British engagement in the slave trade to the West Indies continued, fueling the British economy. The British aristocratic and middle class ladies would have benefited from the exploitation of the colonial "other." Slave trade was legally abolished in 1807.

WORKS CITED

Baldick, Chris. "The Politics of Monstrosity." *Frankenstein*. Ed. Fred Botting. New York: St. Martin's Press, 1995. 48–67.
Bate, Jonathan. "Caliban and Ariel Write Back." *Shakespeare Survey*, 48.155–62.
Bennett, B and S. Curran. Ed. *Shelley: Poet and Legislator of the World*. Baltimore and London: The Johns Hopkins University Press, 1996.
Botting, Fred. *Making Monstrous*. Manchester: Manchester University Press, 1991.
Curran, Stuart. *The Cambridge Companion to British Romanticism*. Cambridge: Cambridge University Press, 1993. 177–95.
Eagleton, Terry. *The Function of Criticism*. London: Verso, 1984.
Hansberry, Lorraine. A *Raisin in the Sun*. New York: Signet, 1994 (includes citation of poem by Langston Hughes, "What happens to a Dream Deferred?").
Haraway, Donna. "Ecce Homo, Ain't [Ar'n't] I a Woman, and Inappropriate/d Others: The Human in a Post-Humanist Landscape." *Feminists Theorize the Political*. Eds. J. Butler and J.W. Scott. New York: Routledge, 1992. 86–100.

Johnson, Barbara. "My Monster/ My Self" *A World of Difference*. Baltimore: Johns Hopkins University Press, 1987. 144–54.

Mellor, Anne. "'Am I Not a Woman, and a Sister?': Slavery, Romanticism, and Gender." *Romanticism, Race, and Imperial Culture, 1780–1834*. Bloomington: Indiana University Press, 1996. 311–329.

———. "Choosing a Text of Frankenstein to Teach," in *Approaches to Teaching Shelley's Frankenstein*. Ed. S. Behrendt. New York: MLA, 1990. 31–7.

———. *Mary Shelley: Her Life, Her Fiction, Her Monsters*. New York: Routledge, 1989.

Poovey, Mary. The *Proper Lady and the Woman Writer*. Chicago: University of Chicago Press, 1984.

Shelley, Mary. *Frankenstein*. Ed. A. Mellor & T. Reyes. New York: Washington Square Press, 1995.

Spivak, Gayatri. "Three Women's Texts and a Critique of Imperialism" in *"Race," Writing, and Difference*. Ed. H.L. Gates, Jr. Chicago: Chicago University Press, 1985, 1986. 262–80.

Williams, Raymond. "The Romantic Artist." *Romanticism: Points of View*. Ed. R. Gleckner and G. Enscoe. Detroit: Wayne State University Press, 1974. 269–85.

Wolfson, Susan. "Editorial Privilege: Mary Shelley and Percy Shelley's Audiences." *The Other Mary Shelley: Beyond Frankenstein*. Ed. A. Fish, A. Mellor and E. Schor. New York: Oxford University Press, 1993. 39–72.

MARK MOSSMAN

Acts of Becoming: Autobiography, Frankenstein, *and the Postmodern Body*

INTRODUCTION

1. My body is a postmodern text. I have had sixteen major surgeries in thirty years and I am about to have a kidney transplant. My left leg has been amputated and I have only four fingers on one hand. I walk with a limp, and in each step my left shoulder drops down lower than my right, which gives me an awkward, seemingly uncertain gait. My life has been in many ways a narrative typical of postmodern disability, a constant physical tooling and re-tooling, a life marked by long swings into and out of "health" and "illness," "ability" and "disability." As I write this I am in end stage renal failure, with about twelve percent kidney function. My body is in jeopardy, running a race to transplantation, a race against dialysis, debilitating nausea, and ultimate mortality.

2. My body is a postmodern text. I play basketball every day; I am good at tennis, racquetball; I garden, walk for miles. I look "healthy," young, and am often mistaken for a student. My life is defined by activity, work, ambition. I write now in the evening, after a day that started with several hours of critical reading, and then included teaching two writing courses and one literary criticism and theory class, meeting individually with four

From *Postmodern Culture* 11, 3. © 2001 *Postmodern Culture*.

freshman composition students, playing an hour of basketball, spending another hour in a contentious faculty meeting, taking a trip to the grocery store, cooking supper, and, at last, talking for a few short but meaningful minutes with my spouse before I scurried downstairs to where I currently sit working in my office in our basement.

3. My body is a postmodern text. When I sit behind a desk, looking out to my class on that first day of the semester, my students think I am a "norm." It is rare in those first moments for students to notice my disfigurement. I usually arrive at the classroom early. I prepare, go over notes for the opening class session. I sit down. Students slowly drift in, and then finally, after taking roll and beginning the arduous process of matching names with faces, I get up and distribute the syllabus. What happens? I see surprised expressions, eyes quickly shifting away from my body, often glancing anywhere but the location, the space where disability is unexpectedly and suddenly being written. I go on and begin my introduction to the particular course, while my students hurriedly attempt to account for difference, to manage the contrast of the literal with the prescribed stereotype and the previous impression. These are the crucial moments that constitute the process of my life; these are the absolutely significant points that define the narrative of my body.

4. My body is a postmodern text. I am aware that I am constantly located in a social space, a gray area where the category of disability is manufactured. My body is deceptive, though, so I can at times escape, slip out of the net of discourses that determine the lives of so many disabled people. I am aware that I am able to have these moments because my body is so pliable in its ability to be normal and then abnormal and then normal again. I live in a space that allows perception, comprehensive awareness. I can feel the colonizing discourses of biomedical culture wash over my body like waves sweeping up onto the seashore. They recede and I am normal; they crash again and I am drowning in stereotype and imposed identity. The unique privilege of my life has been the fact that I am, figuratively, a beach, an edge of something; I know the different spheres of water and sand; I am able to live in both worlds. And as I move through these worlds, as the narrative of my life is constructed around and through me, I am aware of how I change and am changed, written and re-written by the different clusters of discourse that mark all of our lives: at the doctor's office last week, for example, I was "ill," a "patient"; on the basketball court later that day I was "healthy," a "player."

5. The goal of this paper is manifold and ambitious. My intention here is to swirl together autobiography, narrative, and critical analysis in order to

simultaneously create a reading of disability, of Mary Shelley's novel *Frankenstein*, and of the construction of the postmodern body. I acknowledge the irritating impossibility, the bombastic complexity of such a goal for a piece of critical writing. I recognize the likely failure of this project, although I am not going to lie: I am terribly hopeful for it. That hope is tempered by fear, coupled with the risk of it all: it is important for me to record that I write this document knowing of such matters, as I am aware of my own tenuous situation as a tenure-track, first-year assistant professor of English. I am a young professional at the beginnings of difficult career, a career that demands excellence and grinding dedication to work in the classroom, on departmental and college-wide committees, and in the chaotic arenas of published research. At the same time, I am a disabled individual who has been, in one context or another, disabled his entire life and has, therefore, acquired a range of experiences and a distinct knowledge as to what it means to negotiate exclusion and discrimination. My own self, then, presented within the framework of these words and of the autobiographical examples that follow, is at issue here, is vulnerable and open. Indeed, the way that these pressures, histories, and goals pull at each other, contradict and countermine each other in this essay is, in part, the very reason for the paper's existence. Like the creature in Mary Shelley's novel, and like the novel itself for Mary Shelley, this work is understood by its author to be something sewn together, hideously grotesque, monstrous, something that is most likely a powerful failure. My hope, however, is that the very fracturing agents that conflict at the core of this essay will slowly fold into each other, connect, blend together, and produce a reading, and an understanding of my own experience, that ultimately helps to define what David T. Mitchell and Sharon L. Snyder have recently demanded: an authentic, developed "disabled perspective" of culture (242).

6. At the outset my question is, what happens when a disabled individual writes herself? What happens when the disabled person explains and articulates, through either writing or bodily practice, disability? There has been an increasing number of theorists and researchers working in the field of disability studies who have attempted to construct answers to these kinds of questions. In doing so, what critics often discover is a need to expand the emerging field itself. For example, in commenting on the importance of scholars in the humanities working in a field dominated by the social sciences, Lennard J. Davis asserts that narratives written by individuals who are disabled constitute important voices in the workings of culture at large and need, therefore, to be understood through a humanities-centered critical approach:

> Cultural productions are virtually the only permanent records of a society's ideological structure. If we acknowledge that communal behaviors and thought processes have a material existence, then that existence coalesces in the intersection between the individual mind and the collective market. Nowhere can we understand this intersection better than in literary and cultural productions. ("Enabling" 248–49)

Davis continues: "We must examine the process by which normalcy, taken for granted by definition, is shaped into hegemonic force that requires micro-enforcement at each and every cultural, somatic, and political site in the culture…. People learn themselves through consumed cultural artifacts" (250). In the same journal publication, Mitchell and Snyder echo Davis in arguing that

> disability study in the humanities has been critiqued for a tendency to surf amidst a sea of metaphors rather than stand on the firm ground of policy and legislative action. However, the identification of variable representational systems for approaching disability in history demonstrates in and of itself that disability operates as a socially constructed category. The more varied and variable the representation, the more fervent and exemplary disability studies scholars can make our points about the complexity of this social construction. (242)

7. In this theoretical context, writing disability is the (re)production of disability, a potent act of creation. Autobiography by a disabled person is an authentication of lived, performed experience; it is a process of making, of being able to "translate *knowing* into *telling*" (White 1). Using the last two decades of criticism and theory as a map, disabled autobiography can be traced as a postmodern, postcolonial endeavor, for when disability writing constructs the particular self-definition it is attempting to narrate, it automatically resists repressive stereotype at large and attempts to reclaim ownership of the body and the way the body is understood. In other words, writing, autobiography, the narration of an experience by a disabled person to a reader or an immediate listener, enables a marginalized voice to be heard, which in turn causes cultural practice and stereotyped roles to change. The experiences rendered in "illness narratives," as Arthur Kleinmann has named them, work against any kind of essential universalism and instead attempt to demonstrate particularity and individuality in experience. The

writing of illness and the writing of disability, and as David Morris has recently noted the two terms are often collapsed together in postmodern culture, involve new constructions of reality, new categories for the body's performance in cultural practice. Disabled autobiography is a conscious act of becoming.

8. What disability writing constitutes, then, is an unfolding of culture so that, in addition to negative stereotype, liberatory constructs are present and available to the practice of the body, in the body's movement through the different representational systems of general culture. Disability writing, in other words, often takes the instability inherent in the body and spins it into the articulation of a volitional mode of selfhood; writing disability becomes an empowering act of control, a deconstructive critical strategy that attempts to break down oppressive and imprisoning cultural construction. By writing disability, the performance and general representation of disability is re-centered, re-focused on the disabled subject itself, which deflects and displaces the powerful gaze of the "norm." As one critic argues, "as self-representation, autobiography is perhaps uniquely suited to validate the experience of people with disabilities and to counter stereotypical (mis)representation" (Couser 292).

9. For example, one of the students I talked with today is orthopedically disabled. In our conference, I commented on how beautiful the weather has been, and how much I love the springtime. The student responded with a detailed explanation of just how much she hates the spring. She dreads the spring because it is a ritualistic moment in the story or text of her life: each spring she becomes newly disabled. The weather changes, and she is unable to wear clothes that help to conceal her disfigurement. Each spring, then, she confronts new stares, the feeling of awkward humiliation that is attached to being physically abnormal in a public zone where normalcy is in effect. She is undressed by those stares, by the cumulative and constant recognition of difference: she is stripped and re-written with the coming of warm weather; putting on a pair of shorts, a t-shirt, or a bathing suit equates putting on a "disability," dressing down into abnormality.

10. What this particular student experiences every spring is a process of conflict, resistance, and liberation. Again, in the spring, with the eyes, faces, and general behavior of curious and almost always kind-hearted people, this disabled student feels her body, her self, being lifted from her, being re-shaped and re-made because of the recognition of difference and the discursive and perceptual location of abnormality. Her response, however, is to attempt to re-define herself, again to resist the imposition of "abnormality" that comes from the matrix of culture surrounding her. In

articulating her anger to me and to others, in speaking of her lack of control and building up a narrative of her experiences for her audience, she gains a measure of control, takes her body back, realizes a liberation from the construct of abnormality. In this way, she can re-determine and re-write the acts of becoming through which her body must annually move; she can trigger a process of self-definition that works against the subject/object, normal/abnormal polarization of her experience. Her voice, and her body, can claim a degree of power in her ability to narrate her feelings of abnormality. She does not stop wearing the shorts, but instead embraces the perceptual process invoked when she puts them on because she knows that she can define herself, that she can become and re-become what she knows she is.

11. Thinking of this project, I asked her if she had read *Frankenstein*. She had not (again, though she is obviously very mature, the student is only a freshman). When I was her age I had read the book, though, and when I read *Frankenstein* for the first time, at eighteen, I read myself as the creature, as a body that has no place in the world, a body that, in its long twisting scars and attachable prosthetic limb, has the imprint of technology and modernist science written upon it, and seems, therefore, "unnatural." When I read of the creature being built, made from selected parts of dead bodies, I easily read it as an enactment that mirrored my own development as a person: artificial, "fashioned" limbs and transplanted organs create the creature, the daemon; such things also construct myself. At eighteen, again my age at that first reading, I felt all of the resentment of the creature, the anger, the isolation, the loneliness. The creature was the ultimate victim of stereotyped oppression, of a disabling construction of "ugliness"; the creature's response was to torment its author, to triumph in the end by driving its creator and the one who first names it "ugly" to a cruel death. In this way, I vaguely recognized that the creature resisted what it had become and used its disabled body, a body that was incredible and superior in strength, in its ability to experience extremes in cold and heat, to wreck the inscribing process of outside definition. Being constructed in postmodern discourse, being the person I was and am, I read the creature as "powerful" in its resistance: the creature gained power through its disempowered body; it took the imposition of "abnormality" and used it as an articulation of strength and purpose. When I read the narrative, I read these terms into my own body; I used them to explain my own life.

12. Before I move to a more critical discussion of *Frankenstein*, I have one more autobiographical example of this postmodern process of becoming. I love to swim. I love the sun, the exertion of a day of swimming. A few weeks

ago, with a couple of days off for the Easter holiday, my spouse and I spent a long weekend in Florida. We went to a place south of Tampa, to a condo on Indian Rocks Beach. The facility has a heated pool, but I wanted to swim in the Gulf. In order to get to the beach, though, I had to leave my limb upstairs and use crutches (salt and sand sometimes damage the hydraulic knee of my leg, so I try to avoid leaving it for long stretches on a beach). As I passed by the pool on crutches and felt the stares of roughly forty sunbathing, vacationing people, and heard the questions of several small, inquisitive children, I felt deeply disabled. I called that passage, a route I would take probably eight to ten times during the trip, the running of the gauntlet. That was what it was: a painful, bruising journey that simply had to be made. In those moments, I felt vulnerable. I felt angry. I will be honest: I felt hatred. I remember telling myself, on several occasions, that "I didn't care what they thought of me," that "I was going to do this no matter what." I remember trying hard not to look back at them, those innocent people, not to hear the questions, but instead to focus on the goal: the gateway to the beach and ultimately the sea. I knew that making eye contact meant imprisonment, displacement, perhaps even failure. I knew how the process worked: eye contact would equate deep inscription, the aggressive internalization of abnormality and disability, and I knew that too much of that would have meant a decision to just avoid the whole troublesome thing and not swim at all.

13. When I did get to the water, however, I was free again, my disability hidden beneath the waves. And at that point, typically, I felt a rush of emotions. I was thankful and pleased to be in the water swimming. I was embarrassed by my body's power to cause discomfort. I was anxious about the return passage back to the condo. I was ashamed of my profound inability to resist becoming what those stares had made me into: disabled, a person who needs help—the gates opened for him, the pathways cleared—a person who needs kindness and smiles to offset the uncomfortable stares and questions.

14. Of course, as usual these feelings were almost immediately countered by another very different experience. On the first day back from that trip, I went to the dentist for a check-up. Having been out in the Florida sun, I had a tan, and as I sat down in the reclined dentist's chair, ready to be examined, he mentioned that I looked great and had a "healthy glow." I laughed, but what flashed across my mind was what I had actually experienced while I was getting this tan (which has now begun to peel): that is, disability, the constructions of illness. The dentist defined my body and, in turn, "me," as being "healthy." But just the day before at the pool I was certainly defined as "disabled." Any nephrologist will tell you that for the last

three years I have been seriously "ill." My point here is simple: it is clear that the text of my body, which is my body, is profoundly unstable. Again and again I discover how I am both normal and abnormal, both able-bodied and healthy, and disabled and ill. As I will demonstrate, it is this profound discursive indeterminacy that defines the postmodern body and the direction that both body criticism and disability studies are taking as they develop.

15. I will end this introduction with the following description. We have a full-length mirror in our bedroom. I looked in it tonight; I looked in it with the issues of this essay in my mind, with the experiences of the past couple of weeks clicking off in my head. What I saw was a tanned, smiling face, a body clothed in casual khaki Dockers and a light blue buttoned down shirt by Structure, a body wearing comfortable brown leather shoes and tan dress socks. I then took off the shoes, the shirt. The body was different, just slightly, no longer wearing several markers of class, no longer appearing totally healthy—the left shoulder slightly deformed, again lower and smaller than the right; the body uneven, slightly misshapen. I then took off the pants, the undershirt, and then the underwear and the socks. And there I was, stripped, naked. The body had become disfigured, disabled. Scars danced across the abdomen. A prosthetic limb dominated the left side of the body, drawing the eyes to it. I turned and it was apparent that the hips turn outward, the spine curves inward. My body looked bent, odd, strange to me. I took off the limb and the transformation was complete: I had stripped into disability and disfigurement, into powerlessness and vulnerability.

16. I had changed. In the mirror I had morphed from an apparently normal, youngish, tanned person in reasonably fashionable clothing to a nakedly disfigured creature. If only my dentist could see me now, I thought.

THE CREATURE AS MONSTER

17. The first time I taught Mary Shelley's most famous book I was in graduate school, a teaching fellow, and I was teaching my first upper-division course. The class was a junior-level survey of nineteenth- and twentieth-century British literature. The students were mostly sophomore and junior English majors, and there were about fifteen of them total.

18. The first day we took up the novel was surprising, and one of the highpoints in my early teaching experience. My class loved the book, and responded well to it; they overwhelming aligned themselves with the creature. In fact, at one point in our initial discussion, several of them asked me to stop calling the creature "the monster." They claimed that he was not a "monster"; calling it one, they said, was the whole problem.

19. When I walked out of class that afternoon I think you could describe my disposition as jubilant, very happy with the discussion, with the way the students responded. At the time, and with my own biases hovering in the background, I thought that it was only natural that the class, all of whom were young and disenfranchised by definition, could identify as readers with the scorned, lonely creature. The creature is victimized; it made sense to me then and still does now that readers familiar with any kind of powerlessness will identify with the hated and marginalized creature. In truth, I was really just happy that my students had even read the book! The fact that they had had something to say about it, that they had wanted to talk about it and develop an understanding of the world through it seemed to validate my own experience as a graduate student being trained to teach in an English Department.

20. When I read *Frankenstein* now, I read the text and my own sympathetic alignment with the creature in a slightly different light. More than ever, it seems that the novel demonstrates the power of cultural inscription, the way an individual comes to subjectivity through a series of aggressive cultural acts. In his anonymous review of the narrative, Percy Shelley framed the creature in a similar light, as a being who is made into a violent monster. He argues for the following concise explanation of the narrative: "Treat a person ill and he will become wicked" (Clark 307). What the creature experiences through the narrative, from its birth to its last scene with Walton, is a continued repetition of scorn, hatred, and fear, a constant construction of monstrosity. The creature learns itself in this way; it becomes "unnatural," "abnormal," again a monster through its consumption of "cultural artifacts" (to again cite Davis), and through the practice of everyday life. What the narrative enacts, then, is the creature's inability to resist this overwhelming definition of itself by culture. Unlike my student described above, or myself, the creature lacks the postmodern, technologically driven ability to "dress" out of abnormality, but is instead always starkly naked, stripped, openly abnormal. In the end, the tragedy of the creature is that it can see itself as nothing but a monster. In its own self-narration at the center of the book, it claims: "when I became fully convinced that I was in reality the monster that I am, I was filled with the bitterest sensations of despondence and mortification. Alas! I did not yet entirely know the fatal effects of this miserable deformity" (108). And again the creature articulates a self-understanding in terms of abnormality: "I was ... endued with a figure so hideously deformed and loathsome; I was not even of the same nature as man" (115).

21. Arthur Frank tells us that "Repetition is the medium of becoming" (159). The creature is trapped in repeated social construction, is unable to cloak its disability and escape the constant repetition of "monster." The creature attempts to resist this repetition, to become something other than the monster it is constantly being made into. There is, for example, the way it approaches the blind patriarch of the De Lacey family, attempting to lose its body and become simply a voice; and there is its ultimate utopian desire to hide from the oppressive, normalizing sight of humanity, to have a companion or a mate like itself, with whom the creature can run away and live peacefully in isolation. But again it is never anything but nakedly disabled in its "hideousness." It can never hide with clothes or technology or self-narration or any other cloaking device other than the darkness of night. In open daylight, its disfigurement and abnormality are always present, immediate, defining.

22. Jay Clayton has argued the following point concerning the way the creature's body works in culture:

> Although the monster in Shelley's novel is hideous to look at, Frankenstein himself feels more keenly the horror of the creature looking at him. In this respect, Shelley reverses the terms of monstrosity. Frankenstein cannot bear to see the eyes of his creation watching him. Indeed, the eyes themselves seem to be the most horrid organs the creature possesses. (61)

The passage Clayton refers to is the creature's first act in the novel, which is narrated by Frankenstein in the following way: "He [the creature] held up the curtain of the bed; and his eyes, if eyes they may be called, were fixed on me. His jaws opened, and he muttered some inarticulate sounds, while a grin wrinkled his cheeks. He might have spoken, but I did not hear; one hand was stretched out, seemingly to detain me, but I escaped, and rushed downstairs" (57). In this passage, the creature seeks unity, contact, a reception from its parent, and is instead roughly abandoned. This is the first act in the process of the creature's development into a monster: the creature's body, which initiates contact here by reaching out to Frankenstein, causes discomfort and anxiety in the one it confronts, the one it "fixes" its eyes upon. Terror for both Frankenstein and the creature occur most often when the creature looks back, makes eye contact, for that is the moment when construction takes place, when both bodies are written. One body, Frankenstein's, is located in normalcy, while the other, the creature's, is represented as the excluded "Other," as "abnormal." Indeed, it is Frankenstein, the creature's physical author and the first human the creature knows, who gives the creature the first elements of his identity as a monster. Frankenstein again describes his first confrontation with the victimized creature in the following way: "I had gazed on him while unfinished; he was ugly then; but when those muscles and joints were rendered capable of motion, it became such a thing as even Dante could not have conceived" (57). It is when the creature is "capable," then, when it articulates an ability, and worst of all when it looks back at the observer, that it becomes a monster. Thus, Frankenstein can further narrate his understanding of the creature with the deep horror of normalcy, of the oppressor:

> His limbs were in proportion, and I had selected his features as beautiful. Beautiful! Great God! His yellow skin scarcely covered the work of muscles and arteries beneath; his hair was of a lustrous black, and flowing; his teeth of pearly whiteness; but these luxuriances only formed a more horrid contrast with his watery eyes, that seemed almost of the same colour as the dun-white sockets in which they were set, his shrivelled complexion and straight black lips. (56)

23. Rather than attaching special power to the creature through its disfigured body, however, most critics have treated the novel as Percy Shelley does in his before-mentioned review, traditionally reading the creature's body as a representation of marginalization and victimization, of binding cultural construction. For example, one critic argues, "In Nietzschean terminology, the being's problem is that he is so thoroughly creature [i.e., Other] he is incapable of forming his own values. He is forced to accept them ready-made from his creator and his creator's race" (Hetherington 22). Likewise, David Hirsch highlights that first moment when Frankenstein names his creation a monster, and asserts that it "is Victor's baptismal enslavement of [the creature] with an image, a name, an identity which this 'monster' will attempt to erase by manipulating those very same chains of language and image which bind him" (57). Hirsch continues:

> By seeking inclusion into exclusive structures, [the creature] realizes that his reverent attempts to assimilate disempower him as they reinforce the exclusivity of the closed domestic circle. Asking for similar rights by stressing one's similarity to a normal structure does little to alter the norm and demands no reciprocal conversion on the part of the one to be persuaded. (59)

Hirsch and other critics, in both queer studies and feminist theory, often see the creature as the problematic of marginalization, a dramatization of either femininity or homosexuality in a culture dominated by repressive patriarchy and heterosexuality. The creature fails to break out of stereotype and the repressive discourses that define it, but is instead thoroughly and completely shaped by those discourses. The creature's body, its ugliness and abnormality, and the resulting exclusion and disability, become the ultimate symbols of practices of discrimination.

24. These approaches, all of which choose to focus primarily on the creature rather than its creator or the actual author of the novel, give shape and critical substance to my own reading of the book. The creature attempts to break out of this definite bind of stereotype, out of this "principle of disfiguration" (Vine 247), first when it tells its story to its maker, which in the context of this discussion appears as an autobiographical attempt to claim selfhood, to write and perform disability, and then when it makes its final demand for "a mate." Thinking of Hirsch's argument, it seems that both the self-narrative and the desire for a similar companion can be read as tools or strategies that the creature uses to establish some kind of normalcy for itself. A female mate, for example, would destroy the uniqueness the creature feels, would instead create a sense of sameness, a solidarity of experience, a "domestic circle."

25. The creature's self-narrative, which I would like to place more emphasis on here simply because it is more relevant to our discussion, likewise demonstrates the potential power and cultural force the creature possesses. As we have seen, it is when the creature becomes mobile, a potential functional and able member of society, that it becomes dangerous and needs to be, literally, turned into a monster. Power, then, which the creature achieves by simply being able to breathe and live—that is, to perform in everyday life—is immediately repressed. Power is in a measure re-achieved, however, in the creature's narrative of itself. Again, self-narrative is a tool used by the creature to gain self-determinacy. It is an "illness narrative," an act of becoming and re-becoming. Through self-narration the creature can, to a point, re-make itself, re-fashion and re-invent a new understanding of its self. With its story, the creature tries to resist the disabling definition of "monster" and to write itself into rhetorical normalcy, which it hopes will lead to real, if limited, acceptance in everyday cultural practice.

26. The creature does this by attempting to draw pity, a sympathy, out of its audience, and therefore some kind of recognition of sameness, some kind of inclusion. Once again, in part it works. For example, after hearing the

creature's narrative Frankenstein comments, "His words had a strange effect upon me. I compassioned him, and sometimes felt a wish to console him" (140). It is in these moments that it appears that the creature has established some kindred feeling, some sense of sameness. But, even in these moments, the creature cannot overcome its physical hideousness and the resulting sense of abnormality and otherness. Frankenstein's next thoughts are as follows: "but when I looked upon him, and when I saw the filthy mass that moved and talked, my heart sickened, and my feelings were altered to those of horror and hatred" (126). The creature's body, its "filthy mass," is too much in the present and too radically different; it claims too much definition, and cannot be ignored or put aside. The creature's narrative, then, is the fulfillment of a paradigm first outlined by Leonard Kriegel: "the cripple is threat and recipient of compassion, both to be damned and to be pitied—and frequently to be damned as he is pitied" (32).

27. Indeed, in the end, the only real control or power that the creature is able to achieve is not through the rhetoric of understanding or empathy, but rather through its threats and eventual acts of physical violence. It does control Frankenstein, and drives him to death. It can even claim: "'Remember that I have power.... You are my creator, but I am your master;—obey!'" (160). It is key to recognize that that power comes not in achieving normalcy, but in embodying deviance, the violence associated with physical abnormality. Rather than becoming a "person" or "human" through an act of language and rhetoric, the creature becomes a "master" through "monstrous" acts of violence.

28. Eleanor Salotto has written:

> Narrative in this text is divided among three narrators: Walton, Frankenstein, and the creature. This diffusion of narrative voice indicates that the narrative body is not whole, incapable of reproducing a sutured narrative about the origins of one's life.... The frame of narrative thus disturbs the notion of unitary identity, on which the notion of autobiography has rested. (190)

We have seen that autobiography is not a viable strategy in the text; it does not lead, ultimately, to empowerment for the creature. Salotto argues that it is similarly a failure for all of the characters and for the author of the text herself, Mary Shelley:

> As we have seen ... categories break down, and what one character demonstrates at one moment shifts ground continuously, as with

> the creature's innate goodness and his subsequent reign of terror
> ... the introduction concentrates on Shelley looking into the
> mirror and asking the same questions that the creature does:
> 'Who was I? What was I?' and veering off the 'traditional'
> signification of the feminine subject. (191)

Thus, when Shelley writes the narrative, and the introduction to the 1831 edition, she writes herself, just as each of her characters, especially the creature, attempt to write themselves when they in turn write their own stories. All of them, all of the narratives, are not quite successful; they all lack the ultimate self-definition that they attempt to achieve. What this says for our purposes here is that narrative is used as a tool, a technology, that is intended to be a vehicle to freedom, self-definition, and self-expression. Again, the problem that this novel demonstrates is that such technology—perhaps all technology—fails. The monster, for example, tries to un-monster itself with its personal narrative. Because narrative fails, the creature's ability to resist stereotype and construct a new, more "human" identity likewise fails. It is always victim, always resisting the powerful inscription it feels on its body, but never able to avoid the snares of abnormality that trap it and direct its every move. The creature's body is trapped in a kind of profound disability, is transformed into a violent monster and lacks any power to stop this transformation from taking place. It tries to narrate itself out of that construction; it attempts to become something else. It fails.

THE POSTMODERN BODY

29. It seems that we now have a deep contradiction working in this paper. The first section establishes how, through autobiography, the disabled individual can narrate herself into a kind of ability, how the instability of the discourses that presently define the body leads ultimately to possible constructs of freedom and re-self-definition. The next section of the essay then undermines that notion in its assertion that the creature in Mary Shelley's *Frankenstein* is unable to narrate itself into ability and normalcy; the creature attempts to narrate itself out of the disfigurement that defines it as "monster" and excludes it from normal practice, and it is of course unable to do this. What is the solution to this paradox? The answer is postmodernity, or the condition where, according to Donna Haraway, there is "agency ... without defended subjects" (3).

30. I want to refer again to the class in which I first taught *Frankenstein*. In that class the students aligned themselves with the creature, and more

importantly refused to recognize the creature as "monstrous." If I recall correctly, the students in that class looked like many of the classes I have taught during my eight years of teaching experience. Body piercings, tattoos, dyed hair, extremes in baggy and tight clothing—all are characteristics of our students today. Notions of individuality, self-expression, and freedom dominate the self-presentations of our students. Indeed, with the abundance of research on the teaching of writing and literature out there these days, it is no surprise to me that when I teach my writing and literature sections, the work that requires personal narration and experience from my students is always the best, the most rewarding and the most productive writing and speaking. It has been demonstrated time and time again that teaching writing is linked with teaching empowerment, self-exploration and discovery, personal relationships, and the ability to have a voice in the functioning of our culture.

31. But again as we have just seen, narrative, self-writing, and self-presentation or performance are the very tools that fail the creature. I think the answer here is that in the contemporary West there are simply more tools to work with, more experiences to augment narration and the process of self-becoming: today the creature could have plastic surgery, for example, or use its size and strength to play a professional sport, or use its intellect to manage itself into financial and cultural power. Put simply, not only are the times a-changin', the times have already changed. Postmodernism has unhinged the hegemony of culture and stereotype, and has allowed for the development and availability of liberatory constructs and discursive practices that lead to freedom. Indeed, the dynamic of postmodern cultural practice is to center such marginalized subjectivities, to hear voices now that before were not heard. A disabled perspective of culture, then, is now available, possible, likely.

32. In my own research, I know that I am reading more and more autobiographical narratives written by disabled authors offering a variety of perspectives on their experience; and in my everyday life, I am seeing more and more disabled people claiming power in the functioning of culture, resisting stereotype, and re-making the ways in which their bodies are understood by others. A good example here is Sean Elliott, the professional basketball player. Sean Elliott is a transplanted body, a body that is surrounded by images of abnormality and "unnaturalness." He now plays a sport dominated in the eighties and early nineties by images of perfection, ideal normalcy—when one thinks of professional basketball, one thinks of Michael Jordan's athletic body, a body that is often cited by multiple intelligence theorists to be a kind of kinesthetic "genius." Elliott's play,

though, his ability on the court, wrecks the polarization of normal and abnormal that the marketing of Jordan's body seems to establish. Elliott is able to be both extremes of the pole: he is ill and healthy; he is a body that is unnatural and a body that is strikingly natural. He is impaired and disabled and neither all at the same time. He is postmodern. Sean Elliott does not only "look back" at or make eye contact with the defining practices of culture and the stares of millions of people; he redefines himself in those moments, and he succeeds in the re-definition by making himself a viable option for the three-point shot, by being a professional player. When millions of people see him playing basketball on television, what they see is disability becoming ability, again a wrecking of the whole polarization of able- and disabled-body experience. The dichotomy is destroyed because Sean Elliott, a transplanted, reconstructed person—in addition to the transplant, both of his knees have been rebuilt—is able to play the most glamorous, most promoted, and most marketed sport in recorded history. Every night he is in an arena of perfect bodies. His body works, claims the same perfection, without any loss of what he actually is: a transplant patient, a medically maintained body, a professional athlete, a great three-point shooter.

33. Lennard J. Davis has written that, "When we think of bodies, in a society where the concept of the norm is operative, then people with disabilities will be thought of as deviants" ("Normalcy" 13). Though many, if not all scholars working in the field of disability studies will disagree, I am arguing in the end here that we can now foresee the moment when postmodern culture pushes into a realm where disabled bodies are, literally, no longer disabled. By establishing a disabled perspective of culture, the notion of disability itself radically changes, is perhaps lost, for a fully articulated disabled perspective seems to reach beyond disability and into an entirely different conceptual and cultural space for all bodies. Already, advances in technology blur the traditional lines between ability and disability as they blur the boundary between "the natural" and "the artificial." The very notion of normalcy/abnormality, an "able body" and a "disabled body," seems to be breaking down; the "norm" is eroding, and certainly attachments of social deviance are no longer relevant in a cultural environment where those images are embraced.

34. I have already demonstrated here how my own body is often able, with the technology of modernist and postmodernist medicine, to float into spheres of traditional normalcy, zones from which I would have been excluded just two decades ago. According to Jay Clayton and Donna Haraway, most people living today have such technologically dependent,

equalized, postmodern bodies, bodies that are, to use Haraway's phrase, "cyborgs." Clayton writes,

> Think of how one's character has been reshaped by the total integration of technology with the body. Many people would be different beings without the glasses or contact lenses that let them see. How would one's self-conception and behavior be changed without the availability of contraception (one form of which can be permanently implanted in women's bodies)? What about mood-altering drugs such as Prozac or body-altering drugs such as steroids and estrogen? For that matter, what about the far older technology of vaccination? In terms of more interventionist procedures, think of people whose lives have been transformed by pacemakers, prosthetic limbs, sex-change operations, cosmetic surgery, and more. (65–66)

With Sean Elliott's comeback, it is now widely apparent that the transplanted body too has this same indeterminacy inscribed upon it, built inside of it. The suggestion is, I think, that the person, any person, is a system of organs, almost all of which can be either replaced or relocated, depending on the immediate need. In this light, the body itself seems to break down as an absolute posit of selfhood and determinacy. What emerges is a sense of possibility. What emerges is the postmodern body.

WORKS CITED

Clark, D. L. *Shelley's Prose*. Albuquerque: U of New Mexico P, 1954.

Clayton, Jay. "Concealed Circuits: Frankenstein's Monster, the Medusa, and the Cyborg." *Raritan: A Quarterly Review* 15.4 (1996): 53–69.

Couser, G. Thomas. "Disability and Autobiography: Enabling Discourse." *Disability Studies Quarterly* 17.4 (1997): 292–296.

Davis, Lennard J. "Constructing Normalcy: The Bell Curve, the Novel, and the Invention of the Disabled Body in the Nineteenth Century." *The Disability Studies Reader*. Ed. Lennard J. Davis. New York: Routledge, 1997. 9–28.

———. "Enabling Texts." *Disability Studies Quarterly* 17.4 (1997): 248–251.

Frank, Arthur W. *The Wounded Storyteller: Body, Illness, and Ethics*. Chicago: U of Chicago P, 1995.

Haraway, Donna J. *Simians, Cyborgs, and Women: The Reinvention of Nature*. New York: Routledge, 1991.

Hetherington, Naomi. "Creator and Created in Mary Shelley's Frankenstein." *The Keats-Shelley Review* 11 (1997): 1–39.

Hirsch, David. "De-Familiarizations, De-Monstrations." *Pre/Text* 13 (Fall/Winter 1992): 53–67.

Kleinman, Arthur. *The Illness Narratives: Suffering, Healing, and the Human Condition*. New York: Basic Books, 1989.

Kriegel, Leonard. "The Cripple in Literature." *Images of the Disabled, Disabling Images*. Ed. Alan Gartner and Tom Joe. New York: Praeger, 1987. 31–46.

Mitchell, David T., and Sharon L. Snyder. "Exploring Foundations: Languages of Disability, Identity, and Culture." *Disability Studies Quarterly* 17.4 (1997): 241–247.

Morris, David. *Illness and Culture in the Postmodern Age*. Berkeley: U of California P, 1998.

Salotto, Eleanor. "Frankenstein and Dis(re)membered Identity." *The Journal of Narrative Technique* 24 (Fall 1994): 190–211.

Shelley, Mary. *Frankenstein*. Ed. Maurice Handle. New York: Penguin, 1983.

Vine, Steven. "Filthy Types: Frankenstein, Figuration, Femininity." *Critical Survey* 8 (1996): 246–58.

White, Hayden. "The Value of Narrativity in the Representation of Reality." *On Narrative*. Ed. W. J. T. Mitchell. Chicago: U of Chicago P, 1981. 1–24.

FRED V. RANDEL

The Political Geography of Horror
in Mary Shelley's Frankenstein

The monster who startles unsuspecting victims in Mary Wollstonecraft Shelley's *Frankenstein* by his sudden and fatal appearance seems to them to come from nowhere. He steps out of the placeless space of our most terrifying nightmares. For many fans of the novel and its filmic adaptations, the murders of *Frankenstein* are likewise situated in a shadowy land of Gothic fantasy and thrill-provoking manipulations of our unconscious. Thanks to recent scholarship, however, many of the historicities of *Frankenstein*—its interactions with French Revolutionary era discourses about gender, race, class, revolution, and science—are now as recognizable to informed readers as its psychodrama.[1] But we have only begun to decipher the significance of the geography of this novel, the rationale for setting its horrors in particular places, arranged in a specific sequence. Franco Moretti's *Atlas of the European Novel 1800–1900* argues that "in modern European novels, *what* happens depends a lot on *where* it happens," but omits *Frankenstein* from his analysis.[2] Does it really matter that William Frankenstein dies at Plainpalais, Justine Moritz and Alphonse in or near Geneva, Elizabeth at Evian, and Henry Clerval in Ireland? Does Victor's trip through England and Scotland serve any purpose except to evoke personal memories of Mary and Percy Shelley? Why does the novel begin and end in Russia and the Arctic?

From *ELH* 70 (2003). © 2003 by The Johns Hopkins University Press.

Mary Shelley inherited a usage of the Gothic that, in contrast with the expectations of many modern readers, foregrounded history and geography. As Chris Baldick and Robert Mighall have shown, Renaissance humanists used "Gothic" to refer scornfully to the architecture of northern European barbarians (as they viewed them), with particular reference to the Germanic and the medieval, but late eighteenth- and early nineteenth-century English Protestant writers typically set their "Gothic" fictions in Catholic southern Europe, while keeping the term's crucial association with the archaic and oppressive.[3] "Gothic," therefore, was implicated in shifting regionalist, nationalist, and sectarian mythologies, but it was characteristically used to align the author and reader with the supposedly enlightened, against the anachronistic and benighted. "The present study," Robert Mighall writes, "will challenge the notion that settings in the Gothic are its most dispensable properties, by observing how various historical and political factors help to shape the narrative material and determine those settings." He excludes *Frankenstein*, however, from the history of Gothic and from his own treatment, on the ground that its greatest horrors are the product of enlightenment and a projected futurity rather than "legacies from the past."[4] I suggest, by contrast, that Mary Shelley's novel is an astute extension and complication of the political geography of Gothic, as applied to the spread of revolutionary ideas, and revolution itself, in Europe and beyond since the mid-seventeenth century. She complicates the Gothic fear of being pulled back into a despotic past by exposing the despotic residue which, in her view, can shadow—but not stop—a potentially liberating, progressive process. At a time when the Congress of Vienna had just given official status to a reactionary interpretation of the French revolutionary era and a reactionary reconstitution of Europe as a whole, Mary Shelley imagines a liberal alternative through the geographical subtext of a European Gothic fiction. She anticipates Percy Bysshe Shelley's "A Philosophical View of Reform" (1819) by opting for an international and comparatist frame of reference, invoking a relatively long-range perspective, and urging the need for the dominant forces of society to abandon Restoration intransigence in favor of fundamental reform—a liberal version of enlightenment—as the only alternative to the spread of violent revolution.[5]

I. INGOLSTADT AND NORTHERN ICE

Lee Sterrenburg first showed why Mary Shelley chose Ingolstadt in Bavaria, as the place where Victor Frankenstein brought the monster to life.[6] An influential ultraconservative cleric, the Abbé Augustin Barruel, whose

Memoirs, Illustrating the History of Jacobinism Mary and Percy read on their honeymoon, had claimed that the French Revolution was the product of a conspiracy of intellectuals originating in that university town. The novel's indebtedness to Barruel is even more extensive than Sterrenburg suggested. When Adam Weishaupt founded a secret society called the "Illuminees" at Ingolstadt on 1 May 1776, he "formed a monstrous digest," in Barruel's words, of the various kinds of subversive thinking already current in the Enlightenment, much as Victor Frankenstein combines an assortment of body parts to form his monster.[7] Like Victor, Weishaupt led a double life at the University of Ingolstadt: distinguishing himself in respectable academic pursuits while secretly, in the privacy of his rooms, pursuing an invisible project. Both men took intellectual shortcuts: Weishaupt, unable to endure delay, recruited disciples by pretending to have a new "code of laws" that he had not yet formulated, while Victor Frankenstein makes an eight-foot giant, rather than a creature of normal human size, for the same reason (81; vol. 1, chap. 3). Weishaupt's secret society then infiltrated the Freemasons, penetrated France, enlisted the Duke of Orléans, and spawned the Jacobins, "that disastrous monster" which would wreak "days of horror and devastation." But the details of the conspiracy's growth are as mysterious as the comings and goings of Frankenstein's creature: "The monster has taken its course through wildernesses, and darkness has more than once obscured its progress."[8] This sentence, remarkably, is Barruel's, not Mary Shelley's, although it would, except for its neuter pronoun, be as suitable in the novel. No killing occurred at Ingolstadt in either version, but the monster formed in that place eventually causes multiple killings elsewhere. In borrowing from Barruel, Mary Shelley accepts his metaphoric equivalence between the French Revolution and a monster, together with his assumption that ideas can have profound social and political consequences. She also assimilates Barruel's suggestion that the conspiratorial secrecy and deceptiveness in which the monster was formed foreshadow major flaws in its socialization. But she adds a sympathy for the monster and an entrance into his thought-processes wholly lacking in the Abbé's diatribe against the Enlightenment and revolutionary change. She uses a conservative text as a sourcebook for political geography but without accepting its ideology.

Rather than constituting an exception, her method in treating Ingolstadt instantiates her systematic procedure in this novel. For example, her creature not only shares a birthplace with the French Revolution, but also a scene of putative endings. St. Petersburg is the address from which Walton sends off his first letter on the first page of the novel, and St. Petersburg was understood to be Napoleon's initial destination in his fateful

Russian campaign of 1812.[9] The novel's subtitle—*"The Modern Prometheus"*—would have invoked Napoleonic associations for a contemporary audience. As Paulson observes, "Napoleon was associated with Prometheus by Byron and his own propaganda machine."[10] Victor's pursuit of the monster across Russia, as "the snows thickened, and the cold increased in a degree almost too severe to support" (227; vol. 3, chap. 7), would recall for readers in 1818 the Napoleonic army's desperate retreat from Moscow by a northern route as a severe early winter began in November 1812: "The Russian winter, which began on the 7th with deep snow, greatly added to their difficulties and sufferings, and their bulletins acknowledge the loss of many men by cold and fatigue in their night bivouackings." Victor, like the Grand Army, forages for food, and lacks the Russian natives' ability to endure the temperature: "amidst cold that few of the inhabitants could long endure, and which I, the native of a genial and sunny climate, could not hope to survive" (228; vol. 3, chap. 7). The "sledge" (57; vol. 1, letter 4), chosen by Victor and later by the monster for transportation (228; vol. 3, chap. 7), repeats the vehicle reportedly used by Napoleon when he left his army in Russia and headed secretly back to Paris: he "set off in a single sledge under the title of the Duke of Vicenze."[11]

The French army was never trapped amidst ice floes in the Arctic like Victor, his creature, and the men on Walton's ship. But the atmosphere of baffled movement, wintry disorientation, and despair which envelops the novel's characters is a figurative counterpart to the plight of Napoleon's retreating forces. A celebrated account of the latter, published in France in 1824, supports the connection. The Count de Ségur, Napoleon's Quartermaster-General on the Russian Campaign of 1812, invokes the metaphor of a ship on a sea of ice to describe the French decision to throw into a Russian lake the trophies of the conquest of Moscow: "There was no longer any question of adorning or embellishing our lives, but merely of saving them. In this shipwreck, the army, like a great vessel tossed by the most violent storm, was throwing overboard on a sea of ice and snow everything that might encumber it or delay its progress."[12] Although Mary Shelley could not have read Ségur when she wrote the 1818 *Frankenstein*, she and the Count were drawn to similar symbolic seascapes to represent the same momentous historical events.

Against the novel's final setting of Northern ice, one contrasting image has striking force: the monster's planned suicide by fire on the book's final two pages. The comparable historical image is the burning of Moscow by the Russians, as the Napoleonic army prepared to settle into it for winter quarters.[13] The monster's announced motive—that his "remains may afford no light to any curious and unhallowed wretch, who would create such another as I have been" (243; vol. 3, chap. 7)—resembles the Russian action insofar as it immolates something priceless of one's own to deny use of it to another. The novel is not proposing that the monster represents the anti-Napoleonic forces of the Czar. Rather, the creature's trajectory from birth in Ingolstadt to death by fire, amidst Northern ice, is a figure for the history of the French Revolution. Not only Napoleon's victorious career, but also the revolutionary age itself seemed to have met its fatal blow in the flames of Moscow and the consequent retreat. With the Grand Army now severely reduced in size and morale, Napoleon's days were numbered. His message in this period was the same as the monster's inscription on trees and stone: "My reign is not yet over" (226; vol. 3, chap. 7). But for the Emperor of the French, the end was in sight. The dominant powers, which had assembled at the Congress of Vienna, sought to convince the world that the French Revolution itself was now finally over.

But was it? In the novel's last line, the monster is "lost in darkness and distance," producing a sense of obscurity and open possibility, rather than certainty. The monster's inscription echoes beyond Napoleon's fate to suggest the possible return of revolutionary violence. The novel uses the idea of a recently completed French revolutionary history as a point of departure for a sustained confrontation with the international legacy of revolution, including its promise, its violence, its possible continuance, and its geographical emplacement.

II. GENEVA

For the Byron-Shelley circle, Geneva was above all the city of Jean-Jacques Rousseau, the deeply flawed but uniquely prophetic and instigative intellectual father of the French Revolution. During the sojourn of Lord Byron, Mary Shelley, and Percy Shelley there in 1816, they read and wrote about him extensively. Geneva was also the site of actual revolutionary events in both 1768 and 1794. Mary's three and a half months in and near the city gave her an incentive to read about its history and an opportunity to draw upon the living memory of natives and long-time residents. *Frankenstein* puts this geographically specific material to use.

Frankenstein's monster commits his first murder—the killing of Victor's youngest brother, William—just outside the ramparts of Geneva in Plainpalais (98–99, 102–3; vol. 1, chap. 6), to which Mary had attributed political significance in *History of a Six Weeks' Tour*:

To the south of the town is the promenade of the Genevese, a
grassy plain planted with a few trees, and called Plainpalais. Here
a small obelisk is erected to the glory of Rousseau, and here (such
is the mutability of human life) the magistrates, the successors of
those who exiled him from his native country, were shot by the
populace during that revolution, which his writings mainly
contributed to mature, and which, notwithstanding the
temporary bloodshed and injustice with which it was polluted,
has produced enduring benefits to mankind, which all the
chicanery of statesmen, nor even the great conspiracy of kings,
can entirely render vain. From respect to the memory of their
predecessors, none of the present magistrates ever walk in
Plainpalais.[14]

Both Frankenstein's creature and revolution engage in "temporary
bloodshed and injustice," which readily invite a response of wholesale
condemnation. That is precisely the response given to the Genevese political
executions in the source most readily available to an English reader of the
early nineteenth century: Francis d'Ivernois's *A Short Account of the Late
Revolution in Geneva*.[15] Ivernois, like Barruel, was an emigré who had settled
in England, but unlike the Abbé, he had credentials as a political moderate:
a supporter of the Genevese revolutionary settlement of 1768, he was the
principal historian of that earlier revolution, in which his father had been a
major participant. In an emigré society of monarchists, the younger Ivernois
was a republican who supported a somewhat extended franchise, but he
thought universal suffrage inevitably caused mob rule. He was entrusted by
the Genevese government with negotiating a treaty with France, when
Geneva was under siege by a French army in 1792. In July 1794, while
Maximilien Robespierre was at his height of power, an uprising occurred in
Geneva, instigated partly by France and partly by disenfranchised residents
of the city-state. A Revolutionary Tribunal now preempted the constitutional
government. Under the influence of intimidation by "the savage multitude,"
and without credible judicial proceedings or evidence of violation of law,
according to Ivernois, the Tribunal executed eleven persons, including at
least four magistrates, two of whom were ex-syndics or presidents of Geneva.
Ivernois sums up these events—including the executions which Mary Shelley
links to Plainpalais and to William's murder—as a "work of horror" or
"horrors."[16] Mary Shelley, whose only son at the time was also a child named
William, registers the horror; in that sense, she is no apologist for murder.
But she refuses to demonize the revolution or the monster: the first, she

claims "has brought enduring benefits to mankind," and the second, she gives a sympathetic hearing on the basis of Rousseau's revolutionary philosophy.

Plainpalais is the site of a monument to "the glory of Rousseau," whose "writings mainly contributed to mature" the revolution of France as well as Geneva. By locating the novel's first murder at a spot consecrated to the memory of the prophet of revolution, situated just outside the city where he was born and bearing its own history of revolutionary bloodshed, Mary Shelley establishes an equation between the monster's murders and revolutionary violence. Although some recent critics position this novel in a conservative direction, her explicit ruminations about Plainpalais suggest otherwise.[17] *Frankenstein* itself is sympathetic to the monster of revolution and, as David Marshall and James O'Rourke have shown, is pervaded by the philosophy and literary precedent of Rousseau.[18] Even the murder of the child William is seen through a largely Rousseauvian lens. Following the Genevese philosopher's revolutionary premise, that all human beings are naturally good, Mary Shelley claims that the monster is naturally good as well, but society has imposed its evil ways upon him.[19] As in Rousseau's state of nature, the creature's first feeling toward others is pity: he stops stealing food from the De Laceys "when I found that by doing this I inflicted pain on the cottagers," and he gathers wood for their fire to save them labor (137; vol. 2, chap. 4). When his first effort to tell his story is brought to a traumatic end with an unmerited beating by Felix De Lacey, he refrains from striking back though "I could have torn him limb from limb" (160; vol. 2, chap. 7). He saves the life of a "young girl" who has fallen into a stream, only to be shot by her male companion (165; vol. 2, chap. 8). Biased people torment him solely because of his appearance, but he has still not harmed or sought to harm any of them, and he yearns for acceptance in some kind of social unit. He concludes that his only chance for a friend is to talk to a child who is "unprejudiced" because society has not yet corrupted him (166; vol. 2, chap. 8). Young William, however, turns out to be already the product of an artificial and malignant society: he labels the creature with visual stereotypes—"monster," "ugly wretch," and "ogre"—and pulls social rank upon him by insisting that his father is "a Syndic" (167; vol. 2, chap. 8). The creature is finally stained by the social evil that already infects William. By killing the boy, he shows the extremity of social wrong that surrounds him, and he illustrates the need in the novel's implied system of values for profound social and political change, in the direction of greater inclusiveness. But he never ceases to have a core of natural goodness, as his final remarks about his persistent craving for "love and fellowship" attest (243).

Before committing his first murder, the creature resorts on one occasion to violence of a lesser kind. When he learns that he will never get a second chance to try to gain the friendship of the De Laceys because they have permanently abandoned the cottage in fright, he burns the unoccupied structure down at night (163; vol. 2, chap. 8). This episode bears a striking resemblance to a famous event in the revolutionary history of Geneva. In January 1768 the city faced a constitutional crisis, as the patricians who controlled the Small Council were locked in dispute with the General Council of Burghers about the respective rights of each body and how restrictively citizenship should be defined. One night a public building burned to the ground, and it was believed by many that the burgher faction set the fire. The patricians agreed to a major constitutional compromise, which secured the public peace. The incinerated structure was a theater built by the patricians in defiance of the burghers' view, articulated by Rousseau in his *Letter to M. d'Alembert on the Theatre* (1758), that such an institution would corrupt Geneva's republican manners and morals with aristocratic decadence.[20] The first revolution in the post-Enlightenment West—and the first to bear the imprint of Rousseau—had, as one of its central events, a nighttime conflagration similar to that which Mary Shelley uses as the first act of violence by a Genevese thinker's creation.[21] A happy outcome followed in the city-state in 1768: patrician accommodation and a more inclusive political order, which lasted until royalist France imposed the reactionary Black Code on Geneva in 1782. In *Frankenstein*, on the other hand, continued rejectionism and exclusion make bloodshed inevitable.

William's death is followed by another: the authorities in Geneva execute the innocent servant, Justine Moritz, for the crime. This fictional miscarriage of justice is rooted in Genevese political history. The revolutionary executions in Geneva in the summer of 1794 had been swiftly followed by Robespierre's fall and execution, and the Thermidorean Reaction in Paris. Geneva too recoiled against radical excesses and sought scapegoats. Six weeks after Jacobinism seemed triumphant in Geneva, a reactivated Revolutionary Tribunal condemned four members of the radical Mountaineer faction to death although, according to Ivernois, "no positive evidence was adduced" to support the charges, and testimony was introduced implicating the judges in the crimes for which they condemned the defendants.[22] As in Justine's wrongful execution, the institutional punishment for one fatal crime becomes another murder.

The only observer who behaves creditably at Justine's trial is Elizabeth Lavenza. While Victor Frankenstein remains silent, despite his knowledge of who killed William and his own responsibility for making that creature what he is, Elizabeth speaks eloquently in defense of Justine's character. But her testimony fails to overcome the "public indignation" against the defendant (111; vol. 1, chap. 7), and the guilty verdict follows. There is a precedent for this combination of male silence and admirable, though futile, female intervention amidst popular frenzy. Ivernois's account of the history of Geneva in the summer of 1794 includes this memorable episode:

> One generous effort, indeed, was made by the women of Geneva (for the experiment was too hazardous for men to engage in), who, to the number of two thousand, went in a body to the Revolutionary Tribunal, to intercede for them ["the unhappy victims"]; but their tears and entreaties had no other effect, than that of exposing them to the brutal ridicule of the Judges, who ordered the fire-engines to be got ready, in order to administer what they profanely called, the rights [sic] of *Civic Baptism*.

Elizabeth speaks not merely for herself in Mary Shelley's book, but for a multitude of women who, in recent Genevese history, had bravely sought to inject generosity into a dehumanized political context—and who had been spurned for their efforts.

Justine's execution is, in one sense, highly untypical of Geneva's experience in 1794. Ivernois contrasts France's conduct with his own city's:

> In one point indeed, and in one point only, the *French* are still without a rival; for out of no less than 508 persons, on whom different sentences were passed, on the late occasion, there was but *one* Woman, who was condemned to be imprisoned for life, for having given assistance, and forwarded letters, to some *French* Emigrants; and it is more than probable, that even this sentence was obtained by the influence and intrigues of the *French* Resident.[23]

The murdered females of *Frankenstein*, to the extent that they represent revolutionary executions of women, point to French rather than Genevese political history. Yet Geneva does not escape responsibility since its native son, Rousseau, hovers over French as well as Genevese practice, as the monster's involvement with Justine's death reveals. He admits planting on the sleeping young woman the incriminating evidence—a necklace taken from William's body—that led to her conviction (168; vol. 2, chap. 8). But he echoes Rousseau's explanation of evil by shifting the blame onto society. It had deprived him of the love of women, such as Justine, because of his appearance, and through the "lessons of Felix, and the sanguinary laws of man," it had taught him "how to work mischief" (168; vol. 2, chap. 8). Rousseau not only provides a philosophical defense, but a specific precedent for the monster's deed. When Rousseau was about nineteen years of age, he stole a pink and silver ribbon and blamed an honest, young female servant named Marion for the theft. His accusation, he believes in retrospect, probably prevented her from finding another situation, and betrayed her into a life of misery and friendlessness.[24] In occupation, gender, innocence, and unjust fate, Justine is Marion's mirror image. Rousseau professes excruciating remorse for this deed, as does Victor for his silence, but remorse fails to help the two young women. The legacy of Rousseau, including the treatment of women and the sidestepping of personal responsibility, is as Janus-faced and problematic for Mary Shelley, as it had been for her mother in *Vindication of the Rights of Woman*. She is much indebted to the Genevese thinker, but she seeks a more balanced and inclusive way to rectify the social wrongs that he exposes.

The last murder to occur in Geneva or its environs is that of Alphonse Frankenstein, Victor's father. He dies of an apoplectic fit, brought on by grief shortly after learning of Elizabeth's murder (220; vol. 3, chap. 6). From the point of view of political geography, the two most important things about him are, first, that he was a syndic, as William tells the monster just before his own murder (167; vol. 2, chap. 8) and, second, that his death is the indirect result of the monster's killing. Syndics were not merely high public officials, but chief executives, the apex of political authority in Geneva. Two of those executed by order of the Revolutionary Tribunal in the summer of 1794 were ex-syndics, like Alphonse, who has long since withdrawn from public life. To kill a syndic was the closest the republic of Geneva could get to the traditionally most horrendous crime of regicide, the act taken by the French National Convention in January 1793. Alphonse's death in *Frankenstein* carries some of the traditional aura of a *ne plus ultra* insofar as it is a culmination of a relentlessly murderous logic, which carries us through a sequence of victims, beginning with "W" (William) and ending with "A" (Alphonse) in consistent reverse alphabetical order.[25] But the novel rejects both the traditionalist view that killing the king is the ultimate crime and the radical view that regicide is a major ingredient in achieving a just society. Alphonse's end is anticlimactic, briefly told, and lacking in the emotional force and impact on the narrative of all the other monster-caused deaths in the book. Mary Shelley rejects the hierarchical premise that society's happiness depends chiefly on the presence or absence of a king, president, or syndic. She substitutes a more egalitarian model, in which the fate of a child, a servant, or a spouse may be at least as influential.

In the lives of the novel's major characters, the natural death of Caroline Beaufort Frankenstein, Victor's mother, just outside Geneva is more consequential than the death of his father. It helps motivate Victor to master the boundary between life and death by creating the monster, and, by a dream-logic that supplements the literal narrative, it becomes the book's first murder. Victor eliminates the role of the mother in the birth which he causes in his laboratory, and immediately afterwards—as if reaping the consequences—dreams of holding his own mother's corpse in his arms (85; vol. 1, chap. 4). She had died of scarlet fever in the same chapter as, and just one paragraph before, he left home to study in an all-male environment in Ingolstadt (72–73; vol. 1, chap. 2). The demarcation of this chapter so that these two events constitute a unified textual space implies an equation between them: his abandoning female companionship and input at this point is tantamount to killing her. It is the erasure of the mother, not the killing of the father/ruler, which plunges the world of *Frankenstein* into catastrophe. The prototype behind this entire process is the death of one's mother after, but in a sense because of, one's own birth—an experience that happened first to Rousseau in Geneva, and later to Mary Shelley in London. These events left the surviving offspring in situations fraught with a potential for matricidal guilt. Mary Shelley responded by foregrounding the positive value of the maternal role and striving intensely throughout her life to be the kind of mother her mother wanted to be. Rousseau and Victor, by the implied value system of this novel, exacerbated their guilt: Rousseau by taking his five newborn children from their mother and abandoning them to the Foundling Hospital; Victor, his fictional counterpart, by not only eliminating the role of the mother from the birthing process, but also by repeatedly abandoning the offspring.[26] Geneva's eighteenth-century political prophet, from the point of view of *Frankenstein*, has been the source for all of Europe of a salutary revolutionary inspiration—and of a model of society that reinforces longstanding gender-based and dehumanizing suppressions and exclusions.

III. ENGLAND AND SCOTLAND

Victor Frankenstein's "many months" (192; vol. 3, chap. 3) or "nearly a year" (194; vol. 3, chap. 3) in England and Scotland, while shadowed by the monster, are seemingly a respite from murder. Yet Victor agonizes over his fatal past and possible future, mulls over the seventeenth-century killings of King Charles I, Lord Viscount Falkland, and John Hampden (184–85; vol. 3, chap. 2), and physically destroys the female creature that he was laboring to complete on one of the Orkney Islands. The stay in Britain puts special emphasis on the role of the author's country in the development—and retardation—of modern revolutionary thought and practice.

Victor's visit is partly a representation of transnational influences and misunderstandings, in the development of subversive thinking in Europe during the eighteenth century. After promising to make a female mate for the monster, Victor visits England in order to tap the knowledge of "the most distinguished natural philosophers" (183; vol. 3, chap. 2). At this stage, Victor reenacts the French Enlightenment's indebtedness to English science and politics, especially Voltaire's stay in England from 1726 to 1728, which resulted in his *Lettres Philosophiques* (1734), where the celebration of Sir Isaac Newton, John Locke, and English liberty was used to criticize established French practices and institutions.[27]

But in London Victor swiftly finds "an insurmountable barrier placed between me and my fellow-men." His mental state becomes "sorrowful and dejected," afflicted by "extreme anguish" (183; vol. 3, chap. 2), "tormented" by thoughts of the monster's revengeful plots against him and his family, "guiltless" yet cursed (187; vol. 3, chap. 2). He journeys to Derbyshire (186; vol. 3, chap. 2), among other places, and responds to the hospitable invitations of a "person in Scotland" (184; vol. 3, chap. 2), a "Scotch friend" (186; vol. 3, chap. 2), with much less than "the good humor expected from a guest" (187; vol. 3, chap. 2). He craves solitude and eventually finds it on a remote and almost uninhabited island, where he can go about his work "ungazed at and unmolested" (188; vol. 3, chap. 2). In each of these instances, Victor relives Rousseau's tormented visit to England from 1766 to 1767. The latter had been invited by the cosmopolitan Scotsman, David Hume, and he stayed most of the time at a house in Wooton, Derbyshire, isolated from society. His mental condition was unstable, partly because he had been subjected to fierce personal attacks, public condemnations, outlawing, and even stoning on the continent, and he imagined plots by nearly everyone, including his friends, against him. He and Hume had a much publicized quarrel, as a result of mutual misunderstandings and Rousseau's frenzied and unfounded suspicions.[28] He fantasized about the period in 1765, when he withdrew from society to the Island of Saint-Pierre in the middle of Lake Bienne in the Neuchâtel region, as the happiest period in his life and celebrated it at length in his *Confessions* and *Reveries of the Solitary Walker*.[29] Rousseau's recoil against society is itself a form of identification with and adaptation of an English cultural model of individualism, pushed toward solipsism: in the *Confessions* he explicitly resolves to be another Robinson

Crusoe and, in the process, he alienates himself from his British hosts. He reveals what Mary Shelley would see as a defective grasp of human interdependence behind his—and his English prototype's— reconceptualizations of politics and society.

Victor's stay in Oxford constitutes a meditation on English revolutionary history, from the point of view of a narrator who is himself subject to the author's criticism. He lingers nostalgically over the "spirit of elder days" in the Oxford of Charles I and his beleaguered royalist forces and followers, between 1642 and 1645: "This city had remained faithful to him, after the whole nation had forsaken his cause to join the standard of parliament and liberty." The beheading of "that unfortunate king" in January 1649 is the imminent event that looms over an Oxford of "peculiar interest" (184; vol. 3, chap. 2) to Victor, as he reconstructs it. He finds in the king's environment a mirror of his own mood of anxious waiting for an inevitable catastrophe. Instead of drawing practical lessons for himself about what might have been—and what might be—done differently to minimize bloodshed, as Mary Shelley's royalist source, Edward Hyde, Earl of Clarendon's *History of the Rebellion*, attempts often to do, he aestheticizes the scene, making its "ancient and picturesque" college buildings and their "lovely" (185; vol. 3, chap. 2) natural setting into a still visible correlative for an irremediably doomed circle. Victor's naming of "the amiable Falkland" and "the insolent Goring" (184; vol. 3, chap. 2) on the royalist side implies a large moral spectrum within that faction, with much unintended reference to his own ambiguous moral personality. Clarendon, whose history Mary Shelley referred to unmistakably in her manuscript version of the Oxford passage, had vividly portrayed Lucius Cary, Viscount Falkland's brilliance, idealism, absolute integrity, and courage in the years up to his death in battle, as well as George, Lord Goring's irresponsibility, treachery, and insolence, ending in his ignominious desertion and flight.[30] But, from Mary Shelley's point of view, neither character represents a viable option, granted the historical transformation occurring in his time. Both are stuck within too many of the assumptions of a no longer viable, absolutist order. Victor's romantic antiquarianism and morally equivocal life-history replicate what the duo jointly exemplify. The British section of *Frankenstein* faults the monster's creator and recent British society, not for excessive radicalism but for not being radical enough.

Before leaving the Oxford area, Victor sees another spot sacred to English Civil War history, but this one is potentially exemplary for his own life:

We visited the tomb of the illustrious Hampden, and the field on which that patriot fell. For a moment my soul was elevated from its debasing and miserable fears to contemplate the divine ideas of liberty and self-sacrifice, of which these sights were the monuments and the remembrancers. For an instant I dared to shake off my chains, and look around me with a free and lofty spirit; but the iron had eaten into my flesh, and I sank again, trembling and hopeless, into my miserable self. (185; vol. 3, chap. 2)

For the only time in Britain, Victor here experiences the possibility of liberation. Mary Shelley relies on Clarendon's character sketch of John Hampden but not his underlying evaluation of the man. Clarendon pays eloquent tribute to Hampden's reputation for probity and courage, his sagacity and yet modesty in debate, and his unique rapport with the people of England: "He was indeed a very wise man, and of great parts, and possessed with the most absolute spirit of popularity, that is, the most absolute faculties to govern the people, of any man I ever knew." But as an opponent of the radical parliamentary Independent group, in which Hampden was (with John Pym) a co-leader, Clarendon thinks him a subtle deceiver, pretending moderation but instigating root and branch extremism behind the scenes: "he had a head to contrive, and a tongue to persuade, and a hand to execute, any mischieve."[31]

For Mary Shelley, as for her father and husband, Hampden was the supreme English model of political leadership. William Godwin, in his *History of the Commonwealth* published six years later, would treat him as the greatest hero of his period and "one of the most extraordinary men in the records of mankind."[32] Percy Shelley, in his "Philosophical View of Reform," would rank Hampden as one of the four greatest Englishmen of all time, the only one not a major writer.[33] Unlike Charles I, Falkland, and Goring, he had a profound sense of his historical moment, and of the possibilities and promise of radical change. In contrast to Rousseau and Victor, he had a firm grasp of social and political reality, and an unbroken bond with the people. In contrast with Rousseau and Victor, whose irresponsibility toward their offspring is notorious, he was thought so suitable a mentor for a young person that he was proposed by the parliamentary forces as a tutor for the Prince of Wales (later, Charles II), then ten years old—a window on Hampden's remarkable character that Godwin will emphasize.[34] Hampden first came to public notice by defying an absolutist monarchy and refusing to pay thirty shillings for a tax, imposed by the king without the consent of parliament. He died courageously in battle against a royalist army in 1643 before having an opportunity to participate in the execution of the king.[35] He is *Frankenstein's* ideal male revolutionary.

Mary composed the passage about him in October 1817, when she visited his monument in the church at Great Hampden, Buckinghamshire, with her father.[36] In the England of 1817, Hampden was not merely a subject of antiquarian interest. The principal vehicle of organized popular agitation for parliamentary reform and working people's economic relief was the Hampden Clubs, named after the seventeenth-century parliamentary leader and founded by Major John Cartwright in 1812. The first national meeting of Hampden Club delegates was held in London in January 1817, and it was linked to the presentation of a petition, signed by a half million to a million and a half persons, calling for annual parliaments, universal manhood suffrage, and vote by ballot.[37] Percy recalls the episode vividly in "A Philosophical View of Reform": "The people were then insulted, tempted, and betrayed, and *the petitions of a million* of men rejected with disdain." Like the monster addressing Victor for the first time in the Alps earlier in the book, these people craved a hearing.[38] In February and March repressive legislation, including the Seditious Meetings Act and the suspension of *Habeas Corpus*, drove the reform movement underground and crushed the Hampden Clubs. The trip to Greater Hampden by Mary Shelley and her father and the insertion of a paragraph celebrating Hampden into the novel was, in late 1817, a political act implying just the reverse of the conservatism now sometimes attributed to *Frankenstein*.

But Victor cannot sustain his momentary identification with the Hampden model; by the end of the paragraph he relapses into a politically passive pathology. He is still in such a state when he happens upon the Lake Poets in Cumberland and Westmoreland, "men of talent" "who almost contrived to cheat me into happiness" (186; vol. 3, chap. 2). These influential British intellectuals figure as male sirens who lure people away from decisive political engagement. It will take more than aesthetic pleasure, according to Mary Shelley's pointed (but reductive) put-down, to break out of the chains.

On "one of the remotest" Orkney Islands in Scotland, Victor will learn that the monster has secretly accompanied him throughout his travels in Britain (188; vol. 3, chap. 2). Yet the monster has killed no one during this period. This interruption of bloodshed has two distinct referents. If the excluded and oppressed believe their problems are being seriously addressed, as the monster does while Victor works on making a female creature, they will feel no need for violence: this is an argument for political and social reformation, an expression of hope. On the other hand, the remission of killing points to a historical reality: revolution never happened in Britain in the 1790s. There were no executions by revolutionary tribunals, but neither did significant progressive change occur in Britain during this period. The country lurched into reaction and repression. Ultimately, in the book's narrative, what gets killed is the female creature. The explanation for why and how she dies is rooted in the political geography of England and Scotland in this novel.

Victor makes his decision to kill her, while suffering the pathological effects of the island existence celebrated by Defoe and Rousseau. His "solitude" (188, 189; vol. 3, chap. 2) is not just a matter of miles from population centers. He is psychologically remote from the few impoverished inhabitants of the island, whose misery facilitates his isolation by numbing their awareness. He sinks into anxiety, speaking repeatedly of his fear. He will soon let his boat drift at sea, like Rousseau on the lake surrounding his island.[39] He stifles the compassion which had once made him agree to provide the monster with a female companion. In this state, his reasoning is as unbalanced as his emotions.

His analysis of the possible catastrophic consequences of letting loose a female monster on the world depends on two fallacious premises: that a creature's appearance is an accurate indicator of his or her moral state, and that both male and female monsters can be expected to be "malignant" (190; vol. 3, chap. 3) and "wicked" (192; vol. 3, chap. 3). While the monster's earlier narrative had shown him to be naturally good but forced into crime by a biased and exclusionary society, Victor now assumes, in opposition to Rousseau, that both creatures must be naturally depraved. To prevent "terror" (190; vol. 3, chap. 3), he, therefore, reinforces the mistreatment that drove the monster into crime in the first place. By couching his uncompromising rejectionism in the vocabulary of high-minded altruism toward fixture generations, he reverts to the historically obtuse posture of saintly absolutism taken by Charles I. Like Goring, he is a treacherous and insolent promise-breaker. He fails to measure up to Hampden's precedent of adopting new insights and placing himself in the vanguard of history.

By tearing up the female creature, Victor kills society's best hope for deliverance. In Mary Shelley's fiction, she holds the potential of restoring human balance to an all male social formation, by substituting love and caring for repulsion and irresponsibility. She offers human connectedness in place of island disjunction. Her prototype is the author's mother, Mary Wollstonecraft, whose version of revolutionary ideology, in her daughter's estimation, was the best of what Britain had to offer during the 1790s.

Wollstonecraft was sensitive to the wrongs suffered by people excluded from social acceptance and political voice, by reason of gender and class, while also affirming and practicing the nurturing processes that Victor and Rousseau conspicuously failed to cultivate. The description of the female creature's murder reenacts in displaced and inverted form the circumstances of Mary Wollstonecraft's death, shortly after her daughter's birth. Instead of a physician unsuccessfully picking the pieces of a retained placenta out of the birth canal, as occurred after Mary Shelley's birth, Victor dismembers the yet uncompleted female creature and drops the pieces into the sea.[40] As we read the account in the novel, the grown-up offspring of that 1797 birth is telling the horrific story of a quasi-abortion in which her mother was aborted. The agonizing nature of the event has personal roots, but it affects an entire civilization.

When Victor places the "relics" (194; vol. 3, chap. 3) of the riven female form into "a basket," "cast" it into the sea, and "listened to the gurgling sound as it sunk, and then sailed away from the spot" (195; vol. 3, chap. 3), he is enacting a nightmare transformation of what Moses's mother did with him when he was three months old: "And when she could not longer hide him, she took for him an ark of bulrushes, and daubed it with slime and with pitch, and put the child therein; and she laid it in the flags by the river's brink." Unlike Victor, she carefully sealed up the container to keep the water out and placed it near the edge of a river where it would be likely to be found. The Pharaoh's daughter found the child, "had compassion on him," and named him Moses "[b]ecause I drew him out of the water."[41] Victor, lacking such compassion, does precisely the reverse. In the Bible, Moses would lead his people out of bondage. In *Frankenstein*, the female creature had the same potential for liberating a society. Her ending recalls not only Mary Wollstonecraft's catastrophic demise in her most productive years, but also the near simultaneous destruction of her reputation and the elimination from public discourse in Britain of the point of view which she championed. The silencing of her emancipatory voice has, in Mary Shelley's estimate, been climactic in a series of obstructions and choices which have prevented Britain, despite its seventeenth-century revolutionary legacy, from exerting a decisive positive role in the era of the French Revolution.

IV. IRELAND

Just after the novel's treatment of an event of 1797, the monster murders Victor's friend, Henry Clerval, in Ireland. This outbreak of violence is Mary Shelley's representation of the bloody Irish rebellion of May to September

1798. Unique among the important settings in *Frankenstein*, Ireland is not chosen by Victor: a storm drives him there at night, and he assumes when he lands that he is still in England or Scotland. His first human encounter forces him abruptly to change his premises:

> "Why do you answer me so roughly?" I replied: "surely it is not the custom of Englishmen to receive strangers so inhospitably."
> "I do not know," said the man, "what the custom of the English may be; but it is the custom of the Irish to hate villains." (197; vol. 3, chap. 3)

In this exchange, the book posits a new sense of culture clash; previous transitions from Bavaria to Geneva to Britain lacked this sharply contrastive rhetoric. Upon seeing Henry's corpse, Victor is startled to learn that the monster's murderousness—and his own unwitting causality—have reached in an unexpected direction: "Have my murderous machinations deprived you also, my dearest Henry, of life?" (200; vol. 3, chap. 4). The question points, on one level, to historical fact. The most likely landing-places for Victor's boat are Northern Ireland or County Mayo: he is blown to the Irish coast from the Orkneys by a high northeast wind (196; vol. 3, chap. 3), which becomes a "strong northerly blast" (198–99; vol. 3, chap. 4). If he lands in Ulster, his trip points to the role of the United Irishmen in preparing Ireland for revolution. Founded in Belfast, but extending their influence during the next few years over much of Ireland, the United Irishmen distributed selected writings by such authors as Locke, Voltaire, Rousseau, Constantin-François de Chasseboeuf, comte de Volney, Godwin, and Thomas Paine to a wide Irish readership.[42] Victor now resembles the European intellectuals who flirted with or actively promoted radical ideas at home, but were aghast when overseas colonies chose to apply Enlightenment notions of human rights to their own condition. Revolutionary leaders in France, for example, recoiled against the revolutionary aspirations of black slaves in Haiti.[43] The alternate likely landing point for Victor's boat is the Killala region of Mayo, where French forces landed in 1798 to give military support to the Irish rebellion and were ultimately defeated.[44] Most English admirers of Locke, Godwin, and Paine drew back from supporting a French invasion coupled with an Irish rebellion. Murder in Ireland, therefore, adds to *Frankenstein* the reminder and prospect of revolutions and imperial conflicts multiplying throughout the empires of Britain and other European powers. Imperialism and philosophies of popular sovereignty were an explosive mix. Clerval's death extends the book's implied political geography of horror to Asia,

Africa, and the Americas, as well as to the rebellious subjugated people across the Irish Sea.[45]

Conservative Victorian Englishmen regularly turned the monster of *Frankenstein* into a patronizing figure for troubles in Ireland.[46] But it is not generally recognized that the monster, as originally conceived by Mary Shelley, already included Irishness in his hybrid composition. An earlier text resonates behind the creature's first self-initiated action in the novel:

> He held up the curtain of the bed; and his eyes, if eyes they may be called, were fixed on me. His jaws opened, and he muttered some inarticulate sounds, while a grin wrinkled his cheeks. He might have spoken, but I did not hear; one hand was stretched out, seemingly to detain me, but I escaped, and rushed down stairs. (86; vol. 1, chap. 4)

Compare Gulliver's first personal encounter with a Yahoo:

> The ugly Monster, when he saw me, distorted several Ways every Feature of his Visage, and stared as at an Object he had never seen before; then approaching nearer, lifted up his fore Paw, whether out of Curiosity or Mischief, I could not tell: But I drew my Hanger, and gave him a good Blow with the flat Side of it.[47]

Jonathan Swift and Mary Shelley tell of a monster who gestures to signal a wish for friendship, but gets contemptuously rebuffed by the title character. Gulliver will accurately read the extended hand or foreleg as a token of friendship when the dominant Houyhnhnms employ it, or when he uses it himself.[48] The Yahoo's "distorted" face, in this light, may be as much a "grin" as the facial expression on Frankenstein's creature. But Gulliver fails to penetrate cultural differences far enough to translate the body language of the Yahoos reliably or to see their positive humanity. Swift's characterization of these savage creatures was in part his own conflicted representation of the indigenous Irish population that he lived among, condescended to, and courageously defended.[49] As in *Frankenstein*, a refusal of sympathy toward a friendly monster provokes a hostility, which is social and political as well as individual. Where Swift writes of a mob of Yahoos gathering around Gulliver, climbing a tree above him, and discharging their excrement on his head, Mary Shelley imagines a murder which recalls a widespread rebellion.

She alludes to, but rises above, then current English stereotypes about Ireland. The book's first sentence about the place is a concentrated example of a process that will recur during Victor's two months there: "It had a wild and rocky appearance; but as I approached nearer, I easily perceived the traces of cultivation" (196; vol. 3, chap. 3). First impressions focus on "rude" (197, 201; vol. 3, chap. 3, 4) appearances and behavior, "frowning and angry countenances," "ill-looking" faces (197; vol. 3, chap. 3), the look of "brutality" (202; vol. 3, chap. 4). In the most influential account of the 1798 Irish rebellion available to Mary Shelley, the loyalist Sir Richard Musgrave explains that "[i]t was a peculiar favour from heaven to send a civilized people," that is, the English, among the Irish to govern them and thus save them from their "savage," "ignorant and bigoted" ways.[50] A recent historian sums up Musgrave's epithets characterizing the uprising: "Musgrave's aim was ... to paint the rebels in the most unflattering light possible. Terms like 'rabble', 'barbarous', 'ignorant', 'fanatic', 'horrid', 'cruel', and 'vulgar' pepper his descriptions of the United Irishmen and especially their Catholic manifestations."[51] Mary Shelley, however, keeps speaking of a quite different Ireland, evident on closer examination. Victor's initial hostile reception and the witnesses' testimony supporting his arrest turn out to be reasonable human responses to the available information. The Irish magistrate's persistent quest for the facts and his concern for Victor's well-being lead the latter to revise his first impressions of the inhabitants: "These were my first reflections; but I soon learned that Mr. Kirwin had shewn me extreme kindness" (202; vol. 3, chap. 4). It is significant that the magistrate's surname is neither English nor Scottish, but unambiguously Irish.[52] Mary Shelley temporarily posits, then decisively discredits, the stereotypes about the Irish that supported England's colonial dominance. The novel's treatment of Ireland, like its treatment of other places and the monster himself, suggests that violent revolution can best be averted by recognizing the humanity of stereotyped groups, hearing their complaints, and genuinely addressing their grievances.

V. EVIAN

The last of the direct homicides in the novel is the monster's strangulation of Elizabeth Lavenza Frankenstein at Evian, on the night of her wedding to Victor (214–18; vol. 3, chap. 5, 6). The place is a short boat trip from the wedding site at Geneva, but so are other lakeside retreats. Why the murder occurs at Evian, rather than elsewhere, is a function of political geography. Percy Shelley provides the essential gloss in one of his sections of *History of a Six Weeks' Tour*, the collaborative project with Mary published just before *Frankenstein*: "The appearance of the inhabitants of Evian is more wretched, diseased and poor, than I ever recollect to have seen. The contrast indeed between the subjects of the King of Sardinia and the citizens of the independent republics of Switzerland, affords a powerful illustration of the blighting mischiefs of despotism, within the space of a few miles."[53]

The King of Sardinia was the title held since 1720 by the ruling member of the House of Savoy, and, as a result, Savoy itself had come to be called Sardinia. By introducing Sardinian or Savoyard Evian into the narrative, Mary Shelley is establishing an implicit contrast with one of the "independent republics of Switzerland," namely Geneva. The latter had won its independence from the duke and bishop of the House of Savoy in the 1530s and declared itself Protestant in reaction against Catholic Savoy in the same decade. In 1602 Geneva had victoriously repulsed a sneak attack by the Duke of Savoy's forces, who had placed their scaling ladders against the city walls. This event, called the "Escalade," is a much commemorated defining episode in the history of the republic. Geneva was admitted to the Swiss Confederation in 1814, just before Percy and Mary Shelley made literary and political use of a contrast between free Swiss Geneva and absolutist, Sardinian Evian.[54]

When *Frankenstein* was written and first published, the Sardinian regime was especially obnoxious to European liberals: King Victor Amadeus III had led a coalition of Italian rulers against the French Revolution in the 1790s, and after 1802, Victor Emmanuel I became a symbol of conservative resistance to Napoleon by holding out against the Emperor of the French on the island of Sardinia, where he was protected by the British fleet. He was a big winner at the Congress of Vienna, regaining Piedmont, Nice, and Savoy, including most of the south shore of Lake Geneva, and acquiring Genoa at the same time. He would rule autocratically, until a popular revolution forced him to abdicate in favor of his brother in 1821. For the Shelleys in 1816–1818 the Kingdom of Sardinia was a distillation of the most reactionary politics of the European Restoration.

Unlike the earlier murders in the novel, the killing of Elizabeth does not represent some past political execution or revolution. It is an image of an impending future. Revolution, from this point of view, looms within the most conservative European states: not only the Kingdom of Sardinia, but also Austria, Britain, Prussia, and Russia. Although the rulers do their best to keep their populations uninformed about or hostile to the ideas of Rousseau and other protorevolutionary thinkers, the novel suggests that a monster has been let loose which can never again be confined within any set spatial boundary. Although this vision is expressed through fictions of horror, it is not necessarily pessimistic. *Frankenstein*, like the novel incompletely named in Mary Shelley's dedication page to her father—*Things as They Are; or, The Adventures of Caleb Williams* (46)—traces the disastrous consequences of faulty political assumptions held by society as a whole. If those assumptions, "things as they are," can be peaceably changed and the pleas of the stereotyped and downtrodden can begin to be heard, revolutionary violence, according to Mary Shelley's novel, can be averted. As Percy Shelley would write, in his "Philosophical View of Reform," there are only two options for society in the post-Waterloo period: "Despotism" inevitably followed by "Revolution"; or else "Reform."[55]

By the time the second edition of *Frankenstein* is published in 1831, the rightist political meaning of "Evian" has been blurred by the 1821 uprising in Sardinia, and the resignation of an especially reactionary monarch. Yet the kingdom would not become even a constitutional monarchy until 1848. Mary Shelley now has seen firsthand the rising popular tide of Italian nationalism, which is directed not against Sardinia but against a more reactionary and unwanted regime—Austria. Accordingly, she supplies a new political emphasis surrounding Elizabeth's life and death, while leaving the murder itself at Evian. She cannot credibly transport the newlyweds to Austrian territory in the time required by the monster's threat—"*I shall be with you on your wedding-night*" (193; vol. 3, chap. 3)—granted that the wedding itself has to take place in Geneva, the home of Victor's father and the bride. In 1831, therefore, Mary gives Elizabeth origins in Austrian-controlled Lombardy and a honeymoon destination in the same area. Her father becomes an Italian nobleman from Milan who "exerted himself to obtain the liberty of his country." His fate points an accusatory finger towards the Hapsburg empire: "Whether he had died, or still lingered in the dungeons of Austria, was not known." Victor's mother finds the young child living with Italian peasants near Lake Como in Lombardy. As the wedding approaches, Victor's father persuades the Austrian government to restore to her a "part" of her confiscated "inheritance," a small villa on Lake Como, where the couple will go "immediately after our union," though "sleeping that night at Evian," in order to "spend our first days of happiness beside the beautiful lake near which it [the villa] stood."[56] The narrative and the lovers strain toward the idyllic Italian lake but find themselves trapped in a reality—Evian—that falls fatally short of such a recovery. The restoration of Italian liberty is the political prize that hovers just out of reach. In this seemingly temporary state of deprivation, murder, signifying revolution, erupts. The cautionary lesson is much the same as in 1818, but the narrative means have become more complex, as

Mary Shelley attempts to adjust her story to altering political realities. Alphonse Frankenstein's successful negotiation with the Austrians suggests a potential for nonviolent progress, but the novel implies that if change does not come very quickly, it will be too late to prevent catastrophe.

Frankenstein's selection and sequence of places represent the international and destabilizing phenomenon of spreading Enlightenment ideas and revolutionary impulses in the eighteenth and early nineteenth centuries. In contrast to Moretti's model of the solidification of the boundaries and structures of existing nation-states in the nineteenth-century European novel, Mary Shelley's book depicts forces that cannot be confined by the political control or geographic space of French or British power.[57] From initial plotting, at least in reactionary eyes, in Ingolstadt, Bavaria, and by a son of the independent city-state of Geneva, through early outbreaks in French-speaking Europe, with special emphasis on the Genevese manifestations, to abortive British attempts to develop the revolutionary tradition further, followed by a bloody and portentous uprising in the overseas colony of Ireland, to a threatening cataclysm within the homeland of the bulwarks of European reaction, the author systematically places her Gothic horrors within the geographical and political particularities of European and world history. Like Percy Shelley, she views revolutionary thinking and practice as an informed, critical observer and liberal sympathizer who wishes to prevent both continued injustice and revolutionary violence, by motivating readers to overcome their prejudices sufficiently to accept fundamental reform.

NOTES

1. Some important contributions to the large scholarly literature are: Lee Sterrenburg, "Mary Shelley's Monster: Politics and Psyche in *Frankenstein*," in *The Endurance of Frankenstein*, ed. George Levine and U. C. Knoepflmacher (Berkeley: Univ. of California Press, 1979), 143–71; Ronald Paulson, *Representations of Revolution (1789–1820)* (New Haven: Yale Univ. Press, 1983), 239–47; Paul O'Flinn, "Production and Reproduction: The Case of *Frankenstein*," *Literature and History* 9 (1983): 194–213; Mary Poovey, *The Proper Lady and the Woman Writer* (1984; reprint, Chicago: Univ. of Chicago Press, 1985), 114–42; Anne K. Mellor, *Mary Shelley: Her Life, Her Fiction, Her Monsters* (1988; reprint, New York: Routledge, 1989); Joseph W. Lew, "The Deceptive Other: Mary Shelley's Critique of Orientalism in *Frankenstein*," *Studies in Romanticism* 30 (1991): 255–83; H. L. Malchow, *Gothic Images of Race in Nineteenth-Century Britain* (Stanford: Stanford Univ. Press, 1996), 9–40; and Marilyn Butler's introduction to Mary Wollstonecraft Shelley's *Frankenstein or The Modern Prometheus: The 1818 Text* (Oxford: Oxford Univ. Press, 1994), ix–li.

2. Franco Moretti, *Atlas of the European Novel 1800–1900* (London: Verso, 1998), 70.

3. See Chris Baldick's introduction to *The Oxford Book of Gothic Tales* (Oxford: Oxford Univ. Press, 1992), xi–xxiii. See also Robert Mighall's introduction to *A Geography of Victorian Gothic Fiction: Mapping History's Nightmares* (Oxford: Oxford Univ. Press, 1999), xiv–xix, 1–26.

4. Mighall, 26, xx.

5. Paulson proposed that *Frankenstein* "was to some extent a retrospect on the whole process of maturation [of the revolutionary scenario] through Waterloo, with the Enlightenment-created monster leaving behind its wake of terror and destruction across France and Europe" (239), but he did not develop the implications of this insight for the novel's specific settings.

6. Sterrenburg, 155–57.

7. Abbé [Augustin] Barruel, *Memoirs Illustrating the History of Jacobinism*, trans. Robert Clifford, 2nd ed., 4 vols. (London, 1798), 3:2, 9–10, 15–16. Percy Bysshe Shelley used Clifford's translation of Barruel: his copy of the second volume is in the Berg Collection of the New York Public Library, as pointed out in the annotation to *The Journals of Mary Shelley 1814–1844*, ed. Paula R. Feldman and Diana Scott-Kilvert (1987; reprint, Baltimore: The Johns Hopkins Univ. Press, 1995), 18–19, where Mary's reading of Barruel is also recorded. M. W. Shelley, *Frankenstein; or, The Modern Prometheus*, ed. D. L. Macdonald and Kathleen Scherf, 2nd ed. (Peterborough, Ontario: Broadview Press, 1999), 81–82; vol. 1, ch. 3. Unless otherwise noted, all further citations will be of this edition of the 1815 version, and will hereafter be cited parenthetically by page number, followed by the volume and chapter numbers.

8. Barruel, 4:30 ("code"), 3:414 ("disastrous monster"; "days"), 4:2 ("The monster"). For an elaboration on the concept of "code of law," see Barruel 4:30–4:32. On Weishaupt's doable life, see Barruel, 4:22–23.

9. *Annual Register, or a View of the History, Politics, and Literature, For the Year 1812* (London, 1813), 173. I am indebted to Ray Garcia for his insight into the relevance of Napoleon's Russian Campaign to the ending of *Frankenstein*.

10. Paulson, 245.

11. *Annual Register, 1812*, 178 ("Russian winter"), 180 ("single sledge").

12. Philippe-Paul, Comte de Ségur, *La Campagne de Russie*, 2 vols. (Paris: Hachette, 1960), 2:116; Count Philippe-Paul de Ségur, *Napoleon's Russian Campaign*, trans. J. David Townsend (Cambridge, Mass.: Houghton Mifflin, 1958), 178–79.

13. Mellor suggests that "the creature's funeral pyre" refers to "the final coup de grâce of the French Revolution, Bonaparte's coup of 18–19 Brumaire (November 9–10, 1799)" (238). But *Frankenstein*'s detailed chronological focus on the personal and political events of the 1790s, which has been demonstrated by Mellor and Charles E. Robinson, is supplemented by its political geography, which extends the novel's time frame to, for example, events in Ingolstadt in 1776 and Russia in 1812. Incidents in this novel can have more than one chronological referent. Compare with Mellor, 54–55, 233, 237–38, and Charles E. Robinson's introduction to M. Shelley's *The Frankenstein Notebooks*, ed. Robinson, 2 parts comprising vol. 9 of *The Manuscripts of the Younger Romantics: Shelley* (New York: Garland, 1996), 9.1:lxv–lxvi.

14. M. W. Shelley and P. B. Shelley, *History of a Six Weeks' Tour* (1817; reprint, Oxford: Woodstock, 1989), 101–2. The quoted passage is from M. Shelley's letter, dated 1 June 1816, and included within the *History*. The parallel with *Frankenstein* is noted by Jeanne

Moskal in her edition of M. W. Shelley's *Travel Writing*, vol. 8 of *The Novels and Selected Works of Mary Shelley* (London: Pickering, 1996), 46. The editor documents incorporations of sentences by P. B. Shelley but finds no evidence that the passage about Rousseau and revolution was the work of anyone but M. W. Shelley. *Six Weeks' Tour* was published less than two months before *Frankenstein*. For the chronology of publication, see Robinson's introduction to *The* Frankenstein *Notebooks*, xc–xci. The location of Plainpalais is shown on a 1770 map of Geneva, inside the front cover of *Histoire de Genève*, ed. Paul Guichonnet (Tonlouse: Privat, 1974).

15. Francis d'Ivernois, *A Short Account of the Late Revolution in Geneva; and of the Conduct of France Towards That Republic, From October 1792, to October 1794, in a Series of Letters to an American*, 2nd ed. (London, 1795).

16. R. R. Palmer, *The Age of the Democratic Revolution*, 2 vols. (Princeton: Princeton Univ. Press, 1959–1964), 1:111–39, 2:398–402. Ivernois, 22–36, 24, 29.

17. Poovey, 114–42; Mellor, 70–88, 137; William Veeder, *Mary Shelley and Frankenstein: The Fate of Androgyny* (Chicago: Univ. of Chicago Press, 1986).

18. David Marshall, *The Surprising Effects of Sympathy: Marivaux, Diderot, Rousseau, and Mary Shelley* (Chicago: Univ. of Chicago Press, 1988), 135–233; James O'Rourke, "'Nothing More Unnatural': Mary Shelley's Revision of Rousseau," *ELH* 56 (1989): 543–69.

19. Jean-Jacques Rousseau, *A Discourse on Inequality*, trans. Maurice Cranston (Harmondsworth, Eng.: Penguin, 1984), 98–102.

20. Palmer, *Age of Democratic Revolution*, 1:111–39, 2:398–99; Rousseau, *Politics and the Arts: Letter to M. d'Alembert on the Theatre*, trans. Allan Bloom (Glencoe, IL: Free Press, 1960), 113–37.

21. In M. W. Shelley's novel, however, the De Lacey cottage is in "Germany," not Geneva (150, 158; vol. 2, chap. 6, 7). It is, on one level, an idealization of the honeymoon cottage on Lake Uri, in German-speaking Switzerland, that Mary and Percy had sought in 1814: see M. W. and P. B. Shelley, *History*, 45.

22. Ivernois, 46–50; Palmer, 2:401–2.

23. Ivernois, 25–26, 42.

24. Rousseau, *The Confessions*, trans. J. M. Cohen (Harmondsworth, Eng.: Penguin, 1953), 86–88; O'Rourke, "Mary Shelley's Revision of Rousseau," 559–62.

25. Veeder identifies the pattern of reverse alphabetization, but explains it psychoanalytically as M. W. Shelley's device to critique Victor's (and P. B. Shelley's) negative Oedipus complex (152–53).

26. Rousseau, *Confessions*, 17–19, 320–22, 332–34.

27. Voltaire, *Letters on England*, trans. Leonard Tancock (Harmondsworth, Eng.: Penguin, 1980).

28. Jean Guéhenno, *Jean-Jacques Rousseau*, trans. John and Doreen Weightman, 2 vols. (London: Routledge, 1966), 2:160–203.

29. See Rousseau's *Confessions*, 587–602; and Rousseau, *Reveries of the Solitary Walker*, trans. Peter France (Harmondsworth, Eng.: Penguin, 1979), 81–91. M. W. Shelley read both works between 1815 to 1817 (see her *Journals*, 89, 94, 101, 670).

30. "Among others," she wrote, "we regarded with curiosity the press [Clarendon Press] instituted by the author of the history of the troubles" (M. W. Shelley's *The* Frankenstein *Notebooks*, in Manuscripts of 9.2:459–61). Edward Hyde, Earl of Clarendon, *The History of the Rebellion and Civil Wars in England Begun in the Year 1641*, ed. W. Dunn

Macray, 6 vols. (1888; reprint, Oxford: Clarendon Press, 1958), 3:178–190, 2:294, 2:314–15, 3:400, 3:402–04, 3:444–45, 4:23–27, 4:34–37, 4:49–103. Mary read Clarendon's history between late September and late October 1816 (see her *Journals*, 93, 96, 654).

31. Clarendon, 3:63, 3:64.

32. William Godwin, *History of the Commonwealth of England*, 4 vols. (London, 1824–1828), 1:11.

33. P. B. Shelley, *Political Writings*, ed. Roland A. Duerksen (New York: Appleton-Century-Crofts, 1970), 140.

34. Godwin, *History of the Commonwealth*, 1:14–15.

35. Clarendon, 1:85–86, 3:61.

36. M. W. Shelley, *Journals*, 181–82; M. W. Shelley, *Frankenstein Notebooks*, xc.

37. E. P. Thompson, *The Making of the English Working Class* (1963; reprint, New York: Random House, 1966), 84, 191, 607–19, 631–49.

38. P. B. Shelley, *Political Writings*, 147. On the cultural politics of mountains in this novel, see Fred V. Randel, "*Frankenstein*, Feminism, and the Intertextuality of Mountains," *Studies in Romanticism* 24 (1985): 515–32.

39. Rousseau, *Confessions*, 594; book 12.

40. Godwin, *Memoirs of the Author of "A Vindication of the Rights of Woman"* (1798; reprint, New York: Garland, 1974), 176.

41. Exodus 2.3, 2.1–10.

42. Kevin Whelan, *The Tree of Liberty: Radicalism, Catholicism and the Construction of Irish Identity 1760–1830* (Notre Dame, IN: Univ. of Notre Dame Press, 1996), 63, 59–96.

43. Malchow, 11–12.

44. Richard Musgrave, *Memoirs of the Different Rebellions in Ireland, From the Arrival of the English: Also, A Particular Detail of That Which Broke Out the 23d of May, 1798; with the History of the Conspiracy Which Preceded It* (1801), ed. Steven W. Myers and Delores E. McKnight, 4th ed. (Fort Wayne, IN.: Round Tower Books, 1995), 526–93.

45. See Lew, 255–83, and Malchow, *Gothic Images of Race*, 9–40, both of whom demonstrate the presence in *Frankenstein* of systematic allusions to European imperialistic involvements in Asia, Africa, and the West Indies, but they do not relate Clerval's murder to these themes.

46. Sterrenburg, 168–69; Malchow, 34–35.

47. Jonathan Swift, *Gulliver's Travels*, ed. Paul Turner (1986; reprint, Oxford: Oxford Univ. Press, 1998), 216.

48. See Swift, 216, 217, 219, 274.

49. Swift, 351n.

50. Musgrave, 4–5.

51. Whelan, 138.

52. Patrick Hanks and Flavia Hodges, *A Dictionary of Surnames* (Oxford: Oxford Univ. Press, 1988), 298.

53. P. B. and M. Shelley, *History of a Six Weeks' Tour*, 116.

54. See the 9th ed. of the *Encyclopaedia Britannica* under "Geneva," "Savoy"; see also the 15th ed. of *The New Encyclopaedia Britannica: Macropaedia* under "Geneva"; and the 15th ed. of *The New Encyclopaedia Britannica: Micropaedia* under "Savoy, House of." Also, see R. R. Palmer and Joel Colton, *A History of the Modern World*, 2nd ed. (New York: Knopf, 1962), 170–71, 413–17, 480.

55. P. B. Shelley, 132 ("Despotism"; "Revolution"; "Reform"). See also 113–14.

56. M. W. Shelley, *Frankenstein* (1831), 35, chap. 1 ("exerted"; "Whether"), 191, chap. 22 ("part"; "inheritance"), 192, chap. 22 ("immediately"; "sleeping"; "spend"). For the Lake Como episode, see 34–35, chap. 1, from this edition.

57. Moretti, *Atlas of the European Novel*, 11–73.

LEE ZIMMERMAN

Frankenstein, *Invisibility, and Nameless Dread*

Early in Mary Shelley's *Frankenstein* (1831), Victor Frankenstein tells Captain Walton: "No human being could have passed a happier childhood than myself. My parents were possessed by the very spirit of kindness and indulgence" (43). But is what he says true? Is Victor's claim borne out by the details of his narrative? I would like to propose that it is not, that it is idealized and defensive, and that just as the monster suffers from parentlessness, so too does Victor, who is his double. The monster's story of emotional abandonment is Victor's story.

One might suppose this would hardly be worth taking the trouble to argue, given the common view that, as George Levine puts it, "the hero and his antagonist are one" (1973, 209) and "the monster can be taken as an expression of an aspect of Frankenstein's self ... re-enacting in mildly disguised ways, his creator's feelings and experiences" (209–10). But this insight has not informed most readings of Victor's early life. Indeed, a chorus of responses—all notable enough to be collected in the Norton Critical Edition (Hunter 1996) of the novel—despite their differences, unites in taking Victor's glowing report at face value. Strikingly, Levine himself writes that "Frankenstein's father ... in caring for him, behaves to his son as the monster would have Frankenstein behave" (211). Christopher Small sees in Victor's upbringing an "atmosphere of perfect love, harmony, and parental

From *American Imago*, Vol. 60, No. 2 (2003). © 2003 by The Johns Hopkins University Press.

indulgence" (1972, 102), and he calls Victor's father "benevolent ... wise ... altogether un-authoritarian" (103). For Sandra M. Gilbert and Susan Gubar, Victor's "Edenic childhood is an interlude of prelapsarian innocence in which, like Adam, he is sheltered by his benevolent father" (1979, 231); while for Mary Poovey he is "the son of loving, protective parents" who provide the "harmony of his childhood" (1984, 122); and for Ellen Moers he experiences "doting parents" (1976, 98). Typifying the way that Victor is often *contrasted* with his double in this respect, Barbara Johnson sees the novel as "the story of two antithetical modes of parenting that give rise to two increasingly parallel lives—the life of Victor Frankenstein, who is the beloved child of two doting parents, and the life of the monster ... who is immediately spurned and abandoned by his creator" (1982, 242).

In counterpoint to this apparent consensus, Anne K. Mellor draws attention to "the many ways in which *Frankenstein* portrays the consequences of the failure of family, the damage wrought when the mother—or a nurturant parental love—is absent" (1988, 39). Like the above chorus, however, Mellor focuses on the consequences of Victor's absenting himself from the monster. Indeed, she echoes Johnson's opposition between Victor and the monster's experiences of their parents: "Throughout the novel, Frankenstein's callous disregard of his responsibility as the sole parent of his only child is contrasted to the examples of two loving fathers" (43–44), one of whom is Alphonse Frankenstein (the other being the father of the De Lacey family).[1]

Everyone agrees, at least, that the monster suffers a horrible abandonment, and Mellor reads his murderousness as a measure of it, seeing in Victor "a classic case of a battering parent who produces a battered child who in turn becomes a battering parent: the creature's first murder victim ... is a small child whom he wishes to adopt" (43). But why start the chain with Victor?[2] Doesn't this "battering parent" have parents of his own? Does he not himself suffer the absence of "nurturant parental love"?

My approach to the monster's story of deprivation as a double of Victor's own is inflected by a particular psychoanalytic way of thinking. Going against the grain of Freudian and Lacanian readings, I invoke an object relations perspective that explores the centrality of an infant's early experiences with primary caretakers and of the intense feelings of love and hate that, even on the surface, are the main concern of *Frankenstein*.[3] Although Melanie Klein pioneered the notion that the self is constituted by intense early relationships, it was D. W. Winnicott, following the lead of W. R. D. Fairbairn, who stressed how the particular "facilitating environment" shapes these relationships. By, at the outset, supporting the infant's feeling of omnipotence without prematurely abrogating it, and by presenting the external world with a flexibility that accommodates the infant's creativity rather than too rigidly or hastily imposing "reality"—by acknowledging, in short, the authenticity of the infant's being—the parents help to constitute a mediating *"potential space* between the individual and the environment" (Winnicott 1967a, 100). This transitional realm helps "the individual engaged in the perpetual human task of keeping inner and outer reality separate yet interrelated" (Winnicott 1953, 2). The infant's disposition is important, but for Winnicott much depends upon the child's earliest relations with others who may respond either in a "good-enough" way that allows his or her "true self" to emerge or by imposing rigid structures that leave the child in a "false" position, caught between an endangered inner world that can't be made known and an unresponsive external world that refuses to know it.

The latter condition haunts *Frankenstein*. Victor himself stresses the perdurability of early relationships, telling Walton that "the companions of our childhood always possess a certain power over our minds, which hardly any later friend can obtain. They know our infantine dispositions, which, however they may be afterwards modified, are never eradicated" (Shelley 1831, 176). But there is more—or less—to his early years than benevolent "companions" and "friends. "Just as the monster is abandoned by Victor, so too Victor is abandoned—psychically and emotionally—by his ostensibly "doting" parents, who never acknowledge or strive to accommodate his inner world, and instead inflict their own version of reality on him.[4]

This parental world suppresses imagination, desire, troubling emotions, and spontaneity—everything that eludes reason and instrumentality. Victor introduces his father exclusively as a public man, without a private self, and defined utterly by his position in the social order. He had passively "filled several public situations with honor and reputation" (38); he was "respected" for "indefatigable attention to public business"; and his imagination and emotions were prematurely supplanted as "he passed his younger days perpetually occupied by the affairs of his country." When, late in life, he finally marries, it hardly signals a delayed eruption of passion. His "love" for his wife Caroline is a pale derivative of "a sense of justice" and of an accountant's concern with "recompensing her for the sorrows she had endured" due to her father's loss of fortune, illness, and death (39). Alphonse's conviction that all emotions can be trumped by rational appeals to duty and instrumentality is typified in his response to Victor's looming despair after his brother William's murder and the family servant Justine's death:

My father observed with pain the alteration perceptible in my disposition and habits, and endeavored by arguments deduced from the feelings of his serene conscience and guiltless life, to inspire me with fortitude, and awaken in me the courage to dispel the dark cloud which brooded over me. "Do you think, Victor," said he, "that I do not suffer also? No one could love a child more than I loved your brother;" (tears came into his eyes ...) "but is it not a duty to the survivors, that we should refrain from augmenting their unhappiness by an appearance of immoderate grief? It is also a duty owed to yourself; for excessive sorrow prevents improvement or enjoyment, or even the discharge of daily usefulness, without which no man is fit for society." (83)

Such a dismissing not only of the claims of grief, but of all aspects of the nonrational, structures Victor's childhood. "In my education, my father had taken the greatest precautions," he tells Walton, "that my mind should be impressed with no supernatural horrors. I do not ever remember to have trembled at a tale of superstition" (53). The child's primitive fears aren't recognized and negotiated—aren't contained by a narrative—but are, rather, systematically disallowed.[5] Indeed, in describing his "ideal" infancy, Victor inadvertently suggests that this premature dismissal—a kind of emotional abandonment akin to what the monster suffers—marks his experience from the start. I have cautioned against taking him at his word as he generalizes about his childhood, but here Victor thinks he's *praising* his parents:

My mother's tender caresses, and my father's smile of benevolent pleasure while regarding me, are my first recollections. I was their plaything and their idol, and something better—their child, the innocent and helpless creature bestowed on them by Heaven, whom to bring up to good and whose future lot it was in their hands to direct to happiness or misery, according as they fulfilled their duties towards me. With this deep conviction of what they owed towards the being to which they had given life, added to the active spirit of tenderness that animated both, it may be imagined that while during every hour of my infant life I received a lesson of patience, of charity, and of self-control, I was so guided by a silken cord, that all seemed but one train of enjoyment to me. (40)

His father's "smile of benevolent pleasure" and mother's "tender caresses" might ordinarily suggest recognition and love, but that doesn't square with Victor's being objectified as a "plaything" or the sense of "duty" and "owing" that defines his relationship to his parents (and their world-view in general). One might object that this "duty" is merely "added to" a "spirit of tenderness," but look again at how the sentence continues: "every hour of my infant life I received a lesson of patience, of charity, and of self-control."

Is this an ideal "infant life"? "Lessons," passively received every hour, preempt any sense of authentic being. The lesson of "patience" entails the imposition of an alienating structure of time, a premature violation of the sense of early omnipotence; the lesson of "charity" precludes the infant from spontaneously having something to give, so that the claims of otherness disallow those of selfhood; the lesson of "self-control" thwarts playfulness and passion.[6] What kind of self can develop in the face of such an onslaught? Even—or especially—the murderous rage (and guilt) that such self-obliteration is likely to fuel has no standing, cannot be spoken, must be split off and disowned (as the monster); and so Victor defensively idealizes his first hours as an uninterrupted "train of enjoyment."

William Veeder's reading of the passage suggests the way that those who share Victor's idealization of his childhood disregard the undertone of tyranny. Actually, Veeder wants to defend Alphonse from what he sees as Victor's self-justifying attribution of his fate to his father's failures. But while Victor provides copious evidence from which inferences about his father's failures can be drawn, he himself only rarely and mildly broaches those conclusions, insisting, as I have suggested, mostly on his father's goodness and blaming mainly himself. By minimizing Victor's few "complaints" as "convenient pretexts" (1986, 138), Veeder detaches them from the context that would allow us to see them as tips of the iceberg. Despite his important caution that "we must ... remain alive to distinctions between ... Victor's assertion and our experience of it," he takes Victor's word for the overall happiness of his childhood and clings to the prevailing idealization of Alphonse. (Perhaps he does so in part because he assumes a Freudian framework, seeing early conflicts as oedipal and relatively invariant, rather than a relational one that stresses preoedipal experience and its variability.[7]) He does register Victor's discontent in the "lessons" passage, but immediately discredits it:

> "Seemed" and "cord" indicate Victor's sense of insecurity and constraint. But since every child doubts parental love occasionally and since every child is bound to parental will indubitably, the question is whether "seemed" and "cord" justify a sense of estrangement as enormous as Victor's becomes. Is Mary [Shelley]

not insisting upon the facts of life—that even this virtually ideal
home cannot be perfect, that tension will exist in any human
relationship? (142–43)

Veeder can see Victor as having a "virtually ideal home" only by reducing his
"complaint" to the nuances of "seemed" and "cord," while making no
mention of the tyrannical "lessons" of patience, charity, and self-control,
repeated every hour. Indeed, he defines these oppressive conditions as
incontestable "facts of life," as if any such "facts" were not social
constructions and all forms of "parental will" were one and the same.

If we turn from Victor's generalizing about his parents to the scenes he
actually describes, we see the lessons enacted. The first time we encounter
Alphonse in action as a father—and the first time he speaks in the novel—he
dismisses young Victor's "enthusiasm" for an alchemical volume by
Cornelius Agrippa (Shelley 1831, 44). Veeder predictably counts this "a
minor mistake," and normalizes it by asking, "What parent has not missed by
at least this much the proper tone in a random moment?" (1986, 139). For
Poovey, Alphonse "neglects to explain Agrippa's obsolescence," and the
episode is simply an "accident" (1984, 253), while for Mellor he merely
"failed to monitor sufficiently closely" Victor's reading (1988, 50). But what
is at stake in this exchange isn't so much *what* Victor has read, but *how* what
he has read has affected his entire state of mind. The book fires his passion
and imagination, and he immediately wants to validate his intense experience
by making it shareable: "A new light seemed to dawn upon my mind; and,
bounding with joy"—and thus defying the infantile lessons of patience and
self-control—"I communicated my discovery to my father" (Shelley 1831,
44).

Alphonse doesn't get the point of his son's enthusiasm: "My father
looked carelessly at the titlepage of my book, and said, 'Ah! Cornelius
Agrippa! My dear Victor, do not waste your time upon this; it is sad trash'"
(44). By failing to receive his son's eagerly proffered communication,
Alphonse cannot present the external world in a way that recognizes and
affirms the inner one; what might have become a "potential space" between
subject and object instead remains a vacuum. Belatedly, Victor's benevolent
professor, M. Waldman, does recognize some value in Cornelius Agrippa and
modulates Victor's enthusiastic understanding by adding to it his own, more
experienced, perspective. Alphonse, however, flatly denies Victor's passion
and seeks to foist on him his own rigid and narrowly rationalistic world-view.

That this is the first detailed exchange between Victor and his father in
the novel might in itself qualify it as something more than a "minor mistake"

or an "accident." But its significance is crucially reinforced by Victor's emphasis on the inadequacy of his father's *looking*. "My father looked carelessly at the titlepage of my book.... [T]he cursory glance my father had taken of my volume by no means assured me that he was acquainted with its contents" (Shelley 1831, 44). Indeed, *Frankenstein* is pervaded by an anxious preoccupation with glances of recognition. When Captain Walton suffers the absence of someone to "participate [in] my joy" or to "sustain me in dejection," he expresses this absence in terms of not being properly seen: "I desire the company of a man who could sympathize with me; whose eyes would reply to mine" (28). The first thing the just-made monster seeks is just such sympathetic eye contact: "his eyes," Victor relates, "were fixed on me. His jaws opened ... while a grin wrinkled his cheeks" (58). And according to Shelley's introduction, her inspiration for the novel derived from her vision of the pale student's creation "looking on him with yellow, watery, but speculative eyes" (23).

But the monster's predicament, which literalizes Victor's, is precisely that his sympathetic looks *cannot* be returned. After his abandonment and troubled early wandering, he can join the loving De Lacey family only invisibly, as, from his hiding place, he regards their "interchanging each day looks of affection and kindness" (99). He reveals himself solely to the blind father, and when the others return, instead of requiting his kind look, they evince "horror and consternation on beholding" him (117). In some sense, *Frankenstein* takes as its central subject the longing to be truly seen, as well as the despair about whether such recognition is possible; and Alphonse's "cursory glance" epitomizes the self-denying "lessons" that structure Victor's early experience.

The intensity of the novel's preoccupation with sympathetic looking anticipates Winnicott's emphasis on the importance, for the emerging self, of the mother's face. As he describes it, a sense of meaningful selfhood is in large measure constructed from the infant's earliest experiences of being seen and recognized. "What does the baby see," Winnicott asks, "when he or she looks at the mother's face?" (1967b, 112). Optimally, "what the baby sees is himself or herself. In other words the mother is looking at the baby and *what she looks like is related to what she sees there*." Although he calls the mother's face a "mirror," it is responsive to what it reflects, so that the baby gets back not merely itself but also the mother. These early moments of the coming together of internal and external worlds make both seem real.[8] The consequences for babies who "have a long experience of not getting back what they are giving," who "look and ... do not see themselves," are that "perception takes the place of apperception, perception takes the place of that which might have been the beginning of a significant exchange with the world, a two-way process in which self-enrichment alternates with the discovery of meaning in the world of seen things" (112–13).

Thus, while looking is an excruciatingly literal concern in *Frankenstein*, it is also a figure for recognition of all sorts. In this sense, Victor's early "lessons" are lessons in invisibility, and the novel centers on a creature *defined by* the impossibility of being sympathetically seen. On her deathbed, with the incontrovertible authority of last words, Victor's mother Caroline poses his relationship with his adopted sister Elizabeth entirely in terms of their parents' needs: "'My children,' she said, 'my firmest hopes of future happiness were placed on the prospect of your union. This expectation will now be the consolation of your father'" (Shelley 1831, 47). Victor's own desire doesn't enter into the equation, nor, for that matter, does Elizabeth's: she is scripted to be not only a wife but also a mother, who, Caroline orders, "'must supply my place to my younger children.'"

That this union would entail not a fulfillment of his own desire but a capitulation to his mother's is confirmed by Victor's "wild dream" after the monster's birth, where "Elizabeth" is merely a screen for Caroline. No wonder Victor seems not only not drawn to Elizabeth, but consistently drawn away from her. Victor says he loves her, but, again, it's useful to attend to the difference between what he says and what he does: if he were so eager for Elizabeth, there would be no reason to keep on stalling. He finally, reluctantly, goes through with the marriage, but what gets consummated isn't his desire, but rather his unacknowledged rage at seeming to have no other choice.

Victor's procrastination doesn't escape Elizabeth's notice, of course, and she has more than an inkling of its meaning. She writes to him:

> "You well know, Victor, that our union had been the favorite plan of your parents ever since our infancy. We were told this when young, and taught to look forward to it as an event that would certainly take place.... You have traveled; you have spent several years of your life at Ingolstadt; and I confess to you, my friend, that when I saw you last autumn so unhappy, flying to solitude, from the society of every creature, I could not help supposing that you might regret our connection, and believe yourself bound in honor to fulfil the wishes of your parents, though they opposed themselves to your inclinations." (157)

In response, Victor recommits himself to the marriage in terms that evince his early lessons in self-obliteration: "I resolved ... that if my immediate union with my cousin would conduce either to hers or my father's happiness, my adversary's designs against my life should not retard it a single hour" (159). The infantile lessons, indeed, are repeated virtually "every hour" of his adult life. Forgetting them for a moment, Victor finally attempts to give voice to the disavowed intensities of his inner world and the history of its invisibility. In despair that his father "did not know the origin of my sufferings" and that he "sought erroneous methods to remedy the incurable ill" by lamely advising Victor "to seek amusement in society," Victor blurts out, "'Alas! my father ... how little do you know me'" (155). And he voices the consequences of his rage at being so little known: "'I am the cause of this—I murdered [Justine]. William, Justine, and Henry [Clerval, his only friend]—they all died by my hands'" (155–56).[9] Alphonse fails to acknowledge even this overt expression of his son's inner world, dismissing it as madness and, once again, telling him in the most affectionate terms to shut up: "'My dearest Victor, what infatuation is this? My dear son, I entreat you never to make such an assertion again'" (156). When Victor remonstrates, Alphonse "instantly changed the subject of our conversation and endeavored to alter the course of my thoughts. He ... never alluded to [the scenes in Ireland], or suffered me to speak of my misfortune." When, a short time later, Victor lets slip a melancholic word, Alphonse repeats, "'My dear Victor, do not speak thus'" (160). "Such were the lessons of my father," the son remarks, thereby inviting us to read these later episodes as haunted by the infantile lessons.

Another telling instance of how Victor's infantile dilemma haunts his later years involves his awakening from delirium in an Irish jail, imprisoned under suspicion of killing Clerval. His condition here approximates an infant's not only in his helplessness, but also in his having to contend with intense anxiety and guilt and in his difficulty in establishing the external world *as* external: "The whole series of my life appeared to me as a dream; I sometimes doubted if indeed it were all true, for it never presented itself to my mind with the force of reality" (150).[10] While Winnicott stresses the parents' role in helping the child to establish an intermediate realm indispensable to the "perpetual human task of keeping inner and outer reality separate yet interrelated" (1953, 2), the nurse and physician in the jail, like Caroline and Alphonse, do their material "duty" (as the nurse puts it, echoing one of Alphonse's guiding words) by Victor, but staunchly decline to engage with, and thus contain, his emotional state. Indeed, at the center of this breakdown is once again the failure to be genuinely *seen*, and Victor's disappointment centers on cold looks and cursory glances: "The lines on [the nurse's] face were hard and rude, like that of persons accustomed to *see without sympathizing* in sights of misery.... The physician came and prescribed medicines, and the old woman prepared them for me; but utter carelessness was visible in the first, and the expression of brutality was strongly marked in the visage of the second" (Shelley 1831, 150; italics added).

Victor's reproaches echo those of the monster. "No one was near me who soothed me with the gentle voice of love; no dear hand supported me" (150), he protests, just as the monster bemoans that "No father had watched my infant days, no mother had blessed me with smiles and caresses" (107). When, imprisoned in invisibility, the monster watches the De Laceys from his "very bare" room (97), he avers that "my heart yearned to be known and loved by these amiable creatures: to see their sweet looks directed towards me with affection.... I asked ... for greater treasures than a little food or rest: I required kindness and sympathy" (115). Indeed, if we take the monster's tale as the autobiography of the unseen Victor, Victor's traumatic reenactment of his infantile experience in the Irish jail is perhaps as close as he comes to acknowledging the identity of maker and monster—an identity ironically ratified by the pervasive, popular "mis"-naming of the monster as "Frankenstein."

That Victor clings to the idealized version of his early years, which were in reality structured by lessons in invisibility, is evident in the elaboration of the consequences (one could say symptoms) of those lessons in *Frankenstein*. As a child, Victor declares, his "temper was sometimes violent" and his "vehement" passions "by some law in my temperature ... were turned, not to childish pursuits, but to an eager desire to learn, and not to learn all things indiscriminately.... It was the secrets of heaven and earth that I desired to learn" (43). This thirst for knowledge reveals a premature instrumentality modeled on his father's, a "temperature" forced by a rigid "law" to forego the playing that, Winnicott holds, constitutes a precondition for authentic living.[11] The consequent feeling of unreality marks his jailhouse breakdown, but, in less acute form, it pervades his experience in general. Victor experiences the self he presents to others as largely fraudulent; his real need for the world to meet him half way, and his rage at its duty-bound refusal to do so, remains hidden and inexpressible, and is ultimately disowned by being projected into the monster.

Indeed, much of Victor's story seems to foreshadow Winnicott's "Ego Distortion in Terms of True and False Self" (1960). Contrast Victor's infantile lessons in self-control with Winnicott's description of the conditions that allow the "true self" to develop:

Periodically the infant's gesture gives expression to a spontaneous impulse; the source of the gesture is the True Self, and the gesture indicates the existence of a potential True Self. We need to examine the way the mother meets this infantile omnipotence revealed in a gesture.... The good enough mother meets the omnipotence of the infant and to some extent makes sense of it. She does this repeatedly. A True Self begins to have life, through the strength given to the infant's weak ego by the mother's implementation of the infant's omnipotent expressions. (1960, 145)

The "false self," conversely, emerges from just the sort of "compliance" demanded by Victor's early (and later) lessons: "The mother who is not good enough ... repeatedly fails to meet the infant gesture; instead she substitutes her own gesture which is to be given sense by the compliance of the infant. This compliance is the earliest stage of the False Self." Eventually, Winnicott continues, in the most extreme instances, "the False Self sets up as real and it is this that observers tend to think is the real person," especially since its "function is to hide and protect the True Self" (142).

One especially notable moment in this regard occurs when Alphonse strives to talk Victor out of his melancholy, appealing (as always) to his "duty" to "refrain from ... an appearance of immoderate grief," and Victor despairs about any acknowledgement of his true "gesture": "Now I could only ... endeavor to hide myself from his view" (Shelley 1831, 83). Indeed, throughout his history Victor is deeply invested in hiding, whether during his long physical "confinement" (55) in his workroom (which parallels the monster's confinement in his sealed-off room), or in his keeping the monster's existence concealed (sometimes even from himself), or in his response to his imminent wedding to Elizabeth, when the functioning of the false self seems most explicit: "As the period fixed for our marriage grew near ... I felt my heart sink within me. But I concealed my feelings by an appearance of hilarity.... Preparations were made for the event; congratulatory visits were received; and all wore a smiling appearance. I shut up, as well as I could, in my own heart the anxiety that preyed there, and entered with seeming earnestness into the plans of my father" (160–61).[12]

Victor's concealing his extreme "anxiety" under an "appearance of hilarity" also conforms to what Melanie Klein (1935) calls the "manic defense" against the depressive position.[13] Klein stresses that such anxiety pertains above all to one's own destructiveness. But beyond Kleinian guilt or Winnicottian falseness, the most pervasive consequence of Victor's early lessons is his despair about the possibility of meaning. Especially after the killing starts, he suffers the failure of external representations to seem connected to his internal states, that is, from a failure of the potential space that would make existence seem meaningful. Since this is a failure of language, melancholia is by definition a condition, as Victor insists, "such as no language can describe," though this doesn't keep him from trying: "The blood flowed freely in my veins, but a weight of despair and remorse pressed on my heart, which nothing could remove" (Shelley 1831, 83), he tells us, and elaborates: "Not the tenderness of friendship, nor the beauty of earth, nor of heaven, could redeem my soul from woe: the very accents of love were ineffectual. I was encompassed by a cloud which no beneficial influence could penetrate" (86).

Victor tries to respond to such depression in the manner of Wordsworth. Like Wordsworth, he seeks a restoration of meaning in the evocative landscape of his youth, wandering through the Alps as a way of dealing with his dejection after the deaths of William and Justine: "A tingling long-lost sense of pleasure often came across me during this journey. Some turn in the road, some new object suddenly perceived and recognized, reminded me of days gone by, and were associated with the light-hearted gaiety of boyhood. The very winds whispered in soothing accents, and maternal nature bade me weep no more" (87). But such relief is momentary: "the kindly influence ceased to act—I found myself fettered again to grief, indulging in all the misery of reflection."

Why can't Victor, finally, follow Wordsworth? The crucial difference involves Wordsworth's own early lessons. His capacity (at least as he poses it in his poetry), during depressed periods, to conjure what in "Tintern Abbey" (1798) he calls the emotionally and spiritually nourishing "beauteous forms" (l. 23) of a remembered landscape reflects his earliest experience of the external world.[14] This is the case, for instance, in the "Intimations Ode" (1807), where what finally restores the poet to meaning is what remains in the "embers" of the self, the infantile "obstinate questionings / Of sense and outward things" (ll. 129, 141–42). Wordsworth's creative self-assertion is here enabled by the "outward" world's willingness to *be* questioned; being is shaped not by lessons of self-control, but by "primal sympathy" (l. 181). This is true, too, in the second part of the two-part *Prelude* (1799), where, as Peter Rudnytsky elaborates, "Winnicott's vision of the mother–child bond finds consummate expression in Wordsworth's meditation on the 'infant Babe'" (1991, 80), and where the experience of that "infant Babe" seems even more starkly at odds with Victor's:

> Blessed the infant babe—
> For with my best conjectures I would trace

The progress of our being—blest the babe
Nursed in his mother's arms, the babe who sleeps
Upon his mother's breast, who when his soul
Claims manifest kindred with an earthly soul
Doth gather passion from his Mother's eye.
. . . . .
From this beloved presence—there exists
A virtue which irradiates and exalts
All objects through all intercourse of sense.
No outcast he, bewildered and depressed:
Along his infant veins are interfused
The gravitation and the filial bond
Of Nature that connect him with the world.
. . . . .
        From early days,
Beginning not long after that first time
In which, a babe, by intercourse of touch
I held mute dialogues with my mother's heart,
I have endeavored to display the means
Whereby this infant sensibility,
Great birthright of our being, was in me
Augmented and sustained. (ll. 267–73, 288–94, 310–17)

Among the many ways this infancy contrasts with Victor's, perhaps the most salient concerns the quality of parental looking. A far cry from Alphonse's alienating "cursory glance," the "Mother's eye" bestows upon Wordsworth's babe a "passion" that ultimately "connect[s] him with the world."[15] When the poet is later afflicted by inevitable, depressing losses, such connections make possible the recovery of meaning:

For now a trouble came into my mind
From obscure causes. I was left alone
Seeking this visible world, nor knowing why:
The props of my affection were removed
And yet the building stood as if sustained
By its own spirit. (ll. 321–26)

In contrast to the poet who "by intercourse of touch / ... held mute dialogues with my mother's heart," Victor as a baby is forced into the rigid terms of his parents' rationalized world, leaving him with no internal "props," so that in times of trouble his emotional house falls down. There is no "beloved presence" that "irradiates and exalts / All objects"—nothing to underwrite the sort of restorative looking at the world that would bespeak his having once been sympathetically seen. Victor might long for a Wordsworthian recourse to nature, but his early lessons in invisibility doom him to failure.[16]

Victor cannot reconstruct the house of the self, cannot recover the possibility of meaning, and eventually any inclination to do so is eclipsed by his obsession with killing the monster. It isn't until his deathbed that, "examining [his] past conduct" (Shelley 1831, 180), he tries to re-compose meaning—and the meaning he does arrive at is perhaps the most chilling consequence of all his early lessons. When it comes to understanding his relationship to his monster-child, Victor has become his father. Earlier, anticipating the birth of the new creatures he intends to create, he imagines them as *emotional* beings: they will be "happy," feel intense "gratitude," and lovingly "bless" him (55). But, by the end, Victor reconfigures the monster in terms that abolish his inner world. Although the monster has told Victor about his intense—essentially infantile—longing and frustration, and has pleaded only for a mate, Victor defines him here as a "rational creature" from the moment of his creation. In his final construction of the story of maker and monster, Victor resorts utterly to the terms of Alphonse, according to whom relationships can be calculated, enthusiasm is dismissed as "madness," and love, like everything else, is a derivative of "duty": "In a fit of enthusiastic madness I created a rational creature, and was bound toward him, to assure, as far as was in my power, his happiness and well-being. That was my duty; but there was another still paramount to that. My duties towards the beings of my own species had greater claims to my attention, because they included a greater proportion of happiness or misery" (180). In his revisionist account of the monster's history, Victor elides the main point, the monster's poignantly frustrated longing to be seen: "He showed unparalleled malignity and selfishness, in evil: he destroyed my friends; he devoted to destruction beings who possessed exquisite sensations" (180). Despite all he has heard, Victor presents the monster finally as incapable of the same "exquisite sensations" as members of his own species.

Just as Alphonse, from the first, misreads Victor, Victor initially misreads his creature by, for example, seeing his new creation's outstretched hand as seeking not to embrace but to "detain" him (58); and, at the end of the novel, he codifies that misreading by adopting his father's terms. The new-made "eyes ... were fixed" on his maker, but just as Victor doesn't return that first look, his last words render the monster's invisibility complete. The final glance isn't even cursory.

Again, the monster's complete invisibility at the close suggests the degree to which Victor's own inner world remains unspeakable. I have posed his dilemma as a consequence of Victor's early lessons, but what is at stake in the monster's experience of not being seen (and hence, implicitly, also in Victor's struggles) can be understood in terms of what W. R. Bion calls "containment." For Bion, an infant's overwhelmingly intense internal states, especially those of anxiety, fear, and rage, need to be made tolerable by the primary caretaker's taking them in and returning them in a more bearable form. This process, by helping to establish a distinction and relationship between inside and outside, forms the basis for constructing a self that can experience and think about difficult emotions without being dissolved into them. Containment, that is, gives rise to the possibility of meaning. "An understanding mother," Bion writes, "is able to experience the feeling of dread that [a] baby [is] striving to deal with by projective identification, and yet retain a balanced outlook" (1959, 104). So-called "normal development follows" if

> the relationship between the infant and the breast permits the infant to project a feeling, say, that it is dying into the mother and to reintroject it after its sojourn in the breast has made it tolerable to the infant psyche. If projection is not accepted by the mother the infant feels that its feeling that it is dying is stripped of such meaning as it has. It therefore reintrojects, not a fear of dying made tolerable, but a nameless dread. (1962, 116).

Although containment first occurs preverbally, eventually it becomes a matter of language. Bion writes of a patient who was "trying to 'contain' his emotions within a form of words.... The words that should have represented the meaning the man wanted to express were fragmented by the emotional forces to which he wished to give only verbal expression: the verbal formulation could not 'contain' his emotions" (1970, 94).

If, as I have argued, the monster can be understood as Victor's infantile self, Shelley constructs the failure to be seen as a failure of containment, and she elaborates the consequent "nameless dread." Victor consistently links the dissolution of the self—when it is overwhelmed by its intensities, rather than metabolizing them—with its unspeakability. After Justine's death, he is *seized* by remorse and the sense of guilt, which hurried [him] away to a hell of intense tortures, such *as no language can describe*" (Shelley 1831, 83; italics added). In a doomed attempt to enlist the law against the monster after

Elizabeth's death, he tells the magistrate, "My revenge ... is the *devouring and only passion* of my soul. My rage is *unspeakable*" (167; italics added). The magistrate, Victor recounts, "endeavored to sooth me as a nurse does a child" (168), but this scene of potential containment proves catastrophic; rather than taking in or even seeing Victor's anxiety, the magistrate, like Alphonse, dismisses it as "madness" and "the effects of delirium." Thus, the magistrate's failure "to soothe me as a nurse does a child" replicates the primal origins of Victor's rage, and he decries being once again rendered invisible: "'Man.... how ignorant art thou in thy pride of wisdom! Cease; you know not what it is you say'"—a protest that reflects his initial unhousing, as he "broke from the [magistrate's] house angry and disturbed" (168).

Just as Victor finds that "all voluntary thought was swallowed up and lost" so that he is "hurried away by fury" (168), so too in the final pages of the novel the monster tells us he is "torn by the bitterest remorse" (185), and has become "the slave, not the master, of an impulse, which I detested" (182). And just as the monster has become his "uncontrollable passion," he is defined by his invisibility and unspeakability. As Walton's initial response reminds us, the creature is "a form which I cannot find words to describe.... I shut my eyes involuntarily" (181). As such, he is a split-off representative of the "nameless dread" that marks the failure of containment.

Even before he is rejected by the De Laceys, the monster's intense feelings go uncontained: "When I first sought [sympathy], it was the ... feeling of happiness and affection with which my whole being overflowed" (183). The prospect of their sympathy, though, offers a shape for the superabundant self; mere hope sustains the possibility of meaning. But when the De Laceys finally scorn him, the "hell within" (118) breaks loose, and he is "borne away by the stream" of "revenge and hatred" (119) as "a kind of insanity in [his] spirits ... burst all bounds of reason and reflection" (120). The monster's world is thus, in Bion's phrase, "stripped of ... meaning," and though he is free to wander anywhere and wants to flee the scene of his devastating disappointment, "every country must be equally horrible." All places are rendered indistinguishable, flooded as he is by the intensity of his rage.

Under optimal conditions, as Hanna Segal explains, the infant introjects "an anxiety modified by having been contained," but also "introjects an object capable of containing ... anxiety" (1975, 135). Insofar as containment depends on sympathetic looking, we can read the presence of such an internalized object as what allows Wordsworth to survive the loss of the "props of [his] affection": "the building" of the self "stood as if sustained / By its own spirit," and he can then experience nature as restorative.

Without such an internalized, containing object, as we have seen, Victor cannot experience nature in the way that Wordsworth does. And it is just such an internalized object—or, more precisely, a set of internalized relationships—that the monster tries to locate when his own props are lost. When he is deserted by the De Laceys, he is first despondent ("in a state of utter and stupid despair" [Shelley 1831, 119]), then confronted with a rage ("revenge and hatred filled my bosom") that he struggles to contain by evoking an internalized responsive presence: "When I thought of my friends, of the mild voice of De Lacey, the gentle eyes of Agatha, and the exquisite beauty of the Arabian, these thoughts vanished, and a gush of tears somewhat soothed me" (119). Given his invisibility, of course, this attempt—like Victor's endeavor to respond to the "soothing accents" of "maternal nature" in his journey through the Alps—is doomed to fail.

Importantly, the monster's returned rage is turned toward the De Laceys' now-empty cottage. The house is a figure for containment, defining an inside and an outside, and it thus represents the possibility of mental stability. But when the monster's "props of affection" are removed, this house of the self falls down—or rather, the monster *burns* it down. This incendiary act defines the moment in which containment fails, as Walton's summary in the last scene suggests: "'Wretch! ... You throw a torch into a pile of buildings; and, when they are consumed, you sit among the ruins, and lament the fall'" (183).

If the monster's dilemma illustrates Victor's hidden inner world, Victor's final identification with the terms of his father's world implies a complementary dilemma. Which is worse, the novel seems to wonder, a self shattered by its own intensities or one suffocated by the rigid terms imposed upon it? The monster's nameless dread, or the dreadfulness of being named as Victor is named? It is tempting to read Walton as having access to a potential space between these extremes, to a language both internal and communal. He is "led by the sympathy" Victor evinces "to use the language of [his] heart, to give utterance to the burning ardor of [his] soul" (35), but he also "felt the greatest eagerness to hear [Victor's] promised narrative" (37). And it is tempting to see *Frankenstein* itself as Shelley's attempt not only to parse the conditions that construct these dreadful extremes, but also to write her way between them.

But whatever intermediate realm the novel manages to evoke, its deepest investment is in elaborating the quandary itself. Nameless dread or the dread of being named? In *Frankenstein*, this is less a choice than a double bind. Victor dies pledging loyalty to the paternal world that rendered him unseen and uncontained, concluding that he "created a rational creature," while the unhousable monster is "lost in darkness" (185), beyond the reach of even a cursory glance.

Notes

1. Johanna M. Smith does question Victor's claim about his good childhood; but, as she sees it, the problem is that "Alphonse does contribute to Victor's ruin ... because he is a good father" (1992, 278). She usefully evokes John Dussinger's observation that Victor's family is "a paradigm of the social contract based on economic terms" (1976, 52) where affection is subsumed by obligation, but she contrasts the care Victor receives with the monster's abandonment: "while the monster becomes monstrous in part because he has been denied parental care, Victor becomes monstrous in part because he has been *given* care and made subject to the attendant obligations" (Smith 1992, 280; italics in original). My argument is that neither the one nor the other is genuinely cared for: the monster is Victor.

2. Given the well-known facts of Mary Shelley's life—the death of her mother Mary Wollstonecraft shortly after childbirth, the emotional unavailability of her father William Godwin, and the way that the writings of both parents reflect the Enlightenment thinking personified by Alphonse—one might be tempted to wonder: if the monster's story is Victor's story, is Victor's story also Mary Shelley's? To pursue that question would require another essay, and it would require our relying on the various kinds of texts by which we know Shelley's life as adequate representations of her for that purpose, a highly debatable assumption. Indeed, I am inclined to think that it is hard enough to speak with confidence about the inner worlds even of people we know well (or ourselves), much less about historical figures. Literary characters are another matter. Since they have no inner world except ones we can imagine from the texts that constitute them, we can't be right or wrong in our speculations. We can only discuss whether—or to what extent—a particular construction seems to accord with the literary evidence.

3. Broadly speaking, Freudian and Lacanian readings assume a fixed view of human nature. For Freud, this is attributed to the inescapable nature of the drives, while for Lacan it is due to the symbolic order. Object relations approaches see both our internal and external worlds as more malleable and potentially more responsive to one another. See Flax 1990, chs. 3 and 4.

4. My object relations reading dovetails with Jeffrey Berman's (1990) approach to *Frankenstein*, which is grounded in the theories of narcissism articulated by Otto Kernberg and Heinz Kohut. Unlike critics who take Victor's characterization of his childhood at face value, Berman recognizes that it entails "a massive falsification of reality.... Victor sentimentalizes his childhood in order to deny past disappointments" (65). But Berman's emphasis falls less on the dynamics of Victor's early experience than on his "pathological narcissism" as an adult. "The real monster in *Frankenstein*," he begins, "is the scientist whose monstrous empathetic failure comes back to haunt him" (56). Thus, though Berman does see in the novel "the disastrous consequences of not good enough parenting" (55), his primary concern is with Victor as the perpetrator rather than as the sufferer from the consequences of such parenting.

5. I elaborate W. R. Bion's notion of "containment" later in the essay.

6. Winnicott writes: "The mother, at the beginning, by an almost 100 percent adaptation affords the infant the opportunity for the illusion that her breast is part of the infant.... The same can be said in terms of infant care in general.... Omnipotence is nearly a fact of existence. The mother's eventual task is gradually to disillusion the infant, but she has no hope of success unless at first she has been able to give sufficient opportunity for illusion" (1953, 11). He adds that a "good-enough mother meets the omnipotence of the infant and to some extent makes sense of it ... by [her] implementation of the infant's omnipotent expressions" (1960, 145).

7. Dean Franco's Lacanian reading, which also assumes an oedipal paradigm, likewise does not see Alphonse as unduly authoritarian; indeed, he sees him as not authoritarian enough (1998, 95).

8. In articulating his conception of the mirror-role of the mother, Winnicott acknowledges that Lacan's "'Le Stade du Miroir' (1949) has certainly influenced me"; but he adds—with characteristic understatement—that "Lacan does not think of the mirror in terms of the mother's face in the way that I wish to do here" (1967b, 111). Winnicott stresses the variability of the mother's responsiveness, while for Lacan the mirror is inanimate and therefore unchanging.

9. In trying to express his unseen self to his father, Victor—who elsewhere disavows his creation—here for once openly acknowledges his identity with the monster.

10. In "The Use of an Object" (1969), Winnicott suggests that the world becomes external for the infant only if the parent remains psychically available in the face of the infant's fantasied attacks. Hovering behind Winnicott's view is Klein's description of the destructiveness that pervades the earliest months of life.

11. Playing, for Winnicott, partakes both of the child's inner world and of external reality. Its "precariousness belongs to the fact that it is always on the theoretical line between the subjective and that which is objectively perceived" (1971a, 50). Thus, it is crucial to the child's coming to a sense of the aliveness—and meaningfulness—of the outside world. By being prematurely required to accept externality, Victor is placed in a "false position"; and Winnicott observes that the "protest against being forced into a false existence can be detected from the earliest stages," while its consequences "reappear in serious form at a later stage" (1960, 146).

12. The construction of Victor's false self takes place along lines laid down by Winnicott: "A particular danger arises out of the not infrequent tie-up between the intellectual approach and the False Self. When a False Self becomes organized in an individual who has a high intellectual potential there is a very strong tendency for the mind to become the location of the False Self.... The world may observe academic success of a high degree and may find it hard to believe in the very real distress of the individual concerned, who feels 'phoney'" (1960, 144). If the mind is the "location" of such phoniness, we can read Victor's obsession with creating a *body* as a desperate attempt to reconstitute a true self, especially in light of Winnicott's claim that the "True Self comes from the aliveness of the body tissues and the working of body-functions" (148). Victor's sister is similarly driven to a false position. At Victor's departure for Ingolstadt, "she indeed veiled her grief, and strove to act the comforter to us all.... She forgot her own regret in her endeavors to make us forget" (Shelley 1831, 48).

13. Indeed, the first time Victor thinks he is free of the monster he has just created, he suffers what sounds like a manic episode in the clinical sense:

I was unable to contain myself. It was not joy only that possessed me; I felt my flesh tingle with excess of sensitiveness, and my pulse beat rapidly; I was unable to remain for a single instant in the same place; I jumped over the chairs, clapped my hands, and laughed aloud. Clerval at first attributed my unusual spirits to joy on his arrival; but when he observed me more attentively, he saw a wildness in my eyes for which he could not account; and my loud, unrestrained, heartless laughter, frightened and astonished him. (Shelley 1831, 61)

This is followed by a long, confining "nervous fever," the first of what one might call Victor's depressions. The depression seems more deeply rooted to me than the mania, though, as I shall argue below, Victor's inability to "contain himself" underlies both these states.

14. All quotations from Wordsworth's poetry are to the edition (1988) of Heaney, with line numbers given parenthetically in the text.

15. As John Turner writes, Wordsworth is able "to lay firm hands on the inner representation of that lost good object that was his own childhood" (1988, 168–69).

16. It is Clerval, of course, who is directly equated with the Wordsworth of "Tintern Abbey" (Shelley 1831, 133). Clerval's father differs significantly from Alphonse; he acknowledges what he cannot understand in his son, and allows him to pursue his inclinations. "'His affection for me,'" relates Clerval, "'at length overcame his dislike of learning, and he has permitted me to undertake a voyage of discovery to the land of knowledge'" (60).

REFERENCES

Berman, Jeffrey. 1990. *Narcissism and the Novel*. New York: New York University Press.

Bion, W. R. 1959. Attacks on Linking. In Bion 1967, pp. 93–109.

———. 1962. A Theory of Thinking. In Bion 1967, pp. 110–19.

———. 1967. *Second Thoughts*. London: William Heinemann.

———. 1970. *Attention and Interpretation*. In *Seven Servants*. New York: Jason Aronson, 1977.

Dussinger, John A. 1976. Kinship and Guilt in Mary Shelley's *Frankenstein*. *Studies in the Novel*, 8:38–55.

Flax, Jane. 1990. *Thinking Fragments: Psychoanalysis, Feminism and Postmodernism in the Contemporary West*. Berkeley: University of California Press.

Franco, Dean. 1998. Mirror Images and Otherness in Mary Shelley's *Frankenstein*. *Literature and Psychology*, 44:80–95.

Gilbert, Sandra, and Susan Gubar. 1979. *The Madwoman in the Attic*. New Haven: Yale University Press. In Hunter 1996, pp. 225–40.

Hunter, J. Paul, ed. 1996. *Frankenstein* by Mary Shelley. New York: Norton.

Johnson, Barbara. 1982. My Monster/My Self. *Diacritics*, 12: 2–10. In Hunter 1996, pp. 241–51.

Klein, Melanie. 1935. A Contribution to the Psychogenesis of Manic-Depressive States. In *The Writings of Melanie Klein*. 4 vols. Ed. Roger Money-Kyrle, Betty Joseph, Edna O'Shaughnessy, and Hanna Segal. New York: Free Press, 1984. 1:282–311.

Levine, George. 1973. *Frankenstein* and the Tradition of Realism. *Novel*, 7:7–23. In Hunter 1996, pp. 208–14.

Mellor, Anne K. 1988. *Mary Shelley: Her Life, Her Fiction, Her Monsters*. New York: Methuen.

Moers, Ellen. 1976. *Literary Women*. Garden City, NY: Doubleday.

Poovey, Mary. 1984. *The Proper Lady and the Woman Writer*. Chicago: University of Chicago Press.

Rudnytsky, Peter L. 1991. *The Psychoanalytic Vocation: Rank, Winnicott, and the Legacy of Freud*. New Haven: Yale University Press.

Segal, Hanna. 1975. A Psychoanalytic Approach to the Treatment of Schizophrenia. In *The Work of Hanna Segal*. New York: Jason Aronson, 1981.

Shelley, Mary. 1831. *Frankenstein*. Ed. Johanna M. Smith. Boston: Bedford Books, 1992.

Small, Christopher. 1972. *Ariel Like a Harpy: Shelley, Mary and "Frankenstein."* London: Victor Gollancz.

Smith, Johanna M. 1992. "Cooped Up": Feminine Domesticity in *Frankenstein*. In Shelley 1831, pp. 270–285.

Turner, John. 1988. Wordsworth and Winnicott in the Area of Play. In Peter L. Rudnytsky, ed., *Transitional Objects and Potential Spaces: Literary Uses of D. W. Winnicott*, New York: Columbia University Press, 1993, pp. 161–88.

Veeder, William. 1986. *Mary Shelley and "Frankenstein": The Fate of Androgyny*. Chicago: University of Chicago Press.

Winnicott, D. W. 1953. Transitional Objects and Transitional Phenomena. In Winnicott 1971b, pp. 1–25.

———. 1960. Ego Distortion in Terms of True and False Self. In *The Maturational Process and the Facilitating Environment*. New York: International Universities Press, 1965, pp. 140–52.

———. 1967a. The Location of Cultural Experience. In Winnicott 1971b, pp. 95–103.

———. 1967b. Mirror-role of Mother and Family in Child Development. In Winnicott 1971b, pp. 111–18.

———. 1969. The Use of an Object and Relating through Identifications. In Winnicott 1971b, pp. 86–94.

———. 1971a. Playing: A Theoretical Statement. In Winnicott 1971b, pp. 38–52.

———. 1971b. *Playing and Reality*. London: Routledge.

Wordsworth, William. 1988. *The Essential Wordsworth*. Ed. Seamus Heaney. Hopewell: Ecco.

Chronology

1797	Mary Wollstonecraft Godwin is born August 30 at Somers Town to William Godwin and Mary Wollstonecraft (who dies shortly thereafter).
1801	William Godwin marries Mary Jane Clairmont who has a daughter, Claire, and a son, Charles.
1803	Mary Jane Godwin gives birth to William Godwin, Jr.
1805	William and Mary Jane Godwin open a publishing firm and bookshop for children's books.
1811	Percy Shelley marries Harriet Westbrook.
1812	Percy Shelley and Mary Godwin meet for the first time while Shelley studies with William Godwin.
1813	Percy Shelley separates from Harriet.
1814	Mary and Shelley meet again and fall in love; Mary declares her love for Percy at her mother's grave. William Godwin forbids Mary to see Percy. Mary and Percy elope with Mary's stepsister Claire. Mary begins her novel, *Hate*. They return to England. Shelley's estranged wife Harriet gives birth to his son, Charles.
1815	Mary gives birth to a daughter, who dies.
1816	Mary gives birth to son William. Claire begins an affair with Lord Byron. Mary, Percy, and Claire meet Byron in Geneva. At the Villa Diodati, Byron, Percy, Mary and Polidori write ghost stories. Mary begins *Frankenstein*.

Percy, Mary and Claire return to England where Harriet's suicide allows Mary and Percy to wed.

1817 The Shelley's spend the year at Marlow. Mary gives birth to daughter, Clara. Completes *Frankenstein*. Writes with Percy, *History of a Six Weeks' Tour*.

1818 *Frankenstein* is published anonymously with a preface by Percy. Mary, Percy, William, Clara, and Claire sail to Italy. Clara dies in Venice.

1819 Son William dies in Rome. Mary writes *Mathilda*, which was not published her lifetime. Mary gives birth to son Percy Florence.

1820 The Shelleys move to Pisa. Mary writes verse dramas *Proserpine* and *Midas*.

1822 The Shelleys live at Casa Magni at Lerici. Mary miscarries and nearly dies.

Percy Shelley drowns when the boat he is sailing on is lost at sea. Mary writes "The Choice."

1823 Mary publishes *Valperga*. She returns to England with Claire and Percy Florence. She revises *Frankenstein*. Mary collects and edits Percy's unpublished poems into one volume, *Posthumous Poems of Percy Bysshe Shelley*.

1824 Byron dies. Mary begins to write *The Last Man*.

1826 *The Last Man* is published. Harriet and Percy's son, Charles, dies, making Percy Florence the heir to Percy's father, Sir Timothy Shelley.

1828 Mary writes "The Sisters of Albano" for *The Keepsake*, an annual journal.

1830 Mary publishes *Perkin Warbeck*.

1831 Revised edition of *Frankenstein* published with an introduction by Mary.

1835 Mary publishes *Lodore*.

1836 Mary's father William Godwin dies.

1837 Mary publishes *Falkner*.

1838 Mary publishes essays in *Lives of the Most Eminent...Men of France*.

1839 Mary edits Percy's *Poetical Works* and *Essays*.

1844	Sir Timothy dies; Percy Florence inherits title and estates. *Rambles in Germany and Italy* is published.
1848	Sir Percy marries Jane St. John
1851	Mary Shelley dies February 1 in London.
1959	*Mathilda* is published.

Contributors

HAROLD BLOOM is Sterling Professor of the Humanities at Yale University. He is the author of 30 books, including *Shelley's Mythmaking* (1959), *The Visionary Company* (1961), *Blake's Apocalypse* (1963), *Yeats* (1970), *A Map of Misreading* (1975), *Kabbalah and Criticism* (1975), *Agon: Toward a Theory of Revisionism* (1982), *The American Religion* (1992), *The Western Canon* (1994), and *Omens of Millennium: The Gnosis of Angels, Dreams, and Resurrection* (1996). *The Anxiety of Influence* (1973) sets forth Professor Bloom's provocative theory of the literary relationships between the great writers and their predecessors. His most recent books include *Shakespeare: The Invention of the Human* (1998), a 1998 National Book Award finalist, *How to Read and Why* (2000), *Genius: A Mosaic of One Hundred Exemplary Creative Minds* (2002), *Hamlet: Poem Unlimited* (2003), *Where Shall Wisdom Be Found?* (2004), and *Jesus and Yahweh: The Names Divine* (2005). In 1999, Professor Bloom received the prestigious American Academy of Arts and Letters Gold Medal for Criticism. He has also received the International Prize of Catalonia, the Alfonso Reyes Prize of Mexico, and the Hans Christian Andersen Bicentennial Prize of Denmark.

MARTIN TROPP is professor of English at Babson College. His books include *Mary Shelley's Monster* and *Images of Fear: How Horror Stories Shaped Modern Culture*. He is also the author of many articles on related topics.

JOYCE CAROL OATES is the author of many novels, including *Big Mouth & Ugly Girl*, *Freaky Green Eyes*, and her latest novel, *The Falls*. Her novel *Blonde* was a National Book Award nominee and *New York Times* best-seller. A recipient of the National Book Award and the Pen/Malamud Award for

Excellence in Short Fiction, Ms. Oates is the Roger S. Berlind Distinguished Professor of the Humanities at Princeton University.

ANNE K. MELLOR is professor of English and Women's Studies at UCLA. She is the author and editor of a number of books, including *Mothers of the Nation: Women's Political Writing, 1780–1830*; (Editor) *Passionate Encounters in a Time of Sensibility; Romanticism and Gender*; and *Mary Shelley: Her Life, Her Monsters, Her Fiction*.

HOWARD L. MALCHOW is a professor of history at Tufts University. He is the author *Gothic Images of Race in Nineteenth-Century Britain* (1996), *Gentlemen Capitalists: The Social and Political World of the Victorian Businessman* (1991) and *Agitators and Promoters in the Age of the Gladstone and Disraeli* (1983).

MAUREEN NOELLE McLANE is author of *Romanticism and the Human Sciences: Poetry, Population, and the Discourse of the Species*. She's also a visiting media scholar at the Massachusetts Institute of Technology and a Lecturer in History and Literature at Harvard University.

DENISE GIGANTE is assistant professor of English at Stanford University. Her book *Taste: A Literary History* was published by Yale University Press in 2005 and she edited the volume *Gusto: Essential Writings in Nineteenth-Century Gastronomy*.

CYNTHIA PON has published work in Comparative Literature Studies and was a contributor to the volume *Signs of Change: Premodern—Modern— Postmodern*.

MARK MOSSMAN is an associate professor of English and journalism and the Director of Graduate Studies at Western Illinois University. His articles have appeared in *College English, Nineteenth Century Feminisms, Postmodern Culture*, and *Post Identity*.

FRED V. RANDEL, an emeritus associate professor of English literature at the University of San Diego, is the author of many articles about the English Romantic Period, among other subjects.

LEE ZIMMERMAN is an associate professor of English at Hofstra University. He is also the editor of *Twentieth-Century Literature*.

Bibliography

Baldick, Chris. *In Frankenstein's Shadow: Myth, Monstrosity, and Nineteenth Century Writing.* Oxford: Clarendon Press, 1990.

Bloom, Harold. "Frankenstein, or the New Prometheus.'" *Partisan Review.* 32 (1965), pp. 611–618.

Blumberg, Jane. *Mary Shelley's Early Novels: 'This Child of Imagination and Misery'.* Iowa City: University of Iowa Press, 1993.

Botting, Fred. *Making Monstrous:* Frankenstein, *Criticism, Theory.* Manchester: Manchester University Press, 1991.

Bour, Isabelle. "Sensibility as Epistemology in *Caleb Williams, Waverley* and *Frankenstein.*" *Studies in English Literature 1500–1900,* Vol. 45, No. 4, (Autumn 2005), pp. 813–827.

Brewer, William D. *The Mental Anatomies of William Godwin and Mary Shelley.* Cranbury, NJ and London: Associated University Presses, Inc., 2001.

Brooks, Peter. "Godlike Science/Unhallowed Arts: Language and Monstrosity in Frankenstein." *New Literary History,* Vol. 9, No. 3, Rhetoric I: Rhetorical Analyses. (Spring, 1978), pp. 591–605.

Bunnell, Charlene E. *'All the World's a Stage': Dramatic Sensibility in Mary Shelley's Novels.* New York and London: Routledge, 2002.

Gigante, Denise. "Facing the Ugly: The Case of *Frankenstein.*" *ELH,* Vol. 67, No. 2, (Summer 2000), pp. 565–587.

Gilbert, Sandra M. "Horror's Twin: Mary Shelley's Monstrous Eve." *Feminist Studies*, Vol. 4, No. 2, Toward a Feminist Theory of Motherhood. (Jun., 1978), pp. 48–73.

Hustis, Harriet. "Responsible Creativity and the "Modernity" of Mary Shelley's Prometheus." *Studies in English Literature, 1500–1900*. Vol. 43, No. 4. (Autumn, 2003), pp. 845–858.

Ketterer, David. *Frankenstein's Creation: The Book, The Monster, and Human Reality*. University of Victoria: *English Literary Studies*, 1979.

Lamb, John B. "Mary Shelley's Frankenstein and Milton's Monstrous Myth." *Nineteenth-Century Literature*, Vol. 47, No. 3. (Dec. 1992), pp. 303–319.

Levine, George. "'Frankenstein' and the Tradition of Realism." *NOVEL: A Forum on Fiction*, Vol. 7, No. 1. (Autumn, 1973), pp. 14–30.

Levine, George, and U.C. Knoepflmacher, eds. *The Endurance of Frankenstein*. Berkeley: University of California Press, 1979.

London, Bette. "Mary Shelley, Frankenstein, and the Spectacle of Masculinity." *PMLA*, Vol. 108, No. 2. (March 1993), pp. 253–267.

Malchow, H. L. "Frankenstein's Monster and Images of Race in Nineteenth-Century Britain." *Past and Present*, No. 139. (May, 1993), pp. 90–130.

Marshall, David. *The Surprising Effects of Sympathy*. Chicago: University of Chicago Press, 1988.

Marshall, Tim, *Murdering to Dissect: Graverobbing, Frankenstein, and the Anatomy of Literature*. Manchester: Manchester University Press, 1995.

McLane, Maureen Noelle. "Literate Species: Populations, 'Humanities', and *Frankenstein*." *ELH*, Vol. 63, No. 4 (Winter 1996), pp. 959–988.

Mellor, Anne K. *Mary Shelley: Her Life, Her Fiction, Her Monsters*. London and New York: Routledge, 1989.

Mossman, Mark. "Acts of Becoming: Autobiography, *Frankenstein*, and the Postmodern Body." *Postmodern Culture*, Vol. 11, No. 3, (May 2001).

Newman, Beth. "Narratives of Seduction and the Seductions of Narrative: The Frame Structure of Frankenstein." *ELH*, Vol. 53, No. 1. (Spring, 1986), pp. 141–163.

Oates, Joyce Carol. "Frankenstein's Fallen Angel." *Critical Inquiry*, Vol. 10, No. 3. (March, 1984), pp. 543–554.

O'Rourke, James. "'Nothing More Unnatural': Mary Shelley's Revision of Rousseau." *ELH*, Vol. 56, No. 3. (Autumn, 1989), pp. 543–569.

Pollin, Burton R. "Philosophical and Literary Sources of Frankenstein." *Comparative Literature*, Vol. 17, No. 2. (Spring, 1965), pp. 97–108.

Pon, Cynthia. "'Passages' in Mary Shelley's '*Frankenstein*': Toward a Feminist Figure of Humanity?" *Modern Language Studies*, Vol. 30, No. 2. (Autumn, 2000), pp. 33–50.

Poovey, Mary. "My Hideous Progeny: Mary Shelley and the Feminization of Romanticism." *PMLA*, Vol. 95, No. 3. (May, 1980), pp. 332–347.

Randel, Fred V., "The Political Geography of Horror in Mary Shelley's *Frankenstein*." *ELH*, Vol. 70, No. 2. (Summer, 2003), pp. 465–491.

Rose, Ellen Cronan. "Custody Battles: Reproducing Knowledge about Frankenstein." *New Literary History*, Vol. 26, No. 4, (Autumn 1995), pp. 809–832.

Sanderson, Richard K. "Glutting the Maw of Death: Suicide and Procreation in *Frankenstein*." *South Central Review*, Vol. 9, No. 2. (Summer, 1992), pp. 49–64.

Schug, Charles. "The Romantic Form of Mary Shelley's *Frankenstein*" *Studies in English Literature, 1500–1900*, Vol. 17, No. 4, Nineteenth Century. (Autumn, 1977), pp. 607–619.

Sherwin, Paul. "*Frankenstein*: Creation as Catastrophe." *PMLA*, Vol. 96, No. 5. (Oct., 1981), pp. 883–903.

Sharma, Anjana (Ed.). *Frankenstein: Interrogating Gender, Culture and Identity*. New York: Macmillan, 2004.

Small, Christopher. *Ariel Like a Harpy: Shelley, Mary and* Frankenstein. London: Gollancz, 1972.

Thornburg, Mary K. Patterson. *The Monster in the Mirror: Gender and the Sentimental/Gothic Myth in* Frankenstein. Ann Arbor: UMI Research Press, 1987.

Tuite, Clara. "Frankenstein's Monster and Malthus' 'Jaundiced Eye': Population, Body Politics, and the Monstrous Sublime." *Eighteenth-Century Life*, Vol. 22, No. 1 (February 1998), pp. 141–155.

Vasbinder, Samuel Holmes. *Scientific Attitudes in Mary Shelley's* Frankenstein. Ann Arbor: UMI Research Press, 1984.

Veeder, William. *Mary Shelley & Frankenstein: The Fate of Androgyny*. Chicago: University of Chicago Press, 1986.

Ward, Maryanne C. "A Painting of the Unspeakable: Henry Fuseli's 'The Nightmare' and the Creation of Mary Shelley's 'Frankenstein'" *The*

Journal of the Midwest Modern Language Association, Vol. 33, No. 1. (Winter, 2000), pp. 20–31.

Yousef, Nancy. "The Monster in a Dark Room: *Frankenstein*, Feminism and Philosophy." *MLQ: Modern Language Quarterly*. Vol. 63, No. 2, (June 2002), pp. 197–226.

Zimmerman, Lee. "*Frankenstein*, Invisibility and Nameless Dread." *American Imago*, Vol. 60, No. 2 (Summer 2003), pp. 135–158.

Acknowledgments

"The Monster" by Martin Tropp. From *Mary Shelley's Monster*, Boston: Houghton Mifflin Company, 1976, pp. 66–83. © 1976 by Martin Tropp. Reprinted by permission.

"Frankenstein's Fallen Angel" by Joyce Carol Oates. From *Critical Inquiry*, Vol. 10, No. 3 (March 1984), 543–554. © 1984 by The University of Chicago Press. Reprinted by permission.

"Making a Monster" by Anne K. Mellor. From *Mary Shelley: Her Life, Her Fiction, Her Monsters*. Copyright © 1989 by Anne K. Mellor. Reproduced by permission of Routledge/Taylor & Francis Group. LLC.

"Frankenstein's Monster and Images of Race in Nineteenth-Century Britain" by H. L. Malchow. From *Past and Present*, No. 139 (May, 1993), pp. 90–130. © 1993 by Oxford University Press. Reprinted by permission.

McLane, Maureen Noelle. "Literate Species: Populations, 'Humanities,' and *Frankenstein.*" *ELH* 63:4 (1996), 959–988. © The Johns Hopkins University Press. Reprinted with permission of The Johns Hopkins University Press.

"Facing the Ugly: The Case of *Frankenstein*" by Denise Gigante. From *ELH* 67 (2000), pp. 565–587. © 2000 by The Johns Hopkins University Press. Reprinted by permission.

"Passages in Mary Shelley's 'Frankenstein': Toward a Feminist Figure of Humanity?" by Cynthia Pon. From *Modern Language Studies*, Vol. 30, No. 2 (Autumn, 2000), pp. 33–50. © Modern Language Studies. Reprinted by permission.

Mossman, Mark. "Acts of Becoming: Autobiography, *Frankenstein*, and the Postmodern Body." *Postmodern Culture* 11:3 (2001). © The Johns Hopkins University Press. Reprinted with permission of The Johns Hopkins Univeristy Press.

Randel, Fred V. "The Political Geography of Horror in Mary Shelley's *Frankenstein*." *ELH* 70:2 (2003), 465–491. © The Johns Hopkins University Press. Reprinted with permission of The Johns Hopkins Univeristy Press.

Zimmerman, Lee. "*Frankenstein*, Invisibility, and Nameless Dread." *American Imago* 60:2 (2003), 135–158. © The Johns Hopkins University Press. Reprinted with permission of The Johns Hopkins University Press.

Index

Characters in literary works are indexed by first name (if any), followed by the name of the work in parentheses.

00402 1344